CW00684499

T.J. Over the Top

T.J. Over the Top

Best wishes
Ken Piesse

Terry Jenner with Ken Piesse

INFORMATION
AUSTRALIA

Published by
Information Australia
A.C.N. 006 042 173
75 Flinders Lane
Melbourne Vic. 3000
Telephone: (03) 9654 2800
Fax: (03) 9650 5261
Internet: www.infoaust.com
Email: mail@infoaust.com

The National Library of Australia
Cataloguing-in-Publication entry:

Jenner, Terry.
 T.J. over the top.

Includes index.
ISBN 1 86350 271 8

1. Jenner, Terry. 2. Cricket players - Australia -
Biography. 3. Compulsive gamblers - Biography.
4. Ex-convicts - Australia - Biography. I. Piesse, Ken.
II. Title.

796.358092

Page Layout & Design: Ben Graham
Cover Design: inprint design
Cover Photograph: Ray Titus
Printed in Australia by Australian Print Group

Contents

Acknowledgements

The authors would like to thank the following people, in particular, for their help with *T.J. Over The Top*: Wendy & Shane Aston, Dr. Don Beard, Stephen Berry, Ann Blair, Ian Chappell, Lawrie Colliver (statistics), Laraine Coombes, Tony Dodemaide, Ross Edwards, Ashley Mallett, Rodney Marsh, Ken Meuleman, John Rutherford, Alan Shiell, Shane Warne and everyone at Information Australia.

Special thanks to Rex Jory and the staff at The Adelaide *Advertiser* for their assistance with photographs.

Foreword – by Ian Chappell

There are very few guys who walk away from jail and say, "I'm a better man for having been inside". Terry Jenner is one.

Maybe one of the reasons for T.J. "prospering" in jail is because of the way he accepted his punishment. When the term was published in the Sydney papers, a Q.C. who is a member of the tennis club where I play, told me, "The sentence given to your mate Jenner is way too harsh. You should let him know that an appeal would almost certainly get it reduced".

I immediately got in touch with T.J. and passed on the comment. He responded by saying he knew that it was harsh, but he didn't want to get his hopes up and have them dashed so he wasn't going to appeal. He went on to explain that he needed to be put away and he'd just do his time and then get on with life. It was this acceptance of his punishment as a necessary part of his rehabilitation that probably helped T.J. to get through a tough period in his life and come out a better man. Having spoken to him about it since, he talks about how "a great weight" was lifted from his shoulders when he was actually caught. "It put an end to the double life I'd been leading and all the lies I had to tell to cover my tracks."

I can understand how that would have eaten away at T.J.

When he was sentenced, I wrote a column which said in part, "I don't consider Terry Jenner to be a criminal. Never have, never will. In fact, I've always classed T.J. as a very honest cricketer, so honest at times he made life difficult for a captain".

There was never anything behind the back with T.J. If he had a problem that related to my captaincy I'd know about it, usually less than five minutes after stumps. The good thing was once we'd discussed the problem, the matter was closed and it didn't have any bearing on what occurred the next day. I can still hear the sound of that beer bottle thumping down on the wooden table in the middle of the Adelaide Oval dressing room. It was a very definite signal that T.J. had a problem and he wanted to talk it out over a beer. The sound still occasionally wakes me in the middle of the night, probably in the way T.J. shoots bolt upright to the screech of metal doors clanging shut.

Why did I support T.J. when he was going through a rough time? Because of the belief that he wasn't a crook and didn't deserve to go to jail, especially when criminals like Alan Bond and Christopher Skase were roaming free. This offended my sense of fair play. Also, because I felt he needed help, rather than incarceration. And finally I guess because once you're captain, you're their skipper for all time.

It was my job to be there to help and to listen when a player had a problem and in return I expected them to play hard for me on the field.

If you expect 100 per cent you have to give 100 per cent. It was always one of my rules as captain. T.J. had always tried for me when I was captain of South Australia and Australia and he made some monumental contributions. We'd played in three Shield winning sides together (two under my captaincy) and he took more than 250 wickets for SA. He took four wickets in the first innings of the Test we won in Trinidad and five in a drawn game at the same ground. He made a match-turning 74 on a damp wicket at Adelaide Oval in partnership with Doug Walters against England in 1974-75. Those were some of his exploits on the field. As a senior player T.J. didn't shirk responsibility and when I was having a running battle with the South Australian Cricket Association in 1975-76, it was Terry who organized a meeting of the players, which resulted in a show of support for the captain. These things are not easily forgotten. And should never be forgotten.

Off the field T.J. could be excellent company, humourous, observant and full of ideas and always able to express himself; some of the reasons why I wrote in 1988, "He'd make a damn good coach". If he was at odds with the world it was wise to find a different pub and let the mood pass. In short, I'd had a lot of good times with T.J. and a few disappointments along the way and we'd survived it all, so his period in jail was no time to walk away.

There were a couple of things that worried me when I went to visit T.J. at Mobilong. The first was the business of sex in jail and the second was suicide. T.J. answered the first question with typical humour, "Don't worry mate, I'm too old. They want the young, good looking guys".

The second he handled with thought and his usual candor. "Mate, there are 20 questions they ask you on a form and I've always written 'yes' to the first 19 and 'no' to the last one." That was the answer I wanted to hear.

I knew T.J. was going to survive jail when I had a letter from him that responded to my line, "Don't lose your sense of humour".

He told a lovely story about bowling to David "Cracka" Hourn of New South Wales. It wasn't just the hilarious punch line, but the way he was able to weave the story like a good tapestry artist that gave me faith in his future.

Those who have heard T.J. as an excellent after-dinner speaker in recent years will know exactly what I mean.

T.J. didn't lose his sense of humour in jail, but he did find his way. He is a better man for it. And importantly he is helping other people to improve themselves. A number of times since T.J. has been out of jail, I've heard worried people tell me, "T.J's back on the punt". The first couple of times I broached the subject with T.J. and he gave a plausible explanation of how the mistake could have occurred. The last few years I've stopped even asking.

I'm glad T.J. has written a book as he has a lot to offer on a subject (addiction to gambling) about which very little is known. He also has a lot to offer on another subject about which little is known: leg-spin bowling. I'm sure he'll continue to help people in both categories, which will follow a trend in T.J's life. Terry Jenner has helped a hell of a lot more people than he's hindered.

Ian Chappell
1999

Introduction – by Shane Warne

It gives me great pleasure to write this introduction for my mate T.J. He has been a major influence and mentor in my development as a leg-spin bowler.

We first met when I was at the Cricket Academy in 1990-91. At that stage he was going through a tough time and I think his involvement with us was a vital part of his own rehabilitation. Few are as passionate about cricket or leg-spin bowling.

For me, too, it was perfect timing, because I hadn't played first-class cricket at the time. I was like a human sponge trying to soak up as much information about the art of leg-spin bowling as possible.

Our relationship clicked right from the start and we hit it off straight away. We were on the same wavelength.

In my eyes, T.J. is the best spin bowling coach around and daylight is probably second. The reasons are simple. He is a great listener and more often than not, you might just want to get something off your chest, or just lean on those ample shoulders of his.

Other times though he will say you're not quite doing this or that and then his ability to show you really does make a difference. His coaching philosophy is to keep it simple, which I find works very well.

T.J's ideas and ability to come up with something new, have helped countless leg-spinners over the years. One I've employed with great success is when a new batsman comes in at the non-striker's end, I'll immediately bowl a big wrong-un. It doesn't matter if the batsman facing it picks it. You're bowling it for the benefit of the batsman, the non-striker and the other guys sitting in the shed so they can see that the ball is spinning. When it's their turn to face, he's looking for the wrong-un so you starve him of it. It's a plan which consistently has brought me a lot of success.

One thing I really admire about T.J. is that he is always there no matter what.

And over the years T.J. has become a true friend of mine and my family.

We have had some great times on and off the field, so I am sure you'll enjoy this book. He is a character and doesn't hold any punches. It is an intriguing read.

I hope you enjoy it.

Shane Warne
1999

Author's Note

I t seems every time I pick up a Test cricket "who's who", there is a reference to my prison sentence. How events *after* cricket can be combined with my statistical performances are a constant frustration. I felt I should tell the whole story – not just the fact that I was sentenced to six-and-a-half years imprisonment for embezzlement.

I'm not suggesting for one minute my cricketing days were drama and controversy free. On the contrary my aggressive and demonstrative ways continually created obstacles for me. Most I brought upon myself but there were occasions when I was simply misunderstood.

Always a compulsive and reactive personality, my addiction to gambling sent me on a self-destructing path which ultimately led to prison.

I'm not proud of the events leading to my demise. I'm certain a lot of people will find it difficult to understand how someone achieving the dizzy heights of Test cricket could crash so hard. Sporting heroes, even after their careers have finished, aren't supposed to have weaknesses.

Some thought my sentence was harsh and on the surface it possibly was. But, having breached my bond, the judge had little option but to deal with me severely.

In fact, he did me a huge favour because it brought the lie I was living to a halt. Effectively, the prison sentence ended one part of my life and allowed me to begin another. I was off the merry-go-round and my problems were out in the open.

I was done a favour when I was locked up. If I hadn't been, my life would have been shattered and maybe even over. I would have kept on running further away from people because of my shame.

The same friends I'd been dodging were ultimately my salvation. You don't survive all the turmoil and losses associated with prison without friends. I witnessed first-hand the difficulties most inmates suffered because most had no friends. They had lost them along the way to self-destruction.

Initially it was scary and I couldn't see how I could possibly survive the two years I had to serve behind bars.

When I was told Ian Chappell was in the visiting area waiting to see me, I felt more frightened than at any other time.

Facing Ian was to become the true beginning of a new, better life. The truth of our first meeting in prison is that I burst into tears. I told him how ashamed and sorry I was for disgracing him and all my old cricketing mates.

Ian only wanted to know that I was alright and I assured him I was.

After his visit it was easier for me to see others during my sentence.

I get quite emotional thinking about all the people who came to visit and helped me along the way. They gave me fresh hope. This book is for every one of them. God bless them all.

Terry Jenner
1999

CHAPTER ONE

Down and Out

*He said some terrible things about me, calling
me a parasite and a pathological gambler
who had offended again and again.*

It was one of those nights that you didn't want to go to sleep. I didn't
want to wake up and say goodbye. I cuddled up to little Trudianne
not knowing if Jacky was ever going to let me see her again.

As much as I tried to ignore what was going to happen in the next
24 hours, I couldn't. In my own mind, I'd already been sentenced. I
was on death row thinking when I awoke, I'd die.

September 22, 1988, was my day of reckoning. I sat in court while
Michael David Q.C. pleaded for me. He was outstanding. As a
batsman in Adelaide club cricket he'd been cautious, slow, laborious
and hard-to-dismiss, prompting me in one of our games to cheekily
call out to our team that if Michael stayed in, we'd win. Nobody on
our side was allowed to get him out! It was just a heat of the battle
thing and nothing personal. But I reminded Michael before he started
his plea, that today wouldn't be a good day in which to get even!

Others spoke on my behalf. Then it was Judge Greaves' turn. He
said some terrible things, calling me a parasite and a pathological
gambler who had offended again and again. A Good Samaritan had
come to my door, generously given me a job and I'd let even him
down. He was right there.

Including the suspended sentence from 1986, he sentenced me
to a total of six-and-a-half years, with three years' non-parole and no
restitution.

He added, in my case, he could see only a small hope of rehabilitation.

Before being led away, I looked around, saw Jacky and she couldn't look at me.

My mind was racing. What am I going to do? How am I going to survive this? What's on the other side of the door? They hadn't even let me say goodbye to her.

I was put in a small holding cell before being taken downstairs where they took my belt off me and detailed my possessions. Having had five days on remand in the Adelaide jail previously, at least I knew a little bit of the routine. I knew to make sure I had at least some money. I had $20 in my wallet. I was finger printed and handcuffed.

A prison officer, a former cricketer I'd played against, offered to arrange some protection if I wanted it.

I thanked him and said, "No, I'll be alright".

It was the right answer; even if I didn't know it at the time. Later I found out if you go into protective custody it gives the connotation that you could be a child sex offender. They are the lowest of lows in the prison system.

I was steered into a paddy wagon and one of the prison officers started to send me up. "Gee, look what we've got here. Twenty bucks."

I was so low it didn't matter what they said, but I took it all in. I thought to myself when it was all over and I was out, they'd still be living that life.

It was a short drive from the holding cell to the Adelaide Remand Centre. One of the blokes I was with was on charges of smuggling explosives into the Centre to blow it up and escape. He was to get nine years, with seven non-parole. He looked mean.

By now it was almost lunchtime. I went in and stood on a line in front of the counter until told to step forward. I was given a cheese and pickle and a cheese and tomato sandwich and a Granny Smith apple.

They then took some details and gave me some prison clothes to get changed into. Blue everything. Plus singlets, underpants, toothbrush and other incidentals. I was asked if I smoked and before I could answer, a packet of 20 Viscount cigarettes had been thrust my way.

The prison officers watched while I was getting changed. I was to get used to impersonal things like that. I handed in what I'd been wearing and as I was being led away to the cells, a big prison officer with an English accent, "Yorky" Smith said, "You'll find out who your fooking friends are now Jenner".

I'd never felt lower.

CHAPTER TWO

The Corrigin Kid

*One lady, a stern old thing, came into the
shop and asked if we had any straw brooms.
"Yes we do," I said. "Would you like me to
wrap that, or will you ride it away?"*

It's not every day a country storekeeper's son plays for Australia.
Certainly it was a first for Corrigin, a tiny wheatbelt town 250
kilometres from Perth in the West Australian wheatbelt.

There were only several thousand people in our whole district and
in Corrigin itself, less than 500. Bitumen was scarce and it took four
hours to Perth and another four back again on the old gravel roads.

In summer you could experience a week or more of non-stop
century temperatures. In winter it could get so cold sometimes that
the water in the taps would freeze. On occasions there was
widespread flooding.

There was just one school, which catered for primary to high
school aged kids and only a dozen shops or so, including the general
store, A & Q Jenner's, which was run by my Dad and Mum and the
local newsagency which Nana and Grandad owned and operated.

I was born in Mt Lawley and along with my sister Laraine, who is
two years older than me, moved to Corrigin when I was a toddler.
While it was only a small town, it was on the railway line and my
Nana and Grandad saw an opportunity. Nana also bought the
general store for Mum and Dad. They had to pay her back for it. At
that time Dad was working as a foreman at Plaimar and didn't see a
lot of future there.

At birth I was named Kerry Arthur Jenner, but that was changed at baptism to Terrence James Jenner. I was only eight weeks old at the time, so didn't have much of a say! Mum's maiden name was Kerry and Dad's christian name was Arthur, but obviously Mum and Dad were arguing even then as neither would agree to my name. Mum's brother was James Terrence so I became Terrence James.

Dad came from East Perth, a renowned tough area. His mother died in her early 30's and he lost a brother with rheumatic fever at a young age. From the age of 11, Dad was the man of the house. It was a real battle for him.

I admired him in many ways; in others, he disappointed me.

He was brilliant mathematically and could look up and down the rows of pounds, shillings and pence and jot the totals down in an inkling. And he rarely made a mistake.

He was also a good salesman with the happy knack for the right words at the right time.

"Arthur," said a lady to him one day. "Have you got any good quality leather shoes? We bought a pair recently but they didn't last very long."

"Mavis," he said. "The one thing you can be sure of with our shoes and that is our soles arseholes!"

Dad could always pick the right person to joke with and I'd try to copy him. One lady, a stern old thing, came into the shop and asked if we had any straw brooms. I'd heard Dad's response to this question and decided to try it out myself. "Yes, we do," I said. "Would you like me to wrap that, or will you ride it away?" Boy, did it create a stink. No wonder, I was only 14 at the time!

One Christmas, I'd just been given my very first cricket bat and was thrilled. Before I had a chance to use it more than once or twice, Dad came home from the club, pretty full. There was a cat fight out the back. My bat was within reach and he used it to whack one of the cats.

I was awakened by the screech of the cat and Dad walked back inside with my bat all bloodied. Seeing my look of dismay, he said, "Oh well. It was a beautiful cover drive!".

Dad wasn't one to hand out compliments or praise, unless it was to gain continuing custom. Outside the shop, he found it difficult to mix socially with people, especially those who weren't blue collar workers.

The Corrigin Town Hall was a centrepiece for everything in the town, from badminton and the local dance through to the Friday or Saturday night pictures.

Debbie Reynolds was my idol. I collected dozens of photographs of her. One night at the Town Hall they showed Bill Haley in *Rock Around The Clock*. We all wore stove-pipe pants and desert boots. I wore one bright coloured pink and one equally as loud green sock! Talk about rebels! As the movie was finishing, some of the kids ran down the front and started to jive to the music before sprinting off again as if they were going to be arrested and locked up for life!

Mum was a milliner and very talented, too. She used to make all our fancy dress costumes. She loved dancing and it was always great fun to go with her.

Dad, still in his work clothes, would generally come only as far as the front door unless Mum was having a dance with someone. Then he'd come over and say, "You've had your share". It always led to arguments.

If Dad was proud of my achievements, he never let me know. Every boy wants to be close to his father. But as hard as I tried, mine wouldn't let me. I so desperately wanted to be made to feel that I was worthwhile.

One year at the inter-school sports at Yealering, I looked up during the hop, step and jump and saw both my Mum and Dad had come to watch. It gave me a huge lift. In my excitement, I made my best ever jump: 30 feet, three-and-a-half inches, which was a new school record for 12-year-olds.

Unfortunately that was one of the few times Dad ever showed an interest in my sport. "It's always play, play, play. Nothing but play," he'd say to me. I made my highest ever score for Western Australia one day and Dad said, "Notice you made 69. Pity it wasn't 69 pounds".

Sometimes I think Dad would have been happier if I had been a footballer. He taught me to kick left and right foot in the back lane behind the shop. He'd always wear these elastic sided shoes and tie shoe laces around them so they wouldn't come off.

One year I won the Under 12 sports cup at Corrigin and took it home to the shop. I was as proud as punch. Dad was serving so I had to wait. Finally, he acknowledged my presence, saw the cup and said, "What did you get that for?".

"I won it for being Under 12 school champion."

"So you should have."

And on he went with his work. Friday was always our busiest day.

George Holdaway had the green grocers next door. When he saw the cup he warmly congratulated me and filled it with orange fizzy drink. "Well done young Terry," he said, genuinely pleased for me.

I felt good then.

People would come into town, leave their orders with us and we'd make them up for when they returned. I'd take the orders out and stack them in long neat rows, saving the perishables like butter and bacon to last. Nothing was ever pinched. It was a different era.

We lived at the back of the shop, my bedroom doubling as the ladies changing room during the day.

Dad seemed to be working all the time. Only on Sundays would he stop and make the Sunday roast.

There were lots of arguments between Mum and Dad, so much so that my sister Laraine ultimately went and lived with Nana and Grandad in Mandurah.

I also hated the fighting but, being two years younger, I couldn't just get up and leave.

When I was 13, Mum and Dad separated and Mum bought a house in Mt Lawley. It was the first time I could remember living in an actual house.

***

AS A kid, I only ever aspired to running Dad and Mum's store. I never saw a sporting future, even though I loved sports from cricket and football through to tennis and hockey. I could also recite the 1951 Melbourne Cup race, the one in which Delta held out Akbar.

There was no one in Corrigin who had done anything particularly special, though one of the town's footy stars, Maurie Turner, could kick both feet and played down in Perth for awhile. "Ginger" Henderson was another who had a few senior games. My idol was a guy called Rodney Fullwood. He could mark and kick little screwies. Being a kid, I didn't realise that he was too small and not quick enough to succeed in the city.

School sport days, lunchtimes and recess were always my favourite times in any week. A lunchtime game or a kick of the footy would always be going on. Once I was hit on my knee by one of the cork cricket balls which resulted in my not being able to put any pressure on my left leg. At the time, it stopped me from being competitive in virtually every sport except for tunnel-ball.

I could still take a good mark at football, though, as I jumped off my other leg. But I was very skinny, like a matchstick. There were no under-age teams in the town at that time and I was too young to play with the seniors, so only turned out for the school. In one game, in which we were thrashed 30 goals to one by Quairading, a far bigger school than us, I scored our only goal. It was soccered. Years later, when I returned to Corrigin as a 19-year-old, I turned out for Bilbarin, the No. 2 team in Corrigin, just as an interest for Dad. The week after kicking 12 goals in one game, I was targetted and deliberately crunched going for a mark. I kicked only two or three goals and figured I didn't need football anymore. I'd already played for Western Australia at cricket and didn't want to get hurt.

Cricket had always been a priority ever since I'd filled in as a kid for the local cricket team.

I was 14 years of age when I played my first competitive cricket match. I'd played other games, but only as a fill-in. Corrigin was playing against Kondinin and a guy called Rex Growden. Rex was one of the district's star players, a real hero for young guys like me to look up to. The keys and matches in his pockets rattled as he ran in to bowl. I think Rex went easy on me that day. He wanted to get me out, but he also recognised that I was a junior, so he didn't bowl a tough one at me.

Trevor Rogers was another well-known identity. He was Corrigin's wicketkeeper and would stand up to the stumps to virtually every bowler, fast or slow. He'd often leave a lit cigarette going at both ends of the wicket and would take a drag in-between overs!

In my first year, I made five in the Grand Final and we were beaten by two runs by Bruce Rock. Don Langdon who played football for East Perth and Western Australia played in that game

At that age, I saw myself more as a batsman who could bowl medium pacers. My mate from the Corrigin Co-Op, Ray Tyers, and I asked if we could have the old matting which the cricket club was otherwise intending to throw out. An older boy we knew, Errol Henderson, who could bowl "mystery" spinners with an unusual grip just like John Gleeson's, had his own practice net and Ray and I wanted one too.

We'd collect bottles and manna gum and sell the gum to Willcox Mofflin. From the profits we bought chicken wire and posts and established our net. The result was a full-scale pitch, complete with the old matting, on vacant land between the Co-Op and Jenner's. From this time, cricket really got serious. Ray and I started playing test matches and they were full scale affairs. If a fast bowler was operating, you'd bowl as fast as you could. If a slow bowler was called up, you'd try and copy his way of spinning the ball.

Our knowledge of the cricketers was strictly limited and gained only from newspaper pictures and from what "Johnnie" Moyes and the others said about them on the radio. In the old *Post* magazine, Keith Miller had a cricket tips segment and from studying the pictures and taking in Keith's words of wisdom, we learnt to bowl all the deliveries, including off-spin and leg-spin.

In our test matches, Ray would always be "England" and I'd be "Australia" which I thought was pretty smart. We flattened our pitch and eventually got it like concrete before positioning and stretching the matting. Different spots on the net between the posts counted for a certain number of runs, the drives always being the best rewarded. If you nicked one it was an automatic out.

Each and every day we'd play until bad light stopped play – always a controversial time – or until we were told to come in.

On days when it rained or play was impossible, we'd play hat cricket, a game Ray invented. We'd carefully cut cardboard into squares and write numbers or ways of getting out on one side. All the pieces would be placed in a hat and the game would begin, every dismissal, four or six being noted in an exercise book which we'd carefully rule up to look like a score sheet. We didn't play against each other – rather Western Australia versus South Australia or WA versus the Vics.

A batsman would often struggle to get to 100 so we ended up adding more boundary tokens.

We called it hat cricket as we'd put the tokens in an old hat discarded by Ray's father. I'm sure Ray could have marketed the game.

Ray's Dad was very strict. They lived in a house and Ray had his chores to do. Other than chopping kindling up for the fire, my spare time was my own.

One evening after a woodwork class at school had been cancelled, Ray and I called into the Town Hall to see what the Girl Guides were doing. We heard all this giggling so had a peek. The girls finished their game and as they re-entered the Hall, Ray and I hid behind the seats. We must have startled one of the girls, it was Ray's sister, and she screamed! We had to front the headmaster, Don Smith, who gave us a choice of either a letter home to our parents, or six cuts with his cane.

Ray said he'd take the cuts and had blisters for a week. I said I'd take the letter home. Corrigin was a small town so I knew Dad would hear about it anyway. Both Dad and Mum thought the whole thing pretty trivial. But Ray's Dad found out anyway and Ray was punished, not being allowed out of the yard for a month. Our test matches were suddenly on hold!

Years later, when I was looking to get a job with the WA Railways, I wrote to Mr Smith and asked him for a reference. He hadn't seen me for a long time and wrote back:

> *Dear Terry,*
>
> *I'm rather curious why you've left it so long to ask for a reference. However, time does dim memories and all I can recall is an angelic face!"*

***

RAY AND I would go off to the dam and smoke the Turf or Craven-A cigarettes I'd occasionally knock off from our shop. Once at the Corrigin Show, we won a heap of cigarettes and wafer biscuits in a competition where you had to throw a sixpence and make it stick to a cigarette packet. We'd spit on the coins before throwing them and it worked almost every time!

We munched through a mountain of wafer biscuits, but there were too many cigarettes to smoke so we carefully wrapped the packets in plastic and buried them under a tree. Our plan was to have a supply which would last all year! One Friday night one of the kids, Barry Madjen, was caught smoking on the way home from the pictures. Soon I was accused with supplying the whole town's teenage population with free fags!

I told Dad that we had won them, but he didn't believe me. He'd caught me previously with a packet tucked into my pants, so probably had good reason to be suspicious!

As country kids, we never saw ourselves as particularly deprived or missing out on what the city kids had. We went swimming in the dam in summer and never worried about how dirty the water was. We had everything we wanted. We'd amuse ourselves playing badminton and going to the pictures and the dances. I started playing the drums and on several occasions was allowed to play them at the dances, when Mr and Mrs Hancock, who played percussion and the piano, took a break.

The real highlight, though, was school holiday time which we'd spend at Nana and Grandad's at Mandurah. We'd meet up with other kids and do a whole range of different things.

Nana Kerry, one of 13 children, was not well-educated, but she was street-smart and very ambitious. She believed that if you bought it for one and sold it for two everything would be alright. She was particularly big on bricks and mortar. She started with two small flats on the main road into Mandurah before buying a bigger place, Koolyn Flats. We loved going there. We were right opposite an open air picture theatre and we'd all sit out on the front lawn and watch the top half of the movie from over the fence.

The fishing in Mandurah was unbelievable. Laraine and I would also stand in the water and catch crabs and prawns, or if we felt in the mood, nice-sized sand whiting from hand-held lines. It was magnificent.

Nana was always buying and selling property. Grandad Jim was a master builder and would help make the places liveable. They also bought old boats, restored them and offered them for hire. Nana was a real entrepreneur. Later in life, Nana bought a banana plantation in Carnarvon.

She was only 65 when she died, after a massive stroke. Grandad really wasn't interested any more after that. He sold everything off including 300 acres at Furnisdale which Nana had planned to develop as a caravan park. Mum and my uncle Jimmy were given Koolyn Flats. Jim decided he wanted his money and Mum had to sell. They got something like $50,000. Had they held on for only five or six more years it would have been worth at least a million.

***

AFTER MUM and Dad separated and Mum and I moved to Mandurah, I joined Laraine at Pinjarra Junior High.

We stayed at Mandurah before Mum successfully negotiated a loan to buy a house in Mt Lawley, quite a feat in those days for a single Mum. It was the first time my sister and I each had a bedroom to ourselves. Mum took in boarders to help pay the mortgage.

Mt Lawley High was at the end of our street and we were only about three miles from the city. I may have been a dux at Corrigin, but I was a dope at Mt Lawley. I'd been at three different schools in a matter of months. The difference in standards between each of them was dramatic. A further complicating factor was that I started during the second term. Instead of doing General Science or Mathematics, I was suddenly into Physics and Algebra. I never got on top of either subject. At 14 I left school with only average marks and returned to Corrigin where I worked in Dad's shop. He enrolled me in an accountancy course. He thought it was just what I needed if I was to take over the business. God knows how a 14-year-old was meant to do such a complicated course by correspondence, from a country town.

No wonder I felt inadequate. I headed back to Mum at Mt Lawley and wasn't to return to Corrigin until I was 19.

CHAPTER THREE

A Leggie by Chance

"Excuse me son," he said. "Aren't you in the
wrong net?" "No, I'm a wicketkeeper."

I started as an office boy at 15 for the clothing wholesalers Goode, Durrant and Murray. One of my daily responsibilities was to collect and distribute the mail, which saw me make four or five return trips daily to the Forest Place Post office. Often I'd have to wait for the large bag to be filled, so I'd walk across the road to Albert's Bookshop and read cricket and golf books.

At weekends, I used to go and watch Mt Lawley play and was invited to have a game in the Under 15s, as my birthdate was *after* September 1. My only problem was that the team practised immediately after school between 4 p.m and 5 p.m when I was still at work so I'd train with the seniors from 5.30 p.m.

The Under 15s needed a wicketkeeper and I said yes, I could do it. I also volunteered to open the batting. I was the only one in the team who worked and, as a result, the only player who wore long trousers!

During the Christmas holidays, the club sent a few of us to a clinic at the WACA ground. I was in the wicketkeeper's net, just rolling my arm over when one of the coaches walked past just as I was bowling a couple of leg breaks as a loosener.

"Excuse me son," he said. "Aren't you in the wrong net?"

"No," I said, "I'm a wicketkeeper."

"Bowl me another leg break."

I did and it bounced three times. Embarrassed I followed up with an offie.

"A leg break," he said. "Bowl another leg break?"

I did. It must have been a good one. The gentleman introduced himself as Tony Zimbulis. He said he couldn't rate my wicketkeeping skills as he'd never seen me keep, but as a leg spinner, I had a genuine chance. He called the squad co-ordinators John Rutherford and Ken Meuleman over and together they stood behind me as I sent down a few more wrist spinners. It was all very flattering. Until that afternoon I'd never heard of Zimbulis. Apparently he'd bowled against Don Bradman. But Rutherford and Meuleman were true legends in the West. Like me, John was a country kid from the WA wheatbelt town of Merredin. He'd always taken a real interest in the young kids and pricked up his ears when I said I came from Corrigin. In years to come he was to say I had the hardest to pick wrong-un he'd seen.

He immediately okayed my switch across to the spinner's net and I worked with Zimbulis for the remainder of the clinic. They then approached the Mt Lawley cricket club and asked if I could start bowling leg-spin in matches. Without Zimbulis stopping at my net that day, who knows what might have happened? Sadly, he died, aged 45, before I played my first game for WA. As a keen member of the leg-spinner's club though, I know he would have been very proud when I played my first game for the State.

***

SO SUDDENLY I was an allrounder, a batsman who dabbled in leg-spin. I was only knee high to a grasshopper in those days and so thin that one of my teammates dubbed me "sparrow legs".

One of my first games bowling leg-spin was against Tony Mann from Midland-Guildford. He was soon to play "A" grade cricket as a 14-year-old. He showed me how he flicked his wrong-un off his little finger. It was all trial and error, but it seemed to work and it wasn't until years later that I really got the hang of it.

I didn't have a lot of success that year with the ball, but was given the club's most promising junior award.

I found I could curve and spin the ball a long way, but the long hops in-between were exasperating.

I spent the following season in "C" grade under the old master Jack Steel. He was a canny medium-pacer who'd happily bowl both ends had the rules allowed. He took no nonsense. You did what you were told. I bowled only about 100 overs but took almost 40 wickets, Jack never allowing the sloggers to get a chance at me.

By now, I'd also become a member at the Mount Lawley golf club and would play golf in the morning and cricket in the afternoon. There were people who thought I may have been a better golfer than cricketer, but I know I made the right choice. After I'd reduced my handicap to 17 or 18, the thing which tempered my golf was a bout of Bell's Palsy in which my face literally dropped. Mum said I was burning the candle at both ends and not getting enough rest.

One of my "C" grade teammates, John Gill, would come around after practice and be amazed when Mum said I wasn't home yet. John had been home, had tea and was dressed up to go out. "Hasn't he heard of girls yet?" he'd ask.

The reality was that I was a boy from the bush living in a big city because of circumstances and trying to work it all out.

We never felt we missed out on anything growing up in the bush, but in the city there was so much more to do. I played a year of football with the ex-scholars at Graylands, went 10-pin bowling and was into darts and pool. I even found time to go to a health studio, all because someone said I had a frame with nothing on it!

The Bell's Palsy slowed me a little. It's something which has come and gone three or four times. Initially it occurred when I was playing in a junior golf tournament at Mt Lawley. My eye kept running all the time. After the first round we came in for a soft drink and I couldn't close my mouth. The fluid just ran out the other side of my mouth. That was scary. I wore my sunglasses for the second round and had drinks through a straw. A doctor diagnosed some sort of viral infection and prescribed these tablets which I found very difficult to take. They worked that time, but I decided to concentrate on what I did best: cricket. My golf was put on hold.

When I started at Mt Lawley, the club fielded four teams – "A" grade, "B" grade, Colts and "C" grade. Later it became firsts, seconds, thirds and fourths.

I never played Colts and went straight into "B" grade for the new season. During the winter months a group of us had spent a deal of time with Rutherford at Kent Street High. There were no indoor facilities at the WACA in those days and even when it rained, we still all turned up, keen and ready to go.

Mt Lawley had struggled all year and in the second half of the season, promoted a couple of us into their senior side for the last five or six games.

In the final game, I made 60 not out batting at No.11 against Perth and the Rigg brothers, Bert and Basil, at Lathlean Park. It was an enormous boost to my confidence. Trevor Bidstrup was at the other end and a very able partner. I tried to play normally and outwardly exuded more confidence than inwardly I really had.

Again, during the winter months, I worked out with Rutherford at Kent St. High school. Others who were just as keen as me included Ross Edwards, Jock Irvine, John Inverarity, Jim Hubble, Ashley Mallett, Bruce Yardley and "Rocket" Mann. It was a very wet pre-season and come the first game I was promoted to No.4. mainly because I was one of the few to have had any decent practice. Having just turned 18, I made 127 against Subiaco. The following match I made a first-ball duck. What a leveller.

We made the semi-finals and I scored 102 against South Perth after we were something like 6-51. It helped us into the first grade final against Nedlands. We led on the first innings only to be beaten outright.

Tony Mateljan, a Shield-standard left-hand opening bowler, was my first "A" grade captain at Mt Lawley. He was always saying how

I could play for Australia, if only I had more belief in myself. Others could see things in me that I couldn't.

It was a huge summer for the club and a big one for me. One of the old WACA yearbooks I've still got shows that year I scored 515 runs and took 35 wickets. Every young kid wants to belong and at last I did. I remember bowling John Rutherford with my fourth or fifth ball one day. That was a real coup.

Being invited to join Western Australia's Shield squad at the start of the summer, while still an 18-year-old, had given me a tremendous boost. But in essence, I was only a glorified net bowler. They used to ask if we wanted a bat only when it was getting dark. Still it was reward enough to be mixing with some of the "name" players in the State like WA captain Barry Shepherd, who later became our coach at Mt Lawley, Graham McKenzie, Keith "Spud" Slater, Des Hoare and the famed English left-arm spinner Tony Lock, in his first season in Perth. I was only 12 when "Lockie" and Jim Laker spun England to that famous victory at Manchester in 1956. I know one took 19 wickets and the other only one, but Lockie always insisted he bowled far better than his match figures of 1-106 indicated!

Hoare was a very aggressive fast bowler who'd happily bounce the opposition's tailenders, if he felt our tail had been bounced first. Des prolonged his career by dropping his pace and returning as a medium-pacer. One year I copped a reasonable barrage of short balls from the South Australian pair Neil Hawke and "Fritz" Freeman, playing in his very first game. I didn't get hit but it was unwritten law that a bloke batting eight, nine and downwards shouldn't face bouncers. David Sincock came into bat for South Australia and Des went back to his old action where he used to lift his front leg right up in the clouds and sprinted in, slamming bouncer after bouncer at him before finally striking Sincock behind the ear. He lost his balance and almost fell on his wicket. Des was really wound up and coming down the wicket to where Sincock had collapsed, roared in his big, husky voice, "Get up, so that I can knock you down again!". For a kid of 20, I can still remember like it was yesterday!

***

I WASN'T a particularly dominating spin bowler in my early club seasons but the selectors obviously saw something in me. In my era, leg-spinners were never considered to be first innings bowlers. We were meant to bowl sides out on the last day.

The West Australian squad in those days numbered almost 40 and when Ted Dexter's Englishmen arrived, they asked for every available leg-spinner to come and bowl to them. Richie Benaud, Australia's captain, was still considered a genuine menace even approaching his farewell Ashes series.

I knew the members of the English touring party only by name and reputation. Several like Freddie Trueman and Brian Statham had been star players in our backyard tests with Ray Tyers back home. Just bowling in the same set of nets as them was good enough for me. I landed a few and after bowling Dexter with a wrong-un was happy enough to take a rest when the Rev. David Sheppard, who opened the batting, said, "Bring thart laard bark".

I was helped that day by Rutherford who positioned himself behind the nets and told me what to bowl.

Hitting Dexter's stumps made all the papers, here and overseas. Apparently in London, I was referred to as a village storekeeper's son, who travelled huge distances each week to train and play. It was true, too. I'd just turned 18 and was living back in Corrigin with Dad. He had been crook and wanted me to give up cricket and take over the shop. He offered the local milk round as an inducement. Dad was a tough taskmaster and we were so busy that the only day he'd allow me to get away for practice were Wednesdays, as well as Saturday matchdays. Even then he insisted I didn't leave until it was as late as humanly possible to get to training or a game. And I could only go provided I return the same night. I had a green Morris 1100 which could really fly, but even with improving roads it still took me three hours each way.

My cricket was taking off. I was on the verge of being selected for the first time for Western Australia.

***

ASHLEY MALLETT and I were playing in a Sunday game with the Mt Lawley under 21's when my club-mate John McLean rang and said, "How are you, star?" and told me he'd just heard on the radio that I was in the state team to play the South Africans the following week. I couldn't believe my luck. I was only 19.

The South Africans hadn't been to Australia for more than 10 years and there was considerable interest in them, especially the Pollock brothers, Peter and Graeme. One was reputed to be the fastest bowler in the world, right up there with the West Indian Wes Hall; the other a batsman of extraordinary promise.

It was the biggest match of my life. Not only was I playing against a world-ranked Test team from overseas, I was suddenly playing with all these guys who had been my heroes as a kid growing up in Corrigin. I made 21, batting at No. 7 and remember flicking Trevor Goddard, the Springbok's captain, off my toes for a couple of 4s and then wishing I hadn't because he then brought Peter Pollock back! He was so fast. I'd never experienced anything like it before. The WACA was its typical self, fast and bouncy and I soon nicked one chest high straight to Graeme Pollock at first slip. I always say that Peter Pollock bowled the fastest ball I never saw!

In the second innings I was promoted to night watchman and made a duck, being bowled by a big in-swinger from Clive Halse, a reserve paceman behind Pollock and the team's No.1 swing bowler Joe Partridge.

One of the commentators said I should not have been sent in as nightwatchman in my first game. But it was an embarrassingly poor shot. We were trying to save outright defeat and here I was playing a backfoot cover drive before I'd even scored! I took a long time to come off the ground because I was crying at my failure. I had no idea of what a nightwatchman was supposed to do. I'm sure Barry Shepherd deliberately didn't tell me too much in case I became over-awed.

The pitch was like concrete and there was no way I could spin even one ball. Halse was my only wicket, which wasn't much of a wrap given that he seemed well suited to No.11! John Waite, their wicketkeeper and the only member of their side who'd been to Australia before, impressed me as a hard-nosed professional type. He made 93 not out, though we did drop him two or three times.

I re-injured my left knee during the game and it turned out that I had to have my knee drained of fluid three times. I was in the most excruciating pain. "Doc" Irvine, Jock's father, was the WACA doctor and he encouraged me to walk on soft sand to test the knee out. Unfortunately it flared up and with a fitness test scheduled for the next day, Mum and a girlfriend spent all night applying hot and cold flannels to reduce the swelling.

I was picked for my first tour to the eastern states subject to the fitness test. Thanks to the treatment I passed the test and off I went on my first interstate tour. It was a big thrill. In those days the team went away for a month and played all our "away" games in one hit. Our manager Bert Rigg made sure that John Inverarity and I, as the two youngest, had to be in bed by a certain time. If we were all out together, "Invers" and I would be sent home in a taxi at 10 pm. We roomed together for most of the tour, though I remember I also was with "Shep" for a time.

It was a tough tour and our bowling was thrashed everywhere we went. We were twice beaten outright and lost the other two games on the first innings. Even now it makes me wince looking at the old WACA yearbooks. On my Shield debut at the Sydney Cricket Ground, New South Wales made 1-425 and 1-262. Later Queensland made 3-548, Victoria 519 and South Australia 490.

Talk about being touched up! We were sitting in the rooms in Sydney and there was a fair bit of amusement because we'd made 420 and had thought we were some sort of chance at least for first innings points with a score like that, regardless of the strength of the NSW batting line-up. Yet they passed us with only one wicket down and in less than 80 overs! Hugh Bevan had just taken 6-for against South Africa and was on a high. Shep gave him the ball first and his opening delivery was hooked by Grahame Thomas onto the asphalt for six! From that moment onwards they just dominated us. It was the mother of all hidings. The wicket was a beauty, well-grassed and fast, nothing like the dustbowls of recent times. Hughie went for seven an over and I was even more expensive, my first-up figures being: 9-0-76-0!

Even a guy like "Spud" Slater was thrashed and he'd played for Australia. I tried to do my best, but I was so raw, especially when it came to bowling against these great players. "Tonka" Thomas made 127 and Bobby Simpson 247 not out. Together they added 308!

Bobby scored off virtually every ball and expertly farmed the strike, hitting a lot of twos. Either he'd dance at me or step back and cut me. It was an absolute education and further fuelled my feeling of inadequacy and lack of self-belief. "Simmo" had started the season with 359 and followed with 246 against the South Africans and was in awesome touch. The whole NSW side was so strong that Dougie Walters was 12th man. Only two of their team, spinner Terry Lee and wicketkeeper Doug Ford, weren't to play for Australia.

In the second innings, Brian Booth opened up with Norman O'Neill and they put on 127, adding to our humiliation. My nine overs cost 53. And I made only two and 13.

I walked in after Russell Waugh had been caught and bowled for 87, having helped resurrect our innings, with Shep, who made 149. We were four for not many until their stand and for three hours I was padded up, as nervous as I'd been leading into the South African match, especially given the big names we were opposing at the famous SCG.

As I walked in Richie Benaud said, "Hello Terry". Fancy that, I thought, he knows my name! And I haven't even played against him before! All I could see was this great man with the blue eyes and buttons undone to the chest. I was almost looking at him, rather than the ball for the first couple of deliveries. I played and missed at the first and somehow got bat on ball after that. The close-in fieldsmen virtually circled me and Normie O'Neill, at silly mid-on, yelled out, "Hey Rich. See the bottom hand?". It was a subtle sledge, anything to break my concentration.

Grahame Corling, who ended up touring England at the end of that season, got me in the first dig and I fell to Peter "Percy" Philpott in the second, having batted an hour and a half for 13.

We went to Brisbane where Peter Burge made 205 not out and Sam Trimble, 106, before he succumbed to a head-high full toss from me and holed out to our Welsh import, Alan Jones. At least we held the Queenslanders to a draw, but at the end of my first two Shield games, my batting average was 12 and my bowling average 246! And it wasn't to get too much better in Melbourne where the left-handers Bob Cowper and Ian Huntington made centuries and in Adelaide, where Les Favell made 140-odd.

Midway through the New South Wales match, Bill O'Reilly, one of the greats of all time, wrote that I was the most outstanding spin prospect in the country, but it didn't translate into my figures.

Coming into our final game on tour, in Adelaide, I'd taken only two wickets and with a South Australian line-up which included Gary Sobers at No. 4, we all wondered just what else could be in store. Sobers was the world's No.1 batsman. He thrilled Australian crowds in the early-'60s, both with the West Indies and then as SA's overseas player. He was a four-in-one cricketer, great batsman and fielder and a fast medium bowler also capable of bowling quality slow stuff.

Happily for us, Gary was out for single figures, but Favell thrashed us. So did a 20-year-old Ian Chappell who made 75, helping SA to almost 500.

I was bowling to Favell, who was on 99, and I threw one up, he danced and crashed it straight to Slater in the covers. "Spud" has huge hands yet somehow muffed this one. The next one, same ball, same shot except that Les hit it better, a little higher and just out of Spud's reach for his ton. I'd bowled Ken Cunningham for 57 around his legs with a wrong-un and in the finish Les ended up giving me his wicket. He must have reckoned I deserved it. He hit one straight up in the air and walked off. It was the only time all summer I got "2-for" and I was elated.

Making up for his failure with the bat, Sobers took six wickets, sharing the new ball with Neil Hawke and Gordon Brooks. We were beaten by an innings.

We certainly chased leather on that tour. Ian Gallash, who bowled mediums, was our leading wicket-taker with 8 wickets at around 50 apiece. I took 4 but they cost almost 100 each!

For the whole season, I took 7 for 600 at an average approaching 90 runs per wicket. I'd made some runs and also taken a couple of good catches, including a sharp one at slip from Trimble which gave Jones his very first wicket in Australia.

But the catch was only a consolation as I was in the side primarily for my bowling. My confidence needed a lot of rebuilding and there was only one way to do it, via club cricket and even then I was still bowler No.5 and not getting the opportunities I craved. They were difficult times, but I loved cricket and would play anytime, anywhere.

That season I trained or played six and sometimes seven days a week. Monday night was fielding practice, Tuesday and Thursday club, Wednesday state, Friday colts and Saturdays and some Sundays games. For a period, too, Ashley "Rowdy" Mallett and I also had dawn batting sessions on Wednesday and Friday mornings at Shearn Park. There was no financial reward back then. It was all about improving and giving ourselves every possible chance.

At the time I was working for Harris, Scarfe & Sandover in the sports department and someone from the Miling cricket club, about 130 miles from Perth, came in looking for a coach. Their first choice was wicketkeeper Bruce Buggins, who'd only just left State ranks. Bruce wasn't interested and spoke with me. Miling played mainly Sundays and were prepared to pay 15 pounds a week, which was pretty good considering I was getting only 11 pounds working Monday to Friday!

I co-opted "Rowdy", paying him a fiver less petrol. First impressions were lasting. The grass was long and unkempt and growing over and around the concrete wicket.

We soon found that no-one could keep wickets to us, so we worked out when I bowled, he'd keep and when he bowled, I'd keep. There were three brothers, Les, Des and Ray White, and Rowdy and I joked that they would be a good hat-trick to get. Sure enough, the following week, they all fell in consecutive balls! I was batting at the other end and tried to encourage them but one by one they were bowled. You couldn't help but laugh.

We played only five or six games. I made a couple of centuries including 198, my highest-ever score and also took 7-18 in one game and we qualified through to the semi-finals, which were scheduled for a Saturday-Sunday.

Our pennant cricket commitments at Mt Lawley took priority and we left instructions to try and bat first, get as many as we could with nine blokes and we'd come down Sunday and bowl them out. We won the toss only to be dismissed for less than 100. By stumps the opposition were in front and only a few wickets were down. On the Sunday, Rowdy and I took the rest of the wickets, opened up and hit the opposition all over the park. We put them back in again and bowled them out a second time, lifting us into the final. In their second innings, I took three stumpings off Rowdy.

We were playing Moora on a turf wicket and again it was an all-weekend game. It rained on the Saturday which suited us, but a little umpire wanting to make a name for himself gave both Rowdy and I out lbw to a bloke bowling left-arm swingers with a two-piece ball from around the wicket. We were beaten and that was the end of us. The club ran sheep and chook raffles to raise the 15 quid and would pay me immediately after we came off the ground. We'd have a few beers afterwards and then go home. It was good fun, just like being back in Corrigin.

Rowdy and I were virtually inseparable in those days. We even had a late night cleaning job which was going fine until the heavy industrial polisher I was using developed wings and rammed out of control straight through a plate glass door!

Another time we were walking down Hay Street after being at a night club when we saw a guy trying to wrestle a girl into a car.

"Leave her alone," I said. "If the girl doesn't want to go, let her go".

"Mind your own &%#@ business," he said.

Next minute he had tackled me from behind. I never threw a punch but next thing I knew the police had arrived and I ended up being taken to the new Perth lock up, overlooking the WACA Ground.

Ashley came down to bail me out but had only his cheque book with him, which they refused. There was no such thing as ATM machines then. But luckily I had my pay packet in my pocket so I gave them permission to take $10 out for my bail. Nothing too much came of it, or that's what I thought at the time...

T.J. testimonials

JOHN RUTHERFORD
(Western Australia's first Test cricketer)

1963 was a very good year. Among the young men in Western Australia's Under 21 squad were eight who went on to represent Australia: John Inverarity, Ross Edwards, Jock Irvine, Jim Hubble, Bob Massie, Ashley Mallett, a very young Rodney Marsh and a kid from Corrigin, Terry Jenner.

Terry was only a lad, bright-eyed and full of life and boy, could he bowl wrist spin! He ripped a big leg break, his wrong-un turned and his toppie rushed off the wicket. He really put a lot of work on the ball, making it drop and constantly stranding batsmen who had been preparing to drive what they had initially thought to be a half volley only to be beaten in flight.

Terry was also a very attentive listener and along with his mate, Ashley Mallett, would lap up everything I had to say about cricket.

When they came to me, they were both playing at second X1 standard, getting four or five overs per game and batting no higher than No.7 and No.8. Ken Meuleman, also was a mentor for the best young cricketers, and we approached the Mt Lawley selection chairman and asked why he was playing two potential Test cricketers with his second-best side.

"Who are they?" he asked.

When we told him that the two cricketers in question were Terry Jenner and Ashley Mallett, he laughed and told us we had our wires crossed.

I insisted that their talent was special and should be nurtured and suggested that if Mt Lawley didn't want to give them a go, I'd find a club which would. To their credit, Mt Lawley did lift both of them into their No.1 side and in the remaining four or five games, both were very successful, Terry taking 12 or 13 wickets and making a 50.

And in the first game next season he came out in the first match, batted at No.3 and made a century.

In those days the wickets in Perth didn't very often suit the spinners and as I pointed out to both Terry and Ashley, it would help if they could bat as high as possible and score runs consistently.

In those days with the Under 21s, we'd practise directly opposite the State squad boys, which was a big boon. I remember Ashley watching Keith Slater, the Shield team's off-spinner and asking him how he got to drift his off-break away from the right-handers. "Spud" explained, worked with him for a few minutes and away Ashley went with a new bow to his armory.

We arranged country trips for the boys and on one occasion the second car-load took the wrong turn out of Northam and finished up in York, instead of in Cunderdin, where our match was being played. It was almost an hour before they finally made it back to where they should have been. I still blame Terry for that! Another time we'd arranged a 5 a.m. rendezvous at Hungry Jacks on the way up to another game. I was heading out the door at about 4.50 a.m. when there was a phone call. Terry had slept in and would be late.

Eventually both Ashley and Terry went to South Australia where the wickets were more helpful for their style of bowling and they immediately benefited from their inter-action with Les Favell and others.

I always followed their careers with the greatest of interest and I know both gave their utmost every time they went out onto the field. I'm proud to have been a mentor for them both. There are so many talented young cricketers around but only the very elite make it through and for both Ashley and Terry to be among the 380-odd cricketers to play for their country, they have good reason to be very proud.

KEN MEULEMAN
(Former one-Test Australian batsman)

Having played against Terry in his earliest days with Mt Lawley, I considered he had the potential to play Test cricket and so it proved. He was very attacking, possessed two wrong-'uns, his leggie bit and he also could bowl the top spinner.

He was the only leg-spinner who I had genuine trouble in "picking". In one club game I made a century but Terry left me stranded on at least three occasions, only to catch the wicketkeeper going the wrong way as well! Ashley Mallett played in the same game but presented no prob-lems.

Both lads went to South Australia and I followed their careers with great interest. Whether it was by Terry's own choosing or from advice from others, Terry changed somewhat, emulating the Richie Benaud style, becoming more economic, by following a middle and leg stump line.

I never thought he was quite as attacking as he could have been. He would possibly have been more expensive on docile wickets, but on anything that offered the slightest help he would have been sensational. I genuinely believed he had the ability to be a cross between Benaud with his ability to think a batsman out and the little Indian wizard Subash Gupte, who could mesmerise batsmen, especially those loath to use their feet.

It wasn't to be but Terry still played for Australia at a time when the team was the very best in the world and I have no hesitation in rating Terry among Australia's best four or five leg-spinners since the War. He could have played more Tests as a genuine allrounder, too, given his undoubted batting ability which often showed with South Australia.

Terry was always a decent person and once you were a friend, you were a friend for life.

His personality reminds me of the great Keith Miller. Those who really don't know them could be critical but those who really know them won't hear anything adverse said against them.

I can honestly say in all my cricket career I never disliked one person. Maybe at times I haven't liked what some cricketers have done but only a handful of players past or present I have a special feeling for. Terry Jenner is one of those.

Young Bowlers In State Squad

By HARTLEY JOYNT

Terry Jenner, a right-hand leg spinner for Mt. Lawley, and Bob Andrew (Nedlands), a left-hand medium-pace bowler, have been included in a State cricket squad for the first time.

Jenner and Andrew are among 28 players selected to prepare for the 1962-63 Sheffield Shield season under the supervision of coach Barry Shepherd.

The 17-year-old Jenner and Tony Mann (Midland-Guildford), who has lish cricket, has rejoined the squad, which is:

G. Addison (Bassendean-Bayswater), R. Andrew (Nedlands), G. Becker (West Perth), H. Bevan (North Perth), H. Bovell (Fremantle), R. Bowe (Fremantle), I. Brayshaw (Claremont-Cottesloe), B. Buggins (South Perth), D. Chadwick (Nedlands), K. Ferries (West Perth), G. Forsaith (University), I. Gallash (Nedlands), K. Gartrell (Midland-Guildford), C. Harburn (Fremantle),

CHAPTER FOUR

A Tangled Web

*I was trying so hard I lost my leg break and
my sense of humour.*

When I first came into Western Australia's side, I was told to listen and learn. If I had a role, it was purely to light the cigarettes and pour the drinks. We were an emerging side with some great characters, capped off by the arrival of Tony Lock, whose presence was seen as being an enormous boost for spin bowling stocks in Perth. "Lockie" could spin a yarn and was very entertaining, but had little to do with teaching a young spinner how he could better himself. And coming from England where leg-spin had for years been unfashionable, he had little idea about wrist spinners and how they should go about it. What's more, he was so protective of his own place, he showed little enthusiasm for but the most basic teaching.

Lockie never gave Ashley Mallett an inch and when I was asked by the administration if I had been getting any help, I gave the honest reply: "no". Lockie was called in and chastised, but nothing changed too much. He ended up having four years as State captain and didn't finish with the team until 1971, well past his 40th birthday. As good a bowler as he was, few other spinners, other than Tony Mann, were to get a look in.

My second year with Western Australia followed a similar theme to the first, except that I didn't play as often. But in the South Australian game in Perth I did have Neil Dansie stumped and two balls later, Neil Hawke was caught at mid-on during my very first over. I'd never done that before, not for WA anyway.

In the same game the following year, we had a new-look opening attack led by Jim Hubble, playing only his third or fourth game and

Bob "Ferg" Massie, his first. We got away to a reasonable start, with the dismissal of Lyn Marks before Ian Chappell joined Les Favell and immediately took to Jim, Bob and Des Hoare, who followed. They thumped us to all parts of the ground, Les with his magnificent hooks and square cuts and Ian, his majestic and graceful back cuts. I was fielding at third man and in one particular over, I reckoned I just about chased every ball. Some I got to, some I didn't.

At the end of the over I was walking toward mid-on, still catching my breath when Barry Shepherd clapped his hands and motioned in my direction. I looked behind me automatically thinking "Lockie" was around. Whenever "Shep" needed to apply the brakes, Lockie was invariably the man.

"No Ringo," said Shep, "you".

I thought, "Strewth, I'm on!".

I broke out into a huge smile. I just couldn't believe I was getting such an early chance.

"Okay pal," he said, "we'll set an orthodox field. Just relax and be yourself."

Favell was on strike. I flicked the ball from hand to hand and came in, having decided to bowl a leg break. My fingers were tense but I thought the release was good. It had spin and curve. And to this day I wonder how much it would have spun because when it reached Les he was already yards down the wicket, meeting the ball at shoulder height and next minute it was disappearing over mid wicket for four!

I looked back and saw that Shep had dropped his head a little.

Knowing that the leggie hadn't landed, I thought I'd go with the wrong-un. In Adelaide, I'd bowled the last over before lunch and got Ian to play and miss. I thought if he can't pick them, what chance has Favell? After all, he was 36 and had been out of the Test side for years. Released correctly, the wrong-un will curve away before spinning back, hopefully through the "gate". Out of the hand, it felt good. It was doing all the right things, thanks to the Fremantle Doctor, except as I let it go, Les was already advancing and as he hit the ball over mid wicket for four, said "Happy Birthday!".

Eight off two. Suddenly I'm not feeling too good. One of the few blokes in the outer yelled, "Bring him on both ends."

I suddenly remembered what Richie Benaud had said to me in the nets in Perth earlier in the year. I needed to develop something which would skid. He suggested I try a slider, or back-spinner which, if used sparingly, would have an element of surprise and enable me to build the pressure on a batsman. He said it took him a few years to master it and longer to even bowl it in a game. I didn't want to wait that long. I was going for it now. My leg break and wrong-un hadn't landed. Maybe this would.

I bowled it to Les. Again it was released pretty well, but again Les had advanced. Again he said "Happy Birthday". And again it raced to the pickets! 12 off three.

Shep trotted down to me from slip. "Ringo, we're in the shit here. I think we should defend a little."

He put John Inverarity on deep mid-off and told the mid-on to go back. The others also spread out.

I went back to my leg break and this time it landed, but only just. Les had again used his feet, meeting it on the half volley and crunched it to deep mid-off, hitting "Invers" on the chest with such force that it rebounded almost back to me at the wicket. The non-striker, Ian Chappell, said, "Come on, Les. There's got to be one in that".

"No way, son. You don't think you're getting up this end do you!"

I don't know what my figures were for that first over, but I bet Shep does!

Maybe I should have taken a leaf from the book of Peter Philpott, the New South Wales leggie. Often against us he'd start with three off-breaks and a wrong-un, all in the name of getting himself into a rhythm for a long spell. I didn't necessarily subscribe to that, but it seemed to work for him.

Overall I went for 53 from five. I did make 69, however, and at an important time when we were 5-48 chasing 400-plus. I got some runs in the second dig, too. "Invers" got a big one, Ferg stonewalled at the end and we avoided an outright defeat which had seemed inevitable after the first couple of days. That year we actually finished just four points short of the Shield.

Despite playing every game, I still didn't feel that I truly belonged. In those early days, a new ball was available every 200 runs. It didn't leave much scope for the slowies, especially in Perth, the fastest wicket in the country.

All in all, though, it was a reasonable season, especially at club level.

I made a century against Nedlands after Ken Meuleman declared and set us a target. We passed them one down, in the final over. I batted at No.3 and shared a good stand with another young guy, John McLean. We got to the last over needing four to win. John was on strike and I was at the non-striker's end, having made 97. We agreed that John would try and get a single to give me the bowling so I could get back on strike and try and reach my 100. The bowler, Bob Oliver was a very tough competitor, renowned for his habit of "Mankading" anyone who dared back up too far. In my enthusiasm to get down the other end, I forgot about Bob and had already taken off when I realised the ball has not been bowled. Looking back, there he was, with the ball next to the stumps, ready to run me out. "Let that be a lesson," he said.

We got the single we needed next ball and I proceeded to lift Bob back over his head for a six which not only won the game for us, but helped me to 103 not out. Even as the ball was sailing way off in the distance, I'm told I had already tucked my bat under my arm and taken my gloves off. It was the perfect reply.

We had a huge night, but I still had to be back in Corrigin first thing Monday for the milk run.

Coming home that Sunday night, I went to sleep at the wheel and rolled my car. It was lucky for me that the passenger I'd brought down to Perth wasn't with me on the way home. The entire passenger side of the car caved in.

Dad was unimpressed. I don't think he even asked me if I was all right. He said I couldn't continue to play cricket and run the shop. I had to make up my mind. Either I was to stay fulltime in Corrigin, or go back to Mum. I went back to Mum and attacked my cricket with even more purpose.

***

IN 1965-66 in the opening game of the year against the MCC, I took six wickets, including Bob Barber twice, Mike Smith, John Edrich and Colin Cowdrey. Whilst I could rarely repeat this form at Shield level and hadn't done all that much, I felt in time I just might make it.

I still have a cutting where *The Times* cricket correspondent, John Woodcock, wrote:

> *"English cricketers tend to scorn the leg break and anything that may help bring it back into vogue is good for the game. Jenner comes from the bush, bringing with him a lively action, a fair degree of spin and a passable bosie' as the googly is called out here."*

Woodcock said I was a future Australian player and even forgave me for not walking after being neatly taken at slip by Colin Cowdrey off David Allen's "arm" ball.

> *"Nobody is bleating. That was just a small blemish on a good match. It is a pity that more people have not appreciated it. When we arrived we were told our task was to revive cricket in Australia. On today's figures – 900 people paying 128 pounds – we may be too late. It could be a job for the undertakers."*

***

EVER SINCE first playing "A" grade, I regarded my meetings with Ken Meuleman as a real measuring stick on how I was going. Meuleman may have been in his early forties but he was still one of the most consistent club players around and still so nimble on his feet. I'd enjoy our confrontations and would back myself against him.

Invariably, however, he'd still make runs. I'm sure he, too, was motivated by the challenge.

Mt Lawley's wicketkeeper Paul Ronan was a genius who'd squeeze in-between the stumps and the back net at practice and take the fast and slow bowling confidently, even if, at times, in a somewhat unorthodox fashion.

In this game at Inglewood Oval, I was bowling to Meuleman and beat him once outside his off-stump. Encouraged by this I gave Paul my signal for the wrong-un and Meuleman flicked it away as if he'd been tipped off. I waited an over, repeated my signal, this time making sure that Meuleman was watching. Deliberately I didn't alert Paul that I intended to bowl an orthodox leg break.

The leggie pitched perfectly and to my exasperation beat both Meuleman and Paul. "Meulie" had danced, expecting the wrong-un, only for it to initially hold its line, curve and spin away. Paul had gone down the leg-side and missed it altogether! I reckon I could have had Meuleman three or four times that day, but just couldn't cap it off. Paul missed Meulie another four times that day. On reflection, I wished I'd signalled him correctly. Finally, after around 20 overs, I had four wickets to my name but reckoned I needed a 5-for to help me back into the State team. Frank O'Driscoll, our captain, came up and said, "That's enough, Terry. Have a spell".

Frank had always encouraged both Rowdy and myself, along with other young cricketers. He was the man responsible for our dawn practices on Wednesdays and Fridays. He knew how keen I was. I felt he should have known how much I wanted another wicket. I saw red.

"Bullshit," I said. "You're not taking me off now. You owe this to me."

"No," said O'Driscoll. "I'm going to bring Jack Richards on. And if you don't like it, you can piss off!" So I did. I walked off the ground and sat on the hill!

Call it a temper tantrum, call it stupid, but it happened and having done that, I couldn't go back. As was his habit, Richards came in with his left-arm stuff, cleaned up the tail and we won the match. I was cited for my behaviour and had to go down to the WACA to front the selectors and State captain Barry Shepherd. I was severely chastised. I didn't need to be reminded it was very poor conduct. I contacted Frank and apologised and was sincere when I said I was wrong to have walked off.

We finished second last and it seemed to me we weren't going anywhere. In the off season I decided to lobby for the captaincy. I was only 21 but felt we needed a more dynamic leadership style. The extra responsibility would also do me good.

I approached Richards first, saying that if Mt Lawley don't make changes, we could only go backwards. He agreed. "What's more," I said to him, "if I make the State team, someone has to captain the side in my absence. Would you be my vice captain?"

Trevor Bidstrup, who'd represented Western Australia a couple of times, was on the other side of the camp. I never knew whether he had enough votes or not – in those days the players elected the captain. Both Trevor and myself were nominated, but Trevor preferred not to stand. He didn't wanting to fuel any further divisions. He'd been a very loyal member of the club, but my ticket was with Richards and when I won, so did he.

Frank O'Driscoll then had to earn his place in the side which he did. Rowdy and I ceased to become bowlers number 5 and 6. We were first and second change and we had a big year, taking more than 70 wickets between us.

As a team we also had terrific spirit. I was away for three or four games and Jack led us to close wins each and every time and we qualified through to the semi-finals at the WACA. We played Fremantle and knocked them over for 96, only to stumble, having four blokes, me included, caught out on the boundary playing cut shots off Des Hoare. It got to the point where we were nine down with one to tie and two to win. For some inexplicable reason Jack Richards tried to hit his first ball into the vacant mid-wicket region. It went straight up in the air and he was caught. We'd lost by a run. Jack broke down and cried.

We'd been a headlining club all season and not just for our good cricket. On one occasion we were playing West Perth at the WACA and one of their leading players, Derek Woodhead was proving very hard to dislodge. I was fielding at silly mid-off to Bidstrup and crept in closer and closer before going down on my haunches. As Trevor was coming in, I lost my balance and toppled over and called back to Bidstrup, "Don't worry Trevor. He can't hurt me here. He hasn't got any shots". Woodhead got out the very next ball and I was heckled by the West Perth supporters for breaking his concentration.

I had my first real run-in with the umpires, too, when I accidentally walked out after an interval onto the WACA with a still-lit cigarette in my grasp. One of the umpires Warren Carter made a real issue of it. It seemed if there was a storm or two, I'd invariably be involved. I didn't deliberately go out of my way to incite trouble. But I was so competitive and passionate about winning, that it sometimes over-shadowed everything else.

***

AFTER MY initial season in which I played eight games and was 12th man in the last two matches of the summer, I found myself on the slippery dip. I was picked only three times in 1964-65, played every game in 1965-66 but only four in 1966-67. Ashley Mallett did it even harder. At least I'd had 25 games over four seasons. He played just twice – and both times as 12th man, his duties revolving mainly around making Tony Lock his pots of tea!

I was back to Saturday afternoons in the park with Mt Lawley. Nothing seemed to be going right. We rarely won and I was often denied the wickets I reckoned I deserved and so desperately needed. Midway through the hard times, I was trying so hard I lost my leg break and my sense of humour.

Reading articles like one from the vitriolic Jack Lee in the *West Australian* who claimed I was finished at 21, tangled in a web of my own making because of my insistence in bowling so many different deliveries, didn't make me feel any better.

Spin bowlers are like everyone else. They have fragile personalities. I always talk of them having a G-I-F-T and I invariably highlight the "f", as in fragile. Sometimes the gift leaves you and you don't know why. It can happen even in mid-spell. Suddenly you're off and haven't any idea what went wrong.

Keith Slater approached me one day during a game. "I want you to come over to the nets for a minute and bowl me a leggie," he said.

I bowled a leggie. It went straight. I bowled another. Again it went straight.

"Come on," said "Spud". "Put something on it."

I bowled one with so much pep it bounced through head high. But again it was dead straight. I was bowling all top spinners. My leg break had deserted me.

There was no leg-spin coach to consult, especially in Perth. And there were no videos to watch. I looked around at those bowling leg-spin in Australian cricket and "Percy" Philpott was the one who most embodied what I thought I needed. Though he was a smaller man than me and round-armish, he really gave it a tweak. Up until then I'd tried to model myself almost entirely on Richie Benaud. For a whole summer I bowled nothing but leg breaks and deliberately modelled my action on Philpott to encourage more side spin. And what I never let happen again after that was to continue to bowl a period of wrong-uns in succession without also using the leg break.

Our 'keeper at Mt Lawley, Paul Ronan was rapt. He took 13 or 14 stumpings.

***

BARRY SHEPHERD was hugely influential on Western Australia's emergence as a genuine cricketing power. No-one was more parochial towards WA cricket, or possessed more cricketing foresight. He saw the big picture and felt we could win the respect of the eastern states and nurture more Test cricketers by working harder and encouraging risk-takers. Maybe that was why I was given a chance, even when I was only learning the caper.

In the first three years of Shep's captaincy, from late 1961, 17 players new to WA cricket were blooded. Among them, in my first season, were Derek Chadwick, Gordon Becker, Tony Mann and the two overseas imports Alan Jones and Peter Loader.

Shep saw our WACA wicket, the fastest in the country, as a huge natural advantage and started the selection policy which remains today of fast bowling specialists operating down breeze and genuine swing bowlers coming up into "the Fremantle Doctor".

Had Shep been born in Sydney or Melbourne rather than in far away Perth, I have no doubt he would have played more Test cricket. He was a champion batsman and quite brilliant in the gully, especially for a big man.

Many of his ideas were years ahead of their time. He involved us in pre-season training camps long before the football clubs caught on. He was a man on a mission. He reckoned we did not consistently bat and bowl well enough to stay in games, so we had to make up for it by becoming the slickest fielding outfit in the country. Fielding-only nights were incorporated into our weekly programs and the WA sides were soon renowned for their work in the field, a reputation which remains today.

Shep told us to turn up Monday nights and bring old clothes as we were to practise diving. He'd forever be talking to us about the value of saving runs and how not only would they add up on the scoreboard, the efforts would lift the bowlers.

He could be ruthless and at times was scorned by some as he trod on a few toes. On retirement, after all his years of effort and dedication, all the West Australian Cricket Association gave him was an electric jug and some flowers for his wife Audrey.

Shep told me if I ever got the chance to improve myself, I shouldn't hesitate to move on. At the time, I thought it impossible to imagine putting on someone else's cap. But Shep felt moving to better oneself was okay, given his reward. I owed it to myself to go one better.

One of the facts which tipped the balance was Shep's retirement from Shield cricket, aged just 28, in 1966.

Murray Vernon took over and the side not only languished on the field, it wasn't particularly happy off it. Vernon was to last less than 12 months and in my view that was 12 months too long.

I walked into a room once and my name was the centrepiece of the discussion. Vernon said they had to humour me because I wasn't too bright. There was laughter, then he saw me and saw the look on my face. He knew I'd heard what had been said. I don't think I ever recovered from that.

At the close of our eastern states tour, having just played Victoria in Melbourne, I had to withdraw from the team playing South Australia with a thigh strain. Vernon wanted to send me home to Perth. However, I had an Adelaide girlfriend, a lovely girl called Jill, who was a schoolteacher I'd met in Perth whilst she was on holidays. I told Vernon I was staying. I didn't consider it just a coincidence that I failed to make even the 12 for the next two home matches against NSW and Queensland.

While I was in Adelaide, Len Sandford from the Prospect cricket club approached me and said a player of my talent should never be made 12th man, as had happened to me in Sydney just a fortnight previously. He said there were immediate opportunities in Adelaide for quality spinners. South Australia's No.1 spinner was Colin "Blackstick" Harrison, who bowled in a cap and had a low round-arm action, not unlike the legendary Clarrie Grimmett. At best, however, he was a reluctant leggie and known for his nervous disposition.

Rex Sellers had played only one match in three years after touring England in 1964 and David Sincock, the most prodigious spinner of a ball I've ever seen, had just left for Sydney.

We were watching Blackstick bowl and Len said, "surely you can see an opportunity here".

Legend has it that after Blackstick took a wicket one day against NSW, Norman O'Neill came in to bat. The next two balls were wides prompting Barry Jarman, the 'keeper to call out, "Come on Blackstick. Get em on line".

"Jar" knew Blackie well. They were teammates at Woodville.

Blackstick nodded, went back to his mark, took a deep breath and then bowled an even wider wide.

With that, Les Favell, the captain, walked up and said to him, "What's gone wrong?".

Blackie replied, "Every time I get back to my mark I turn around, look up and there's Norm O'Neill standing there. How are you bloody well supposed to bowl to him?".

On return from Adelaide, I spoke to Ashley about the Prospect offer and asked if he, too, would be interested. He said he was keen to go across and speak with Grimmett, who lived in Firle. There would be an opportunity, too, to meet the people from Prospect. We ended up going together. It was fascinating speaking with Clarrie. He was 75 and in total control. He advised me to toss them up, bowl with a deep mid-off and deep mid-on and let them have a go.

I wasn't selected for WA again until the very last game of the season, against South Australia. I bowled only 11 overs for the match. Tony Lock had 45 and Tony Mann 34. Even John Inverarity got a bowl before me.

Vernon wanted to protect his mate, the former New Zealand Test opener Bill Playle and sent both Ross Edwards and myself in as nightwatchmen on the first night. We added 39, the second best stand of the innings. Playle was better equipped to go in and combat the new ball more than we were. He ended up making a pair.

In the second innings, we were again together at stumps on Day 3, and this time put on almost 100. I got 45 and "Rosco" 52. We lost the game easily, but at least I went out with my head high.

We had an enormous time, especially on that month-long tour to the east. Rosco, a good mate, was our songster and composed a drinking ditty which would get a run most nights:

"Listen to the jingle, the rumble and the roar as yet
another schooner goes CRASHING to the floor.

"We're a team of individuals and glory is profound because we are local yokels hailing from the WACA Ground."

Each of us had a verse. Mine was:

"Now T.J. has a complement of drives and cuts and hooks, but if he plays them like he says, we'd read of it in books.

"He's constantly reminding us of his South Aussie flame, but if she is a nice girl, we're sure he's not to blame!"

If Vernon didn't rate me, I let him know that he wasn't high on my popularity stakes either. Ever since I'd heard his deprecating comment, I'd lifted a notch whenever we played his club, South Perth. One day at Richardson Park, I deceived him with the wrong-un and he top-edged a dolly of a catch to Frank O'Driscoll at slip. To this day it remains an embarrassment to Frank that he turfed it. What a disappointment for me!

Another time, I beat Vernon in a single wicket competition at University. Vernon batted first and I deliberately stood beside him and placed Ross Edwards in the short on-drive position. Incredibly Vernon holed out to Rosco for a duck! It took me an over and a half to push the single I needed to win, but I couldn't afford to lose

After that 1966-67 season, it was clear to me that I had to move on. I was 22 and in and out of the side. Vernon was captain and one of our leading batsmen.

Rowdy was also in a no-win situation. "Lockie" was impossible to shift as the No.1 spinner. He'd looked around the states. There was no standout finger spinner around, other than the Queensland veteran Tom Veivers, on the verge of retirement. If he could only secure a regular berth and win the confidence of his captain, he believed he had a genuine chance of making the 1968 touring team to England. It was fairly ironic. Rowdy was probably more likely of playing for Australia than he was his own State.

A season with Ayr in Scotland matured his bowling considerably. He returned a different player. He was quicker through the air, had more grunt and looked every bit a Shield and Test cricketer.

Initially Rowdy returned to Perth hoping to make the State squad. He was overlooked and immediately took the East-West Express and headed to Adelaide, Prospect-bound. I met him at the station. The spin twins were back together again knowing full well that had we stayed in WA, we were never going to make it.

CHAPTER FIVE

In the Right Place at the Right Time

*"I sat in Frank's room with tears running
down my face, still clutching the telegram I
hadn't dared look at."*

For once in my life, I felt I was in the right place at the right time. Adelaide was a land of opportunity, especially if you happened to be a spinner like Rowdy and me.

While Colin Harrison had just been a fill-in at Shield level, there were two emerging wrist spin brothers, Peter and Paul Curtin from Port Adelaide who were just beginning to show promise. Daryl Lambert, a slow left-armer, was also to be selected, but not until he was 30. Basically our arrival shut the door on the spinners in Adelaide. We gave no-one else a chance.

Prospect was a powerful, successful club, having won four "A" grade pennants in the '60s. Conditions were good, the players switched-on and the administration strong. There was a bubble of confidence. Everyone expected to win. It was a huge, uplifting experience.

Graeme Farrell was captain and the team included Bob Blewett, Bob Gilbourne, Jeff "Bomber" Hammond, Barrie Robran, Graham "Clacka" Clarke and many more experienced guys. Apart from the fact that he liked a beer and a bet like me, Clacka would get really red-faced and start to puff even after just an initial over or two. Early in our first game against University, I went to Farrell and said to him that I thought Clacka had had enough.

"No," he said, "he goes that way all day. That's just Clacka."

He also insisted on these funny field placements, including a bloke at deepish backward square in what I frankly thought was no-man's land. Next minute Clacka bounced Rick Drewer, a left-hander and he hit it straight to the bloke!

Clacka knew exactly what he was doing. Rowdy got 6-for, I bowled okay and we were well and truly alive in South Australia.

There was a real feeling of camaraderie among the blokes. Being so successful, they played like winners. And never before had I come across a team with so many blokes keen on the punt! Our opening batsman Kevin Jones doubled as a mid-week bagman for one of the well-known bookies. There was never a shortage of formguides. We were playing Salisbury in a two-dayer, dismissed them cheaply and then batted out the rest of the match. I was heading for a good score on the second day but felt certain that a declaration would be forthcoming. I looked towards the rooms enquiringly and Graeme signalled to me to continue. A wicket fell, and instead of Graeme joining me, Clacka came out.

"What's going on," I said.

"Oh, Luigi (Farrell) has got the second leg of the double coming up in Sydney. He doesn't want to miss it!"

I went on to make 104, my first century with Prospect. It was probably the only time the punt ever did me a favour!

***

LIFE CHANGED for me totally in Adelaide. Getting to know Les Favell, South Australia's veteran captain, was a privilege. He was something special, flamboyant, cocky and charismatic. He backed his men and always played to win. It wasn't a coincidence that Ian Chappell, one of the best Australian captains of them all, learnt the ropes under Les.

My first couple of overs for South Australia, in the opening game of the year against the Vics in Adelaide, were ordinary and I was smashed. Walking in, reluctantly, for my third over, I thought if the punishment continued, that'd be it for me. Les wandered over and said, "You're not playing for WA now, son. You're playing for me.

Give me something to build on. Relax a bit. You can bowl all through this session if you can bowl me a good over".

I did bowl better but didn't take a wicket. However, true to his word, Les let me continue for the rest of the session. Late in the day after the Vics had given us a bit of a pasting, Les took Neil Hawke off just so I could bowl at their No.11 Alan Connolly.

"You should be able to get this bloke," he said. "You deserve a wicket. I'm going to get you one."

Connolly chanced his arm and smashed a couple before holing out to "Hawkey". It was my first wicket for South Australia and while it was the opposition's No.11, it meant the world to me.

From day one, I was very aware that I'd always get the chance for SA if I could produce. If I happened to bowl a few bad ones, Les would come and have a chat and settle me down. "Just bowl me some good overs," he'd say. "Go for three or four an over. Don't try and do too much. Toss 'em up."

My reward was immediate and Les often allowed me to bowl right through a session. Always he'd be at mid-off or mid-on encouraging me and urging me to back myself.

Les didn't treat us like boys. He gave us the chance to be men. We went with him on coaching clinics. He'd drive and the talk would always be cricket. It was priceless. We got to know each other so much better. He loved to attack and his effect on the players around him was infectious.

Not long after arriving in Adelaide, the entire South Australian Shield squad went to Millicent for the opening of a new oval. The Premier, Don Dunstan, attended and played the first ball bowled by Les. It took him quite a few attempts to actually hit it, but eventually he made contact. It was on that trip back to Adelaide where Barry Jarman, who was vice-captain, made it clear to everyone in the squad how united we needed to be and how we should stick together on and off the field. You had a choice after a game; either be a drinker or a punter. Gambling didn't mean much to me, then. Being a drinker meant going to the parties. And parties meant girls. That suited me down to the ground. We developed a terrific fraternity and to this day, "Jar" remains a dear friend.

During one of my early games in Adelaide, Brian Taber made a century for New South Wales. Twice he lifted me over cover for six and Les decided to go to Greg Chappell, who in those days bowled leg breaks. They didn't land an awful lot, but he could spin them prodigiously. I was fielding at cover and Les at cover point. "Tabsy" was 90 odd and Greg dropped one short and Tabsy crunched it straight at me, waist high. And I dropped it!

Les wore this cap which reminded me of a blue engine driver's hat. He tossed it onto the ground in his disappointment. "Geeezzusss," he exclaimed. I'd only been around for five minutes and didn't know where to hide. Several deliveries later, with Taber still short of his ton, Greg dropped another one half deck and you could see Tabsy thinking to himself to hit it a bit squarer. It bounced more than he expected and instead of it flying in my direction, it went to Les. Incredibly, he put it down. It was pretty surprising considering Les had played championship baseball and had a beautiful pair of hands. I could see the funny side of it and grabbed my blue cap, just like Les had done and was about to mimic the toss-to-the-ground when he said, "If that cap hits the ground, son, you'll never play for South Australia again!". I put it back on my head quickly and got on with the game.

We won five games in that 1967-68 season, the same as ultimate winners Western Australia. The following year we did it again and this time won the Shield. It was as much a triumph for Les as it was the players. We all loved him, me particularly. For me he was the encouraging father I never had.

Les started the practice of "Rowdy" and I bowling in long spells in tandem. With 30 wickets in his initial year of Shield cricket, having been 12th man in the first game, Rowdy did enough to make the 1968 tour of England. His sweetest moment came against Western Australia in Perth when he took eight wickets, including 6-for in their second dig. Tony Lock had boasted the very night before that he could play Rowdy until the cows came home. When an off-break ripped back to bowl him, Rowdy couldn't help but let Lockie know that the cows had arrived early! The following weekend we beat Queensland in Adelaide on a wet one. We batted first and collapsed immediately. I couldn't remember ever losing two wickets in the first over of a game, but we did, Ashley Woodcock and Ken Cunningham both falling to Peter Allan. Les turned to me and said, "Pad up. I want you to do a Fritzy," which was his way of saying I should wave my bat and hopefully play some shots like Eric "Fritz" Freeman, who loved to hit the ball hard and often.

I got 24 which wasn't bad considering the next best score was John Causby's 7! Les declared our first innings closed at 7-40, but somehow we got up to win. It was one of the greatest moments of Les' career and he celebrated by skulling a full bottle of beer, an amazing feat considering he rarely drank. Our lowpoint came against New South Wales in Sydney when we were bowled out for 95 and lost easily. On the first day we must have dropped at least a dozen catches, including Geoff Davies, who made 76, six times! We all rotated in the slips and one by one the catches went down. Les was so upset he marched into third slip, dropped two in three balls from Alan Frost's bowling and trudged, redfaced, back into the covers muttering! I went in there and the very first ball, from John Benaud, was edged straight to me. It hit me on the chest long before my hands had got into position. Down it went. And off I went – to third man!

I took 17 wickets for the year, including two 5-fors in consecutive innings against New South Wales and the touring New Zealanders, which earnt me an extra $30 in Harris Scarfe vouchers from the SACA. The game against the Kiwis was remarkable for an astonishing hitting blitz by the big NZ fast bowler Dick Motz, who on the final morning, made 82 in an hour, including 56 (of 62) from three Ian Chappell overs. He literally pummelled the bowling.

Funnily enough, even after doing so well in these games, I still wasn't 100 per cent sure that I would keep my place in the side for the following match. I was 12th man in Perth, which wasn't unexpected given that three pacemen should probably always play there. But it was good to get back home and even better when we knocked them over.

It was particularly disappointing to be made 12th in the final game against the Vics. Several of the cricket writers had included me in their likely touring teams to England. It gave me a huge lift. I knew if I could have a good last game I may have some chance. I was sure Rowdy was already in. Other than Lockie, who wasn't eligible anyway, he was the best finger spinner in the country.

Les called the blokes together in a group and asked, "Are we playing for first innings points or outright points here?".

Someone said first innings points, which bewildered me as we were then sitting second, just two points behind the Western Australians. Like us, they had one game to play. The Victorians were also a danger as they had 36 points, with two games left.

Les said, "Okay, first innings points it is. Does everyone agree with that?".

Most put up their hand. "Okay," he said to me. "Terry, you're 12th."

Les wanted to go with three pace bowlers, "Hawkey", "Fritz" and Frost. It was a bad break for me. Les won the toss, sent Victoria in and we were beaten outright. It was one of the few downers in what had been a terrific year.

We also lost the first grade final to Port Adelaide after Hawkey and Fritz, both selected for England, each took 5-for and we collapsed for 50-odd chasing less than 100 to win.

A second touring party, under Les' captaincy, was named for a short tour of New Zealand and I missed out on that, too, the chosen spinners being the Victorian "wrong-foot" bowler Bob Bitmead and the NSW pair Peter Philpott and John Gleeson.

Preparing for our final, having easily defeated Glenelg in the semi, I was bowling to Clacka Clarke in the nets and he stopped for a moment and said, "Do you know, T.J, that the ball is coming down all messy, instead of seam-up?".

I bowled again and the same thing happened. We talked about it and Clacka said as a medium pacer, unless he released the ball correctly and it regularly hit the seam, he was dead in the water.

I'd been told previously my grip was unorthodox. Remember I was self-taught. I tended to position the seam parallel to my fingers, instead of at right angles. As a result, I didn't always get a lot of "drop" but I felt comfortable.

After years of bowling one way, it was difficult to change and the first night I bowled little else but head high fullies. I was scared to overly experiment. Missing out in Melbourne had battered my confidence, especially after I'd been rated some sort of chance for the Ashes tour.

From that Shield game on, despite Les' reassurances and Ian Chappell's unequivocal support, I never saw myself as a permanent fixture. I'd refuse to take risks. I was too scared to even attempt a flipper. I'd be bowling in a net alongside the young University spinner Nafty Vander Hoek, who hadn't really done much but spun it a lot, and would deliberately find a reason to leave his net to bowl in another so I couldn't be compared to him. Even though he was a left-arm chinaman bowler, I saw him as competition.

***

FROM DAY one at the Adelaide Oval, I felt an affinity bowling there. I loved operating from the scoreboard end into the south-westerly breeze. However, Rowdy Mallett usually had first go from that end and more often than not I'd have to bowl with it.

The wicket was always regarded as a batsman's paradise but Rowdy and I learnt to bowl on it.

I loved watching the lefties march in and look longingly at the square boundary just 50 metres away. They were forever trying to clunk you over the top. Rather than bowl away from the short boundary and give them the width to swing, I worked on the theory you should always keep giving them a look at it. But if you pitched middle and leg to a leftie, you had to make sure it was the wrong-un and it had plenty on it so they would be hitting against genuine spin.

I found I had to adjust my bowling style and use far more top spin than side spin in Adelaide. The wickets were slower and you wouldn't get the same bounce as in Perth.

For the first 18 months there, I lived with Bob Gilbourne and his Mum, Lorna, who was a terrific cook, so much so that I went from 71 kg (11st. 2 lb) to 82 kg (13st)! Rowdy also stayed there, before going off with the Ashes touring squad to England. We didn't do as much pre-season work in Adelaide as in Perth. It seemed to be wetter and we started later.

Ahead was the tour by the West Indies, which included some of the game's big names like Gary Sobers, Rohan Kanhai, Wes Hall and Charlie Griffith.

Sobers, the West Indian captain, had started with a dazzling century against Western Australia in less than two hours. He was the player everyone wanted to see. I was still disappointed at being made 12th man in the last Shield game and therefore missing any chance for a tour and went into the West Indian game keen to prove it was a mistake.

Sobers didn't come in until No. 6 and there was great anticipation of what was to come. Having only made a dozen or so, he caressed a ball to cover, saw me but ran anyway. In a flash. I'd picked it up and shied at the stumps, scoring a direct hit. There was no third umpire in those days, but he wouldn't have been needed anyway. The great man was well short of his crease. Afterwards I even apologised to him, thinking the crowd had come to see him bat, not to watch me field!

He said, matter-of-factly, "You just did what you had to do".

Ian Chappell made a century, as did Kevin McCarthy, our fast bowler, batting at No.9.

The Windies were trying to save the game on Day three and I was bowling in tandem with Rowdy from the Torrens end. There was a nice south-westerly blowing and Sobers was on strike. He'd made only five or six and hadn't quite started to middle them. I troubled "Sobie" a couple of times and Les brought himself in from behind backward square to leg gully. I couldn't work that one out. I then bowled my orthodox leggie. Sobers went to drive, putting his foot to where he thought the ball was landing, but it curled away late and spun back between bat and pad and snipped the middle and off stumps. It was a pearler, not quite the ball of the century, but the best of my life! Col Egar, the umpire, looked incredulous. I couldn't stop grinning. You dream about deliveries like that. Sobers had been the greatest batsman in the world for years. Clean bowling a player of his calibre with a genuine good one was a fantastic fillip for my career. I felt all the years of toiling were at last paying off.

Bob Simpson was watching on and said with deliveries like that I was good enough to play for Australia. It was just a matter of becoming more consistent.

I also had Rohan Kanhai caught by Ian Chappell at slip in both innings with deliveries which bit and spun. "Joey" Carew, a left-hander, was eyeing the short square boundary but holed out to Greg Chappell. I took two wickets in their first dig and five in the second and we beat them by 10 wickets inside three days. It's always special knocking over a touring team, especially when it's the Windies. Big Wes Hall was resting but Griffith played and the top-order contained all their big guns except for Basil Butcher.

We also had a wonderful season at Shield level, and by taking the points against New South Wales, we won the Shield for the last time under Les' captaincy.

Between us, Rowdy and I again took more than 60 wickets. He had a 7-for and made the Test team for the first time in Australia. Barry Jarman also kept for much of the Test summer.

"Jar" was always at me to bowl higher and shorter. Wicketkeepers loved that. It meant more stumpings. Brian Booth was on strike the first time we played New South Wales at home. I bowled higher and shorter to him. He advanced, it spun across him and he was stranded only for Jar to fumble. Without delay he threw it straight back to me. I was standing, disbelieving, in the middle of the wicket. "Get on with it," he growled. The old pros...they don't let you put on a show.

For the first time I played the entire Shield season, my only stint as 12th man being when SA played the Windies the second time around.

***

SEASON 1969-70 was purely a domestic year with the Australian side away in Ceylon (Sri Lanka), India and South Africa. It was a marathon tour, which all-up went for seven months. The phone bills back home must have been enormous.

South Australia had a mediocre year, but guys like Greg Chappell really came on. He'd had two years playing county cricket in Somerset and was a class above almost everybody in Australia that summer. Lance "Sunshine" Gibbs, the West Indian off-spinner, also played with us that year, but not with a great deal of success. I took 34 wickets in eight matches. One of my mates kept game by game statistics and I was our most-used bowler, taking 17 first innings wickets and 17 in the second. I felt fitter than I ever had before and could bowl longer spells, maybe because of all the off-season basketball I'd played alongside a number of the SA team including Ian Chappell, Rowdy, Ashley Woodcock, Kevin McCarthy and Clacka Clarke.

My confidence was at an all-time high, but it still didn't guard against a thrashing or two. We played New South Wales in Sydney and Tony Steele, in only his fourth or fifth game, made a century between lunch and tea on the opening day on his way to 152. The ground was fast but he played absolutely flawlessly. If he wasn't driving you, he was caressing you past slip with a back cut. It was impossible to bowl to him. It was his second century in a week and lifted him into the Australian "B" team visiting New Zealand from late February. He was to disappear almost as quickly as he arrived, but I rate that innings right up there with the best five or six in my time.

A week later, John Maclean and a fastish bowler called Sandy Morgan got into us, bringing off quite a rescue mission, lifting Queensland to first innings points after they'd been 5-69 chasing 388. It was one hell of a fightback. At the end of my 30th over, my figures were 0-99. I'd never before conceded 100 runs without taking a wicket and the Gabba crowd was delighted. I was fielding close to the scoreboard and one bloke yelled out, "It won't be long now T.J.".

I was slowly coming up for my 31st over when Sam Trimble, bless him, came out the front of the old viewing area, clapped his hands and called everyone in. He'd declared! It's said that you're not a batsman until you get a pair and you're not a bowler until you get 0-100. At the time I was just glad to get off the ground. We'd fielded for the best part of two days!

Those setbacks didn't preclude me, however, being selected for New Zealand. After years of being on the fringes only to be passed over, I was one of the chosen spinners, along with Kerry O'Keeffe and the batting all-rounder from New South Wales, Geoff Davies, who also dabbled in leg-spin. The team was announced on the radio, in alphabetical order. As it came up towards the "J's" I held my breath: "DAVIES, INVERARITY, JENNER". I was in! Like everyone else, I looked upon my selection with the greatest of pride. I was playing for an Australian side, albeit the seconds.

Dennis Lillee was on that trip. So were Greg Chappell and John Inverarity, who were quality players, even then. "Invers" had already played Test cricket, as had Dave Renneberg and Graeme Watson.

I took three wickets in each innings at Eden Park and followed with 7-84 from almost 30 overs in a rain-ruined unofficial test on a real spinner's deck at Lancaster Park. Straight after lunch on the opening day, I bowled their master batsman Glenn Turner. I went wide on the crease, angling it in. He shouldered arms and lost his off-stump.

Dick Brittenden, the senior NZ cricket writer, wrote in *Wisden* that I'd been the bowler of the tour. In seven games, I took 32 wickets and on return, Frank Bryant, our team manager, said in one of the papers Mum kept that I'd been magnificent.

It was an eventful tour in more ways than one. I twice conceded 18 runs from an over. You tend to remember things like that. Bruce Taylor did it to me at Canterbury and Bruce Murray in the second of the unofficial tests at Christchurch. He went from 82 to 100 in the same over.

During the very first match of the tour, at Lancaster Park, a telegram had arrived for me at the ground and the delivery boy said, "Whoever this is for, it's not good news". Bryant intercepted it and took the liberty of opening it. The news wasn't good. Four years earlier, he'd been managing the Australian side to NZ when Bob Bitmead's father died. Bob immediately went home.

We were playing Canterbury and after the day's play were back at the motel bar having a drink when Frank asked if he could see me in his room.

Being me, I immediately thought I must have done something wrong.

"I'll be there in a minute."

"No right now."

"Okay."

I went to his room and he said, "Terry, I have known you for a long time".

Blimey, I thought. I *have* done something wrong.

Frank kept talking. "I know how much you have looked forward to this trip and it has taken you a while to be selected. But I have some news. Your Dad has passed away. I hope you don't mind but I took the liberty of opening the telegram because they told me it was bad news. I understand that you are going to have to re-gather yourself. There is some Swan Lager in my fridge. You're welcome to it. Just sit there and think it through. When you're ready, give me a yell and I will do whatever you need to put things in place. You may want to go home, whatever."

I sat there with the telegram in my hand. Immediately I thought of the shop in Corrigin. Then there was a flood of sad thoughts. I'd never had the chance to square the ledger with Dad. We'd never had a close relationship. In times like these, most people would say something like how their Dad would have wanted them to play on.

But it was different with mine. He'd never wanted me to play in the first place. The only thing I could do was talk to my mother and sister about it. But with the four hour time difference, it was still working hours in Australia. I sat in Frank's room with tears running down my face, still clutching the telegram I hadn't dared look at. Finally, after an hour, maybe two, I rang Perth and got my sister, Laraine.

I said, "Hi Sis. It's me".

"What are you doing ringing, money bags?" International phone-calls were a rarity in those days.

"I've rung about Dad."

"What about Dad?"

"Don't tell me you don't know?"

"Don't know what?"

"Dad is dead."

"But I was only talking to him yesterday."

"Well this has only happened today, Sis. I don't understand how you don't know."

"Are you sure?"

Suddenly the penny started to drop. A "Dad dead" telegram could only have come from my sister or mother.

"Just a minute. Didn't you send me a telegram?"

"No."

"Hang on a second," I said reaching for the telegram and finally reading it. I read it quickly. It said: "Dad passed away today, love Jo".

Jo was a girl that I was taking out at the time. It was her father who had died. I'd had two hours of sadness and anguish, needlessly. I wrote to Dad and told him what had happened. He sent back a letter, signed, "O Ghost who walks!".

It made me realise that no matter how many times I'd blued with Dad over the years over so many different things, we were family. Petty differences were inconsequential.

On with the tour I went and the more success I had, the more confident I became.

I don't think I'd started any season so full of enthusiasm as in 1970-71. I wanted to play for Australia, *the* Australia and not just the seconds. It was important for me to get early wickets. I'd spoken with Sir Donald Bradman after the NZ tour and talked frankly to him about my future. I was unsettled job-wise and one option was to put cricket aside and try and establish myself in business. Sir Donald gave me an excellent hearing. Without guaranteeing me selection, which, of course, he couldn't, he encouraged me to think that I could play against Ray Illingworth's Englishmen.

Luckily for me I seemed to have a knack of getting wickets against touring sides. After taking seven for the match and making 60 not out against Western Australia in our first game, I took four against the MCC on a batsman's paradise. I was particularly glad to dismiss Geoff Boycott, who was caught for not many in their second dig having made a big 100 in the first. There were some tall scores. As a team we made almost 650, including 224 from Barry Richards, the champion Springbok and still the best batsman I've ever seen. Just over a fortnight later in Perth, he was to make 325 in a day's play against McKenzie, Lillee, Mann and Lock. He treated them all with absolute disrespect. I have never seen a batsman so much in control of the bowlers. We made 500-plus in a day's play!

John Snow was England's pace gun that summer and he went for plenty in our match. I made 28 not out at the end and just before Ian Chappell closed, one short one from Snowy hit me on the gloves and dollied to Alan Knott the 'keeper, who didn't bother to even appeal. He just casually threw it to Colin Cowdrey at slip. Everyone was waiting for me to walk, but I stood my ground. You either are a walker or you're not. Cowdrey finally appealed but umpire Ron Joseph said, "not out".

A drink's break was taken almost immediately and Snowy, who'd disagreed with Joseph over earlier no-balls, was clearly unhappy. "Are there any more like you out here?" he said.

"If you don't appeal, you won't get any wickets," I replied.

"I'd love to get you on a grass-top," said Snow.

Next over, I took off for a run and he stood in front of me, glaring. I had to run around him to make my crease. I didn't think anything of it at the time, but as I was to soon find out, fast bowlers have long memories.

***

A FORTNIGHT later we were on the overnight train to Melbourne for the match against the Victorians and I said to Ian, in his first year as captain, "I think I know how to bowl to Ian Redpath".

"How?" said Ian.

"I won't encourage him. I'll deprive him," I said, and explained about how I'd force him back and back with my slider, rather than letting him run at me.

"If it works," he said, "I'll say you've come of age."

Ever since I'd learnt to control my back spinner, I'd been a different bowler. In the past players like Redpath, who could use their feet, could always get to me. "Redders" loved to dance straight at me and he'd hit me down the ground. But ever since developing my back-spinner, I'd been able to dictate and force even the quality players back onto their stumps. Then I'd gradually increase my length again and bring my leg-spinner or top-spinner back into play.

Redders had toured with Bill Lawry's team to India and South Africa and started the new season off in dominant style with a couple of 50s the previous weekend against the MCC.

He was in at first drop, after Bill Lawry pulled a thigh muscle and had to retire hurt. Jeff Hammond had only a few overs, followed by Greg Chappell with some of the mediums he had developed at Somerset. With Redpath in, Ian threw me the ball and said, "Here's your chance. What field would you like?"

I'd got the ball ahead of Rowdy which was unusual. I worked at depriving him just as we'd planned before throwing one up and he lifted it at 100 miles an hour straight to Greg Chappell at cover. I took eight for the match, including five of the Victorian top six and felt 10 feet tall. I'd been playing for seven years and finally gained enough knowledge to start implementing my own strategies. A key to it all was finally knowing how to defend myself and I tell kids now unless they can defend when necessary, they don't truly know how to bowl. As I was coming through, there were no academies or expert coaches to help. I was thrown in the deep end and despite the best intentions of guys like Barry Shepherd, I very nearly drowned. I was smashed and had nowhere to hide.

Without developing and learning to control my slider, I had no second answer when guys like Redpath or anyone else came at me. Basically, I was defenceless. No wonder Les Favell had said "Happy Birthday" that early afternoon in Perth!

Until that day at the Melbourne Cricket Ground, I didn't truly know what I was doing. While this was the beginning of my very best years as a wrist spinner, it was also the start of a bad habit. I was to become too dependent on the back spinner and turn to it too often, rather than bowling my leg break. At the time though, it was quite a breakthrough for me.

Ian Chappell was just as delighted as me. From Day One as captain, he'd always said his door was open and in my case, he never refused me a hearing. On the few occasions when things did go wrong he accepted the responsibility. Mainly, however, he did all the right things. He was always very loyal to me and everyone else who played under him.

Given that Ian had a lot more ability than I did, one of the facts that I cherish very much is the respect that he gave me regarding my knowledge of the game. He made it clear on many occasions that he thought I was the best thinking leg-spinner he'd played with. I didn't have the ability to always do exactly what I wanted to do with the ball, but I could quickly assess a batsman's strengths and weaknesses and how we could effect a dismissal. It's a strength which happily has remained with me as a coach.

T.J. testimonials

ASHLEY MALLETT
(Former Australian Test off-spinner)

T.J. and I go back 40 years. He turned up at Shearn Park in his Corrigin cap, faded brown. He was tallish and thin and the cap seemed too big, rather like the SACA "engine driver's" blue cap we both were destined to wear one day.

T.J. was a 'keeper who could bat. His leggies came steadily from about 1960.

He was too old for the Under 15s, so played in the thirds. I played Under 15s in the mornings and fourths in the afternoons.

Our paths were heading in the same direction, but it wasn't until we both became sort of fixtures in the "A" grade teams at Mt. Lawley in the early 1960s that we began to knock around together.

I didn't get my first car, an F.J. Holden, until I was 19. It cost $90. It ran on petrol and virtually nothing else, for unless my Dad gave it water or oil, the old F.J. starved. Before it finally collapsed with a cracked head, I chauffeured T.J. and his Mum to Scarborough beach one frightfully hot summer's night. We were only a few miles from the water when there was an almighty bang and three of us found ourselves floundering about on the back seat, the front bench seat having given away!

To finish the journey I had to maintain a position where I held onto the steering wheel lest I end up in the back seat again, where Terry and Queenie nervously sat.

Not long before we left WA, T.J. and I played for Miling, a little town miles up the track, north-east of Perth.

The area was famous for wheat and the town's cricket team well known for never in 50 years having reached the final four in a five-team competition. T.J. was appointed captain of the team and I accompanied him. We were both paid to play, although T.J. reckoned the bulk of my payment would be needed to help pay his petrol bill, a Morris 1100.

We got Miling into the four. In one match T.J. made 199 and I got 133 not out, my only century in any form of cricket.

T.J. had a brashness about him. He exuded confidence and always seemed to be one-up on whoever was about at the time. Initially, I envied that confidence, but gradually realised that there was more than a share of bluff. The outward show was something of a façade.

The need to be top dog was heriditary, on his Dad's side.

We were in Corrigin one weekend, the first time I met his Dad, Arthur. Confident, brash Arthur Jenner.

No weekend was complete without a game of darts at the local pub. So down we went. Arthur was pretty good, or so he said. During one unforgettable game, Arthur threw two successive triple 20. As every dart player worth his salt knows, you follow your dart, you don't lose momentum. Not Arthur! Wearing the biggest smirk of all time, he yelled out to the entire bar, "Come and watch a man score 180!"

The bar-flys came running. They knew their Arthur and hoped to see his smirk fade. When everyone was gathered around, Arthur threw and turned his back as the non-plussed crowd saw the dart go straight into the triple 20!

T.J. worked hard on networking and getting people on side. He was a lobbiest and networker long before such terms became commonplace. But he also had a need to be top dog. In the early days he was even more confident than he was later. Pressure of first-class cricket may have had a hand in it. But he never let a chance go begging. He was a great opportunist. Once at Shearn Park, Jim Hubble was bowling. A fairly quick left-hander, Hubble played against me years before at the WACA: I was 11. He was 15. He kept belting them back so hard, I once took refuge behind the umpire! This day, however, I was at the non-striker's end. Hubble was bowling quick and short, forcing T.J. further and further back, until he inadvertently trod on his stumps. A bail fell, T.J. grabbed it, looked at the square leg umpire, who was probably Warren Carter so he may have missed it, and calmly replaced it. In apologetic tone, he said, "Oh sorry, the wind" and kept on batting!

The umpires were so taken aback they let him continue!

T.J. had played State cricket and I was 12th man twice, but we both came to the realisation that Tony Lock was the spinner and all others would remain lesser lights while Tony remained.

We arranged to go to South Australia, which had no spinners at all. We needed money for the train trip across the Nullabor and got a job as cleaners. Our task was to clean all offices in a three-storey office block.

T.J. was top dog. He delegated me to security officer: the keeper of the keys. West Australian batsman Peter Kelly worked as an accountant at the venue, so vanity dictated that Kelly and all others leave before we start cleaning. Day 1 went well. Almost. The small offices and large drafting office needed sweeping and polishing. There were the downstairs toilets and large plate glass windows to clean.

It took hours to clean and upon leaving, the security officer (me) tossed the keys to T.J. as we entered the lift on third floor. He tossed them back, unfortunately straight between the gap in between the door and the lift straight to the bottom of the lift well!

Next night, we polished the drafting office, but used too much gear and the floor was sticky and slippery. We also found an improvised cricket bat and soft ball. Not all work for the draftsmen! I happened to be bowling and T.J. was batting when a bloke suddenly burst into the room and slipped on the floor, falling heavily on his back.

"Sticky wicket, old son!" we said in one voice.

Next day T.J. put the heavy polishing machine through the drafting office plate glass window. We got our dough. Insurances covered breakages!

Once in Adelaide, South Australian captain Les Favell gave us every opportunity. If we made early inroads, Les would give us the opportunity to bowl at the tail and get a "five-for".

We complemented each other in attack as our styles were different.

Never did we sit down and talk tactics about how to bowl to so and so, or when it was right to keep one player from getting a single off the last ball of an over to ensure I bowled to a leftie and T.J. to a right-hander. That sort of thing was ingrained. We instinctively knew the importance of building the pressure and what was required.

T.J. was a clever, very shrewd leggie. However, a lot of the time he bowled too many deliveries out the front of his hand. That strategy told me inwardly he was nowhere near as confident in his bowling than he showed. Too few balls he looped – and he could loop a ball.

T.J. has always taken himself seriously, sometimes too much so. Once in the nets, up-and-coming quick John Wheelock was bowling on green turf. Balls were whizzing around T.J.'s head and he asked Wheelock to ease up on the short stuff. The Shearn Park nets were situated about 100 yards from a railway line. Another ball whizzed past his nose. He called out, "Another one of those and I'll hit you down to the railway line."

Wheelock shrugged, threw his head back and laughed. The next ball was another bumper. T.J. ducked, picked up the ball at the back of the net and facing the railway line, he threw the ball up with his left hand and hit the ball down Central Avenue! There were laughs all around as the ball bounced down to the railway line.

Once in an "A" grade game, T.J. walked off the field and sat in the outer when captain Frank O'Driscoll made a bowling change. He talked himself out of that one. Damage control on a Sunday morning.

CHAPTER SIX

Australia's 248th Test Cricketer

*One of the selectors Neil Harvey once told
me he could play me with one hand tied
behind his back. He probably could, but I
wish he hadn't said it.*

We hoped to hear the Test team by the time we left Melbourne at 9 p.m. to return home. I was hopeful, even optimistic but the Overland left on its 12-hour journey to Adelaide before the announcement came. I went to sleep easily following a reasonable drink and was oblivious to the newspaper under the carriage door. Suddenly I was awakened. Eric Freeman was holding the Adelaide *Advertiser* in front of me. On the front page the headlines were: JENNER & GREG CHAPPELL NAMED FOR TEST DEBUTS. If it hadn't been so early, I would have called for drinks all around.

Picked for Australia! You can't have a prouder moment than that. I'd never taken 19 wickets in the opening three games of a season before and felt I was at my absolute peak. John Gleeson from New South Wales had also been chosen, but importantly so had seven batsmen. All four bowlers had to play.

Alan Barnes, the secretary of the Australian Board of Control, issued an official invitation. My match fee was to be $240. When I'd first come to Adelaide in 1967, we were getting $5 a day and $20 a match at Sheffield Shield level.

It was a big week of congratulations with lots of telegrams and phone calls. Tony Zimbulis would have been rapt. He'd been the first to spot my leg-spinners back in the nets at the WACA in 1959.

Come match week and I wasn't quite as relaxed. We all assembled in Brisbane and it was impossible not to be nervous. Apart from Greg and I, also into the squad for the first time were Rod Marsh from Western Australia and Alan "Froggie" Thomson from Victoria. The selectors hadn't taken kindly to the thrashings in South Africa. Greg had been brilliant the previous summer when everyone was away. It was clear he was going to be a great player. "Marshy" had kept wickets to me way back in 1960, during a zone match. He was very agile despite his chunky build and hit the ball as hard as anyone going around. Froggie had made a spectacular entry into first-class cricket with a heap of 5-fors. He had a peculiar windmill action and had good stamina from his wintertime weekend hobby of boundary umpiring. He picked up a 7-for against us which saw him selected ahead of Alan Connolly, "Fritz" Freeman and Laurie Mayne, all of whom had toured with the No.1 team for Tests in India and South Africa the previous summer.

Practice was incredible. I couldn't believe I was there amongst so many champions. Greg and I roomed together at the motel in Kangaroo Point, within walking distance of the ground and walk we did.

I can still remember my nervousness come match day. In almost 100 years of Test cricket, less than 250 players had represented Australia. I was Test player No. 248. It was an unforgettable moment. My hands were shaking as I tied up my boots. Luckily I remembered to put my socks on inside out, an old superstition.

Greg was named 12th man and he was very disappointed. He expected to play and it took a few days for him to settle.

Bill Lawry won the toss and we batted first. I wasn't sure what I would have preferred to have done, get out there and field or sit back a little and watch on. "Phanto" (Lawry) was out early before Keith Stackpole, Ian Chappell and Dougie Walters took control, helping us to more than 300 for the loss of just two wickets at stumps. A third umpire would have judged "Stacky" run out before he'd made 20, but Lou Rowan, at the bowler's end, said it was too hard to call and gave Stacky the benefit of the doubt. Boy, the English press jumped up and down about that one, especially when a side-on photograph of the incident clearly showed Stacky short of his crease. He went on to make a double century.

That first night I sat in the rooms wondering what everyone would do. Phanto was first out of the blocks, quickly followed by Paul Sheahan. The others hung around and had a drink and a chat. It was natural for me to go with the flow.

The next day we collapsed badly, our last seven wickets going down for just 15. I got a duck, caught by Colin Cowdrey at slip. As soon as I came in, John Snow went around the wicket and bowled consecutive bouncers before pitching one up, faster and wider and I did the rest, going for a big heave and nicking it straight to Colin. It was a shocking shot, a typical tailender's dismissal. "Snowy" loved a wicket at any time but he was particularly happy about this one. With Alan Ward's breakdown, he was clearly the fastest bowler in England's side. He seemed to thrive on the extra responsibility. He'd remembered my refusal to "walk" in the tour game. No one went around the wicket in those days unless it was to deliberately intimidate.

In his book, *Captain's Outrageous?* the flamboyant R.S. "Dick" Whitington wrote: "

> *"Snow joined the beanfest to bump a roaster past one of Terry Jenner's side whiskers and I hadn't seen the like of Jenner's "stroke" at the third ball he faced since I watched a few Australian batsmen in the Bodyline series."*

It was a very docile track and while I took a wicket in each innings – John Edrich and Geoff Boycott – I didn't feel I bowled particularly well. As we took the field, I was so jittery I was almost hoping that I wouldn't get to bowl. I couldn't seem to get my hands dry enough to grip the ball, even if it was thrown to me in the field. The sweat was running down my arms to my hands. Psychologically I thought I'd only be able to roll it, rather than rip it. I always found it humid at the

Gabba. Peter Philpott advised me later to use resin to keep my hands dry. Brisbane was the only Australian city I ever had this problem in.

The Gabba was never to be a favourite ground of mine. The crowd often seemed to be very indifferent toward me. One year there, I was booed just because I'd been picked ahead of their local hero, Malcolm Francke. You don't easily forget things like that.

As I was preparing to bowl my first ball, John Gleeson, the team's senior spinner, gave me some advice: "Take 'em one wicket at a time, mate". I appreciated his support. Unfortunately, Bill Lawry, our captain, didn't say anything.

My early line was not particularly good, yet I bowled three or four consecutive maidens and six overs for hardly anything. Geoff Boycott was a champion opener but he'd rarely hurt you. The figures flattered me because Boycott hardly had to play a ball.

I just wasn't comfortable with my field. At Sheffield Shield level, Ian Chappell would always give me the field I wanted. Normally it would be 5/4 – five on the off-side and four on the on. But Lawry was captain and he wanted 6/3 which meant I had to concentrate on and outside off stump. It made me more conscious of bowling on one side of the pitch, rather than attacking the stumps.

Alan Knott was nightwatchman and ended up making 70-odd. He used to love playing a lap shot. Ian suggested I should try and get him on the sweep. My plan was to bowl top-spinners in the sweep zone looking to induce the top edge.

I wanted Graham McKenzie at 45, but Lawry disagreed and put him at backward square. He wanted the man on the boundary. Sure enough, Knott went for the sweep, it caught the top edge and dollied high into the air. It would have landed down McKenzie's throat if I'd had my field. Unfortunately "Garth" was 25 metres away and despite sprinting for it, he could only get to it on the half volley. It would have been my first wicket in Test cricket and a huge boost, especially as it would have been planned.

Lawry gave me an early bowl in the second innings. The game wasn't going anywhere. Boycott was on strike and John Gleeson came up and suggested I go around the wicket and bowl into the footmarks as Boycott was only trying to get the not out. The very first one landed right in the middle of them and Boycott clipped it right back to me for a caught and bowled.

There was a huge roar as Boycott was renowned for batting and batting and batting. Immediately following his dismissal the game was called off. Rumors were rife that Boycott was seen that night hanging from the Storey Bridge!

Afterwards Richie Benaud said he would have been happy if he'd bowled like I did in his first Test. That gave me a lift. But it was to be my only match under Lawry. We went to Perth where I was 12th man. This time Greg Chappell played and made as memorable a debut as you could ever see. His century was a masterpiece.

My gear was next to Bill Lawry's and, after the game, as we were all packing up, "Phanto" came back and found his Australian blazer still on a hook, which was right next to where all my gear was. He saw me and stopped what he was saying in mid-sentence, before spotting Ian Redpath. "Red, can you bring my blazer to Melbourne". Obviously I wasn't going.

I was in the nets back in Adelaide when Sir Donald Bradman, the chairman of the selectors, came over and said, "We're not picking you for the next Test (in Melbourne at Christmas time). We think the form you were showing at the beginning might have tapered off a little. You've got a couple of matches including Queensland before we pick the next teams. Get some wickets and I'm sure you'll be back".

I was disappointed, but I also appreciated Sir Donald letting me know. Over my career he was the only selector to do that. Others had plenty of opportunities. One of the selectors Neil Harvey once told me he could play me with one hand tied behind his back. He probably could, but I wish he hadn't said it. My confidence was fragile enough as it was.

I had two matches, a return match against the MCC and another against Queensland in which to get enough wickets to force my way back into the team. I bowled like a desperate man trying to respond to the challenge. My figures were ordinary against the MCC and I hoped that Ian would give Rowdy and I a real crack against the wooden spooners.

We won by an innings, Queensland lasting for just under three hours in their first innings and just over three in their second. The seamers did not dominate but Ian did give Ashley Mallett 20 overs for the match – and he took six wickets!

In the first innings I didn't bowl a single ball! I was as angry as I could get. I wanted that bag of wickets but I couldn't even get on. Ian tells the story of hearing the clunk as a bottle of Westend was whacked onto the table beside him at the end of the day's play. Automatically he knew it was me. "Yes, T.J." he said. "How come I never bowled a single ball today?"

"Do you want the truth?" he said.

"Yes."

"I forgot you were out there!"

It was an honest reply and the conversation ended there. I looked to the second innings with anticipation. The result was only marginally better.

Ashley went for almost five an over in the second dig. Granted he'd also got some wickets. But how come I got just one full over?

Again I approached Ian. Was it just me, or was Rowdy really getting a better deal?

Ian looked me straight in the eye and said, "Rowdy is a better bowler".

When your captain puts it on the line like that, there's little recourse. We had a few more beers and left that discussion in the dressing room.

***

JOHN SNOW took 7-40 in the second dig in the Sydney Test and after draws in Melbourne and Adelaide, England led the series 1-0 with an extra Test, the seventh of the summer, to play in Sydney. The scheduled third Test in Melbourne had been abandoned without a ball being bowled.

Bill Lawry's axing in-between Tests was the biggest cricketing story for years. He wasn't bringing out the best in the players, so it wasn't a shock that he lost the captaincy. But it was a surprise that he wasn't retained in the X1 as the opening batsman, especially for the deciding Test.

I had a feeling that I'd be in that side. Just a week earlier, against New South Wales, I'd taken 4-39 in their second innings. Even though Sydney wasn't then regarded as a spinner's haven, I knew the selectors had to go all out to win the game by playing their most attacking combination.

It was exciting to go to Sydney and to have a new captain in Ian Chappell. We had two first-gamers, the tall Queenslander Tony Dell and the Victorian left-hander Ken Eastwood, in for the only Test of his career. What a challenge Ian had been set. Our entire attack, Dennis Lillee, Dell, "Skull" O'Keeffe and I had played just three Tests between each other! With two raw quickies and two unproven wrist spinners, it didn't seem to be the perfect combination. It's no wonder Sir Donald resigned.

Ian won the toss and dobbed them, a rarity in Test cricket, let alone in your first Test as captain!

He wanted to utilise whatever life was in the wicket.

Ian went to me first, ahead of Skull. England couldn't have been even 50 at the time. Coming into the game Les Favell had said to me that the selectors wanted me "to throw them up" and that's exactly what I did after Dougie Walters had picked up an early wicket.

It was a wet deck and naturally slower. My natural instinct was to bowl quicker, but instead I remembered what Les had said and gave them plenty of air.

After three or four overs, Ian came up and said, "Why are you bowling these &%#@ing donkey drops? What's brought this on?".

"Les told me that Harv told him they were expecting me to toss them up. They felt I was a bit too defensive."

"Right," said Ian. "If you were playing for South Australia today on this pitch, what would you be bowling?"

"Zooters."

"Well bowl &#$@ zooters."

I dismissed three of the Poms, Ray Illingworth, Snow and Bob Willis. All were bowled. From the press box, Bill O'Reilly described my deliveries as "magnificent wrong-uns, absolutely undetectable," when in essence they were back-spinners, or as Richie Benaud called them when he showed me the delivery, sliders.

In essence, when properly released, the ball curves in towards the batsman and continues off the pitch. This day, with the pitch damp, they scurried through creating the illusion that they were wrong-uns.

We dismissed them for 184, O'Keeffe also taking three. There were big crowds, 29,000 and 30,000 and much anticipation for the weekend's play. We had to win to retain the Ashes.

After losing our first three wickets for 30-odd, it was 7-178 when I joined Greg Chappell. Remembering Brisbane and how I'd self-destructed, my every desire this time was to get behind the line of the ball and show I wasn't frightened of Snowy. He bowled me a couple of short ones and I managed to fend them off and get off strike. We needed every run. Soon I was facing again and being bounced.

Snow had taken the new ball and given our score-line, the stakes could not have been higher. The field was closing in around me, looking for a catch. Snow went wide on the crease and again pitched it in short. This time, with the brand new ball, it came onto me a lot quicker. I'd stepped across to cover my stumps and in the split second saw the ball coming at my head. I had time only to turn my head and half duck. It was like a car accident. Unavoidable. The ball thudded into my skull, just above my left ear and as I fell to the ground my natural reaction was to reach for my head.

Later I was told the ball actually rebounded to cover.

It stung at first but when I saw the blood from the cut it really hurt. I was feeling numb all over and putting the gloves I'd borrowed from Dennis Lillee to my face, covered them both with blood. I was assisted off, put on a bench and given some smelling salts as "Doc" (Brian) Corrigan patched me up.

As all this was happening, umpire Rowan, a Brisbane detective, was warning Snow for excessive short pitched deliveries. Snow and Illingworth apparently remonstrated with Rowan and at the end of Snow's over, he headed down to fine-leg, waving his hands and conducting the crowd's chanting. One spectator reached out over the fence to shake his hand, but instead grabbed his shirt. It was an incredibly volatile situation. All hell broke loose. Cans were hurled onto the ground and amidst volleys of boos, Illingworth led his side off in protest.

In our rooms, someone was yelling, "We've won, we've won. They're forfeiting".

My immediate thought was that I'd won a Test match for Australia. But what a way to do it!

However, the Poms were only off for a short time. All through the break while the cans and rubbish were being cleared, Greg Chappell and Dennis Lillee stayed in the middle. We got to stumps at 6-235 with Greg having made a gallant 50 and Dennis still not out. I'd been stitched up and was padded up ready to go out again.

After the day's play, several of the English players came into the rooms to see how I was. Colin Cowdrey was genuinely concerned and Illingworth asked if I was alright. Even Snow came in. "You alright then?" he said. "Let's have a look. Oh, I only grazed you."

I was back to our hotel very early and thought I'd see the highlights on the news, but went to sleep before they came on. Greg and I were rooming together and next morning we were driving to the ground when we ran into a huge traffic jam. We sat there for half an hour without hardly moving. There was only an hour to go before the game actually started.

I saw a policeman, so got out of the car and said to him, "Greg Chappell is here. He's not out. We have to get to the ground, quick." He immediately provided us with the escort we needed, lights flicking and all. Five minutes later, we were coming in the members' gates. It was another full house.

Doc Corrigan assessed my cut and said I'd need to wear some protection. Helmets were unheard of then, so I borrowed Keith Stackpole's cap, which was bigger than mine. I very rarely batted with a cap because I always felt I could see its peak.

Dennis was out to the very first ball of the morning and taking a few deep breaths, down the pavilion steps I went. By the time I'd walked the short distance from our rooms to the members' gate, everyone was standing and applauding. It was exhilarating. I felt like Bradman but I was only doing what I had to do.

Surviving the first ball was important and after doing that and seeing Greg Chappell go out, I managed to hit a couple of 4s and added 22 to my original score (8) before our innings ended. Snow kept the ball up to me generally, but occasionally did what all fast bowlers had to do. I knew if I kept swinging what the consequences would be! We'd extended our lead to 70 or 80. It would have been nice to have had an even bigger lead, but frankly, I didn't want to get hit in the head again!

England did better in their second innings, making just over 300 and setting us 223 for the Ashes. Having dismissed Eastwood for a duck, Snow caught his hand in a picket and wasn't able to bowl again. At 5-123, we still needed 100 but after Greg Chappell was stumped for 30, we were always going to be in trouble. Illingworth and Derek Underwood bowled superbly, keeping the pressure on. I was last man out, caught by Keith Fletcher, with us still 60-odd runs short.

It was such an important Test and such a disappointment for us. Everything had gone our way, with Boycott being injured on the eve of the game and not being able to take his place. Snow hadn't been able to bowl at all on the last day, yet they'd managed to roll us for 160. Granted it was a bowler's wicket and Underwood, in particular, had been deadly, but it was still an incredibly hollow feeling.

Ian learnt a lot from that game and it was the beginning of the rise for Australian cricket.

Since then, John Snow and I have become good friends and done a couple of talks about the incident. On one occasion, in Brighton, he said he was aware that I could be dangerous with the bat. His only goal had been to get me out. Never was it his intention to hit me. He knew that I wasn't that good against the shorter ball. His best method was to unsettle me.

CHAPTER SEVEN

Tour of a Lifetime

Keith Stackpole lined me up and told me a few home truths. "T.J, you've waited a long time for this trip. Don't waste it."

I've always liked to have a drink and a good time. Having made the Test team for the first time, I know, deep down, that I didn't make enough sacrifices or was sufficiently disciplined. I probably thought it wasn't going to last. I may as well make the most of all the fun which went with both international and interstate cricket while I could.

The options were clear: either follow "Phanto" (Bill Lawry) down the road to the pictures eating an ice block, or join Ian Chappell, Dougie Walters and Johnny Gleeson at the pub for a beer. By now, you'd know which I one I went with!

I had a season of Lancashire League with Rawtenstall in 1971 (making 480 runs and taking 65 wickets) and while the cricket was serious enough, so were the distractions! Fellow West Aussies Neil Hawke, Tony Mann and Dennis Lillee also played for other teams. It was weekend cricket only and during the week I represented Cambridgeshire (making 245 runs and taking 32 wickets). It was one of the wettest seasons on record and the wickets didn't harden up until July.

On return to Adelaide, I completed a change of clubs from Prospect to Kensington on the promise of a job and I worked as a sales representative with Hall's, the soft drinks manufacturer.

South Africa was due to tour in 1971-72, but following the anti-Apartheid demonstrations which dogged the 1971 South African rugby tour, it was felt a cricket tour following immediately afterwards would be a logistical disaster. It was impossible to ignore the politics of it all – or guarantee the players' safety.

Instead, a Rest of the World team gathered, led by Gary Sobers and including such greats as Zaheer Abbas, Tony Greig, "Sunny" Gavaskar and Graeme and Peter Pollock, who would have been here anyway with the Springboks.

Five full-scale internationals were scheduled. They were Test-standard matches without official status. Other than being a guide to selection for the Ashes tour in 1972, the only thing the games counted towards was our player provident fund where the Board allowed us full benefits. I played four of the five games and was one of only three bowlers to take 10 or more wickets for the series, along with Dennis Lillee and Bob Massie. At times we all took plenty of stick. Fellow wrist spinner Kerry O'Keeffe played all five games, for eight wickets at more than 50 apiece. Ashley Mallett played once, for four wickets at almost 40.

The summer highlight was Sobers' 254 for the Rest of The World against Australia in Melbourne. And I witnessed much of it from 22 yards. For six hours, Sobers was all but faultless. I did have him dropped early on the fourth day, but he'd already made 140. It was a glorious display by one of the legends of the game.

Having been beaten by an innings inside three days in Perth, the Rest of the World XI was clearly primed to do better. Sobers had made a duck against Dennis Lillee in the first dig and from the time he marched to the wicket, you could tell he was ready to throw everything at us.

He played majestically, one straight drive against Dennis rebounding from the fence behind him just as he was completing his follow through. Surely no ball had ever been hit harder. He got into Massie and thrashed O'Keeffe. He also hit me a few times through the covers early on, but strangely enough, having reached three figures, he tended to score only singles off me, via drives to deep mid-on or sweeps to backward square. My figures were a respectable 4-87 from 20.3 eight-ball overs.

I was coming of age. I'd worked out the way to bowl to Sobers was to get him up the other end!

A documentary of his knock was made, including commentary from Sir Donald Bradman and it seemed every second Rotary and Lions Club around Australia had a copy. Many asked me to come along and speak and describe the slaughter. I'd sit through the film, listening to Sir Donald obviously delighting in the strokeplay which was regal. He would say things like: "Now here's Jenner bowling a long hop to Sobers. Now let's see that again now again, in slow motion". I felt as if I'd taken 4-187. But it was a great innings and I was glad to be there.

Earlier in that tour, I'd got Sobers with my wrong-un for a duck, stumped by Marshy in a 40-over exhibition match put on after the Perth international finished early. It didn't count for much, but you tend to remember dismissals like that. He was such a great player.

***

GIVEN THAT three spinners Kerry O'Keeffe, Ashley "Rowdy" Mallett and I had been selected for international duty in a season when an Ashes party was being named, it was reasonable for me to be optimistic about my chances of selection. Yet, in a short few weeks from January when I was a member of the team for the Sydney international, I went from being in Australia's best X1 to outside the best 17. It seemed I was expendable and it really hurt.

I had no quarrel with Rowdy's selection for England. He deserved his place. He'd taken more than 50 first-class wickets, better than anyone else all summer. I'd always considered him a class act. But John Gleeson, from New South Wales, hadn't played an international all year and having just turned 34, his career was winding down. He was such a natural, uncomplicated bloke and played the game with such a happy flair, that it was impossible not to be pleased for him.

What disappointed me was that it had been normal practice to name three specialist spinners. This is the way it had gone for each Ashes squad bar one, since 1948 and the days of Don Bradman's Invincibles.

But this time, only two were chosen, Mallett and Gleeson. Rowdy played four of the five Tests, but John played just three, for three wickets and never represented Australia again.

Instead of being on the tour of tours, I went back for a second stint at Cambridgeshire (for 287 runs and 28 wickets). While I was overseas, Coca-Cola took over Hall's and on return I was initially told there was no longer a position available. Greg Chappell was working for the company and they didn't really didn't need me. I'd come home early because of a back problem, which made it impossible for me to get out of bed or an armchair without using my elbows. I was strapped into machines and there was talk about injections so I came home and slept on the floor and didn't do anything until the first ball of the club season. I was so stiff from bowling that the next day I had back spasms just from bending over. For a time there, I even resorted to fielding the ball with my foot.

Thanks to a regular diet of Indocid tablets, my back seemed to settle and I was able to take my place from the opening Shield game of the 1972-73 season. In one game that season in Brisbane, Rowdy and I took 17 wickets between us. He got five in the first innings and I got five in the second. The team then went onto Bundaberg while I went to Sydney for treatment.

Other than a solitary appearance in the 12 in the first Test against Pakistan when I came in as a replacement for the injured Keith Stackpole, I didn't play a Test and by now was learning not to take anything for granted.

While Rowdy's career had taken off, mine seemed to be stagnating. My confidence was at such a low ebb, that it was almost as if I couldn't let the ball go. It didn't help getting the ball late and bowling with the wind. On Day One in a Shield game in Sydney it was embarrassing the way I bowled and I told Richie Benaud of my problems. He said early in his career he'd been hit for 45 runs from three overs. He told me to forget about what had gone before, get in the nets and practise hard. I'd get over what he termed a "spasm". I got three cheap wickets in the second innings, including Richie's brother, John, for a duck.

Corrigin days. Yours truly, aged 3 with my sister Laraine.
Sis was a real power for me when I needed most help.

*A rare photograph of my Mum and Dad together,
taken at the Corrigin ball.*

*Playing dress-ups
in Mum's bathers.
What a strapping yo
man I was!*

With a mate Brucie Collard near our shop in Corrigin.

Dressed to impress: with Laraine at the town's fancy dress ball.

n the backyard swing with Laraine.

With Mum at my 21st, in Cottesloe.

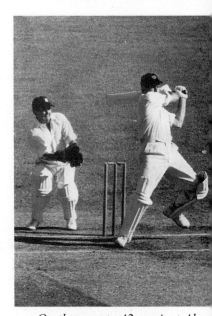

Posing in the backyard at Mt Lawley before my first big game, for Western Australia against the Springboks, 1963-64.

On the way to 42 against Alan Connolly and the Victorians in Melbourne in 1966-67. For once "Slug" Jordon, the Vic keeper, isn't saying a thing!

Learning the ropes at the WACA with cricket legends Tony Lock and Garry Sobers, who were two overseas champions to make such an impression on the Australian scene in the early '60s. That's me on the far left, with Ian McLachlan, Les Favell, "Lockie", Sir Garfield and John Inverarity.

My favourite bowling picture: at practice at the WACA Ground.
Just about the perfect leg-break action, wouldn't you say!

The 1968-69 South Australian team which won the Shield thanks to the positive outlo
of our great captain Les Favell and the runmaking contributions of our all-stars Ian c
Greg Chappell. Back row, left to right: Rex Blundell, Kevin McCarthy, Ashley Woodcc
Greg Chappell, "Rowdy" Mallett, Alan Shiell, Eric Freeman, yours truly and "Clacke
Clarke; Sitting: Graham Stanford, John Causby, Barry Jarman, Les Favell, Ian Chapp
Ken Cunningham and Dave Mundy; Front: Bob Gilbourne and Paul Galloway.

Australians to New Zealand, 1970. The big mutton-chop sideboards were obviousl
the fashion, especially among the quicks! Back row, from left: Kerry O'Keeffe, Denn
Lillee, "Froggie" Thomson, Dave Renneberg, Greg Chappell, Geoff Davies, yours tr
and Tony Steele; Front: John Maclean, Graeme Watson, Frank Bryant (manager), S
Trimble (capt.), John Inverarity (v-c), Derek Chadwick and Alan Turner.

With "Rowdy" Mallett at Prospect C.C. for the first time.

12th man for Australia, second Ashes Test, Perth, 1970-71.

Going for my shots against my old side. "Invers" is at slip and Rod Marsh keeping.

A screamer to dismiss Queensland's John Loxton, Adelaide, 1969-70. I took seven wickets for the game and made 43.

The team was touring the West Indies from February and to my joy, I was picked. I'm sure I was the last guy chosen. Had Rowdy been available, I'm sure I wouldn't have gone. He'd taken something like 60 wickets for the season, more than anybody else, even Dennis Lillee. John Benaud was in the same boat. He got a game when Paul Sheahan withdrew.

Compared to Rowdy, my returns were modest. I didn't play a Test all summer, but I did take eight wickets in the Queensland match in Brisbane, a match notable for all three Chappell brothers playing together for South Australia for the first time. And in Sydney, Rowdy and I took seven wickets between us as New South Wales collapsed for not many in their second dig, setting up our six wicket win.

Having been on only one representative tour previously, in 1970 to New Zealand with the Australian "B" team – as we were called – it was a thrill of a lifetime to make the No.1 squad. Peter Philpott had been highly successful there last time Australia toured in 1965.

When the side was announced, the chosen 15 assembled in Sydney at the headquarters of the Australian Board of Control in George St.

Ian Chappell announced the room pairings and reserved a comment for each: "Stackpole and Redpath two Victorians you belong together", "Benaud and Massie", "Hammond with Watkins", making little one-line comments all the way through. Finally he said, "Walters and Jenner – you can stuff each other up".

As we were soon to find, the West Indies is as close to a cricketing paradise as you'd ever find anywhere. The leading cricketers are treated like Gods. In places like Barbados, home of Gary Sobers, Wes Hall and so many other legends, there's a turf wicket on virtually every clearing. Pick-up games happen all over the tiny island, seven days a week, the majority of the year. The Bajans are just mad about the game.

Despite being stung by a bee at Kingston, I bowled pretty well in the lead-ups, especially at Montego Bay where we first encountered a young Viv Richards. I gave them air and the wickets were turning.

But the selectors went with (Kerry) "Skully" O'Keeffe, ahead of both myself and (John) "Wock" Watkins, who'd played only the opening one-dayer at a small place called Mona, in Jamaica.

I had been the second spinner behind Skully in NZ in 1970, so I wasn't that surprised the way selection panned out. To me, Watkins was also competition. At his best, with his confidence up, he could be formidable. Unfortunately for him and I know the feeling, they never came out on this trip. He played only four games all tour.

After missing out at Kingston, where three pace bowlers were named, I played the next four. Bob "Ferg" Massie and Wock were also left out of that first Test squad and on match-eve that night, we all sat around the bar, feeling sorry for ourselves, but nevertheless drinking copious amounts of beer! We were in seventh heaven in many ways, given where we were and what we were doing, but it was disappointing knowing that we weren't going to be part of it all the following day.

The high-scoring first Test was drawn, the game most notable for Gary Sobers' omission, through injury. We were told it was the first West Indian representative match he'd missed since 1955.

We moved onto Antigua, where Dougie, Ferg, Wock and I wound up with some American sailors having a few drinks and enjoying a sing-a-long. It was a huge night. None of us realised how late it was and we ended up walking home just as the sun was rising. We'd barely closed our eyes before jumping on the bus to St John's. Ferg's first over was a classic. The first delivery cleared the batsman and lobbed into Ross Edwards' gloves on the full; the next landed with "Stacky" at second slip! Finally his third pitched somewhere on line. But it was clear he was struggling with his co-ordination and when someone gently lobbed the ball back to him from cover, he raised his hands to catch the ball and it struck him full on the chest! It's said that figures can sometimes lie, but they didn't in Bob's case: eight overs, none for 56!

The sun was really belting down and there was a lot of glare. I was at mid-on when Bob bowled a full toss and I realised late that the bloke had hit it straight at me. Instinctively, I covered myself and it went right over my head. I indicated the sun had got in my eyes but I knew it was my lack of sleep and the many rums and Red Stripe beers we'd been downing. I hadn't fooled everybody though. Keith Stackpole lined me up that evening and told me a few home truths. "T.J, you've waited a long time for this trip. Don't waste it," he said.

"It's not like playing at home. Over here the tour selectors pick the team and they pick it from the best available. We're definitely looking at (playing) two spinners for Barbados, so it's up to you. I don't think you will ever get a better chance than this."

"Stacky" had always been very supportive of me. I appreciated him taking me aside. I went to Dougie and told him what happened. He was famous for having led one or two room mates astray without ever giving them up. "Don't worry T.J, everything's sweet," he said.

They covered for me and Ian didn't find out until our reunion in Adelaide 20 years later!

***

IF THERE'S meant to be a limit on fun, someone forgot to tell us during that tour. At Kingston, Red Stripe provided us with several kegs of beer. It was decided they should be set it up on our ground floor balcony. Room 9 was suddenly Club 9. Dougie and I were in our element.

I had a good game in Barbados and took three wickets in each innings. Ian allowed me more than 60 overs for the game. I was in good rhythm, my confidence was high and I was taking Stacky's advice!

The Test pitch at Bridgetown was a belter and given the quality of the batsmen on both sides, a draw was always likely. I took 3-65 from almost 30 overs in the first innings. My first Test wicket on tour and one of my most memorable was a Jamaican by the name of Maurice Foster, who possessed such a big back lift that I reckoned I could get him.

I said to Ian that I may be able to get a slider through him and after he played back to a couple of leg breaks, I let my faster one go and sure enough, he edged it back onto his stumps.

Keith Miller, who was in Bridgetown, covering the Test for his newspaper group wrote:

"Jenner took three wickets and certainly earned them. I have always liked his intelligent bowling and it makes me wonder why he has not represented Australia more often."

At Port-of-Spain, I got Foster again, this time lbw, after pushing him back with some quicker leg breaks and then releasing a wrong-un with as much pep on it that I could muster. When you have a plan and everything falls into place against a bloke who bats in a Test top six, it's particularly satisfying.

I also dismissed Alvin Kallicharran with a wrong-un which he lifted to mid-on. The media said it was a poor shot. I actually liked the dismissal, because it was planned. It curved late and spun back, creating the error.

It was an incredible Test match. We were down and out at lunchtime on Day Five. The Windies, set more than 300 to win, were just 66 runs away with five wickets in hand with Kallicharran on fire. We were all pretty despondent because we had been playing pretty well up until then. We had a feeling that the West Indies had been gearing themselves for Trinidad. The first two Tests had been played on absolute batting paradises. This was the one they intended to win and had loaded their side with three spin bowlers for the occasion. Veteran Lance Gibbs was joined by Elquemedo Willett from Nevis, who bowled orthodox left-arm. There was also the local twister Inshan Ali, who bowled left-arm "chinamans". He'd all but destroyed New Zealand the previous year at the same venue. Now he was gunning for us.

An unbelievable century-in-a-session from Dougie Walters split the game wide open. No-one had counted on anyone producing an innings of such breathtaking quality on such a wicket. If it had been played in Australia, everyone would still be talking about it. Because it was in the Caribbean with no TV and the minimum of press, Doug didn't receive the credit he deserved He eventually made 112 and with Ian making 97 in the second dig, we looked good with a 333 run lead.

Thanks to "Freddo" Fredericks' 76 and Kallicharran's 91 not out, we went to lunch on the last day in a whole heap of trouble. Most of us honestly felt as if we'd fired most of our shots. Seeing how dispirited we looked, Ian went for the jugular, giving us an almighty spray. "I can't believe you guys are down and out and already beaten," he said. Actually it was a tad more colourful than that. No-one could swear like Ian. "All we need is another &%#@ wicket," he said. "We're not &%#@ giving this up. No &%#@ way." It was good stuff and 25 years on, I'm still stirred by it. Ian would have revved us for only two or three minutes but it was the turning point.

"Tangles" (Max Walker) was fired up big-time. You could sense his determination as he marched back to his mark and charged in. The very first delivery was as quick as he could bowl and a little wider. Kallicharran, had been seeing them like beach-balls, but after the break, his feet didn't move quite as positively and the resultant snick flew through to "Marshy" who hurled the ball skywards, chased it and caught it again. "We've got em, we've got em," he yelled. I'd never played in a winning Test before. I couldn't believe that Rodney could be so positive. They only needed 60 more. An hour before, they'd been creaming us. History says he was right. Foster was taken by Greg Chappell at short-leg and within an hour it was over. We'd won by 46 runs and were 1-up.

Everyone had lifted. I bowled a full toss which was smashed down the ground and Kerry O'Keeffe sprinted after it, threw himself into the red clay around the boundary and saved it from going for four. It was terrific stuff.

When the last wicket fell, appropriately to an Ian Chappell catch at slip, it was quite a celebration in the middle. Dennis Lillee, who'd been unable to play, came charging onto the ground, closely followed by Stacky, who'd been struck in the face while fielding at short-leg and had returned from hospital all stitched up, still with blood all over his clothes.

It was an unforgettable moment. We'd climbed the mountain that day, all because the captain had given us a blast and we'd all played like our lives depended on it. The elation and joy back in the rooms was sensational. "Redders" brought out this huge cigar, much to everyone's merriment. His wife, Christine, was just about to deliver their second daughter back in Melbourne and "Red" had bought it in anticipation. It just meant he had to buy another, a week later, in Guyana!

I would have loved to have done more on the last day, but when I really wanted another bag of three or four following up my success from the first innings, I went wicket-less. It was incredibly hot, especially early in the game and I was very satisfied to take four wickets. Among them were the top three in the order, Fredericks, Foster and Kallicharran. Coming off the ground having bowled nigh on 40 overs, I tumbled into my seat and next minute there was someone taking my boots off and putting an icy wet cold towel around my face. I just assumed it was the room attendant. I wiped my face and looked down and there was "Fot" (Lillee). Talk about a team man. It was only a little thing, but it gave me such a lift and made me feel like I belonged.

We moved on to Guyana and as the game unfolded, there were quite a few footmarks coming into play. I was on my way home from the cricket one night and stopped in at the bar. Alan McGilvray, the ABC's broadcasting doyen, was there and said to me, "Jenner, Keith and I would like to have a chat to you in my room".

"Keith" was the great Keith Miller, one of my all-time favourites. "Mac" loved his whisky and a bottle was soon produced. I wasn't a scotch drinker but I wasn't game to ask for any coke and patiently worked my way through it.

"How does it feel to know that tomorrow you can win a Test match for your country?" he said.

"That would be terrific," I said. "But I thought I could do that in Trinidad and got none."

"No, no. This is perfect here. You have got the situation now where you can bowl into the footmarks. Keith and I have looked at them and it's absolutely perfect for you."

You always dream about winning a Test match for your country.

"It would be fantastic and the culmination of my career," I said. "I'm nearly 30 and on my first full tour with the Australian side. It would give my career a big lift."

"All you need to do tomorrow is spin the ball into those footmarks."

I thanked them both for their encouragement – and "Mac" for his scotch – went back to my room, thought what tomorrow could bring and started to feel pretty excited. I had to talk to someone about winning the Test. Dougie was still downstairs. So I decided to ring my old writing mate Alan Shiell from the Adelaide *News*, time difference or no time difference. No one loves cricket more than "Sheff". It took ages to get through. It was a very old phone system in the Caribbean in 1973. It was almost like you had to pedal to keep the line open. You'd talk and then have to wait five minutes for the feedback. Sheff's wife, Jill, answered. On hearing it was Guyana calling, she immediately said, "Who's paying?".

I yelled, "I am".

Eventually we got the conversation going and I shared all my thoughts with Sheff. I'd bowled well in Trinidad and hadn't got the rewards, especially late in the match. Tomorrow was going to be the day. "You should see the footmarks, Sheff. The footmarks mate."

I hung up and eventually got off to sleep that night. Next morning I was unusually bubbly and excited. I couldn't wait to get to the ground and warm up. First I wanted to have a look at the wicket. Ian Chappell was there, too.

I looked up at the media area and there was "Nugget" Miller and Alan McGilvray standing together. I gave them a knowing nod and walked up to one end and studied the footmarks.

"Which end do you want to bowl from?" Ian asked.

"I reckon I would like to bowl into these footmarks" and as I looked up I saw Nugget and Mac shaking their heads. "But perhaps it would be better if I bowled to the other end."

"Oh, I thought you'd prefer this bit of breeze," Ian said.

"No, I've got the feeling that I will be able to explode out of those other footmarks."

"Okay, no problem."

We went off, warmed up and went inside for a cup of tea before going out. Ian could sense my nervousness and said, "I think I'll bring Dougie on for one or two from that end and switch Bomber' (Hammond) and Tangles' (Walker) around. You can follow them".

Great, I thought. That'll do nicely.

Would you believe it – I never bowled even one lousy, rotten ball that day!

Dougie got a couple and Walker and Hammond the rest. We bowled them out for 109 and had won by late afternoon, with Stacky and Redders hitting off the runs!

I was rapt for the guys. It meant the series to us, and a rare victory in the Caribbean against the soon-to-be world champions. But given my big build-up, I felt inner dismay and embarrassment. Here I was trying to cement my spot and I couldn't even get a trundle on a wearing pitch.

We finished at Trinidad where I took my first-ever 5-for which ensured a sizeable first innings lead. The resultant draw was enough for us to clinch the series 2-0. A mate presented me with a copy of *Wisden* covering the tour and I still enjoy looking at that scoreboard, especially the entry: R.B. Kanhai, b. Jenner 3.

Years before when Rohan was playing for Western Australia, part of his deal saw him go around to the various clubs, have a net and give some tips. I was only 17 at the time but keen as mustard to have a bowl to him. The locals reckoned I'd knock him over with my wrong-un, but every time I bowled it, he belted it into the houses. I asked him how he knew and he said he smelt it! Seeing my bewildered expression, he smiled and said, "It's your periscope, your little finger. It comes up when you bowl it!". Talk about life being a great education. No-one had ever before said I telegraphed my googly.

Come Port-of-Spain and Rohan is captain of the West Indies and I'm Australia's senior spinner. It's amazing what flashes through your mind. I replayed that conversation with him from 12 years earlier, came in, bowled the googly, he went to hit it out of the park, missed and it took middle and leg. How sweet it is! Rohan said later he'd picked it, but hadn't counted on as much side spin. It was one of the personal highs for me all tour. Keith Miller wrote:

> *"Poor Kanhai had no chance. Jenner flung down what looked like a faster top-spinner. It pitched short and Kanhai rightly shaped to pull it for 6. But the ball dug into the pitch and came through so slowly that Kanhai had finished his shot before the ball hit the middle stump. But good for Jenner. There have been times in this series when Lady Luck has let him down. But she was with him here. Ross Edwards and Jeff Hammond took two stunning catches to send him back to the hotel a very contented man."*

All up, I took 13 wickets in the four Tests and felt as much a part of the team as at any time in my career. Others thought it too, and at a South Australian Cricket Association function soon after our return, one of the selectors Phil Ridings said to me, "It must be a good feeling to know that you are starting next season within the team".

Come November and guess what? I wasn't picked! And again, I didn't know why. Maybe an incident, for which I was wrongly accused, at the conclusion of the West Indies tour had something to do with it. But no-one will give me a straight answer, even now.

It was the second last day of the tour in Trinidad and there was some sort of ruckus at our farewell party. Our team manager Bill Jacobs marched over to me and sternly said, "I want to see you in my room at 9am tomorrow?".

"What for?"

We were making speeches at the time. Apparently someone had put their hand on a lady's bottom and I was being accused.

I wasn't very impressed and told "Fagan" (Jacobs) what I thought. From early in the tour I felt he had doubts about me and at times seemed hard on me without justification. Perhaps I was overly sensitive, but that's the way it seemed. This was the last straw, being accused of something I didn't do, and I defended myself aggressively.

John Benaud stepped between us and told us both to grow up. "You be there too," Bill told Benaud.

"Rosco" Edwards suggested I ask Bill to have a drink and talk it over with him. But Bill made it clear that he chose who he had a drink with. And I wasn't on the list that night.

Bill and I get on fine now. All this is history and I believe him when he says no-one's behaviour was questioned in his report to the Board. "As far as I know, everyone was praised," he said.

But at the time, I felt I was being picked on, yet again. I'd just played four Tests in a row for Australia and instead of being congratulated, I was being castigated. Rosco tried to smooth things over. He told Bill I'd been a pleasure to tour with. And he was speaking on behalf of everybody. If some had thought I was going to be difficult to handle, they were wrong.

On retirement, through Sheff in the *Sunday Mail* and in Perth's *Sunday Independent,* I did a series of articles and talked about being framed at Port-of-Spain. Bill's response was that I was confused about the lady's anatomy; the inference being I'd put my hand on her breasts. It was a disappointing way to end the tour of my life. The hand-on-the-backside *did* occur and the player responsible for it owned up at our reunion in Adelaide. I just wish he'd done it 20 years earlier!

And I still don't know whether it is true or false that my file was marked "never to tour again".

CHAPTER EIGHT

Ambushed, Yet Again

The problem was if you were seen talking to someone, you were supposedly sleeping with them. If you were having a drink you were apparently drunk.

I was once asked if I played cricket for the love or the money. It was a question which hardly needed an answer given the meagre rewards on offer prior to World Series. The opportunity to have toured more would have been a compensation, especially for a single bloke like me. Little did I know that my trip of the lifetime to the Caribbean was going to be my last as an Australian player.

I would have loved to have gone to England in either 1972 or 1975, or New Zealand in 1974. It would have capped off everything. But it wasn't to be.

Back from the "Windies", I started slowly before finding some form at last in the New Year but not in time, the selectors deemed, to get a Test against the visiting New Zealanders. In the match against Western Australia in Adelaide in early January, I made 59 and 47 and took 4-43 and 7-127, the finest match of my career. It was the first time I'd ever taken 10 wickets in a match before and the first time anyone had done the match "double" in Australian cricket – 100 runs and 10 wickets – in more than 40 years. The following weekend, I got a 5-for and made 86, my highest first-class score, against Queensland and soon afterwards won the Lord Hampden Trophy for South Australia's outstanding player.

Mum kept a story from the *Sunday Times*, written by Richie Benaud:

Jenner batted under the pressure of needing a good batting performance to keep his name in front of the selectors who have left him out again from the Test beginning in Adelaide next weekend. From the first ball he looked a competent player and his strokeplay on both sides of the pitch can hardly have failed to impress Phil Ridings (the Test selector) who was watching the match. He cleverly kept control of the bowling when lesser players were at the other end and in all, it was one of the most impressive batting efforts I have seen from Jenner since he began playing Shield cricket. He has turned in similar batting shows this season and his bowling against WA could hardly have been better timed for both his team and his chances of selection in the touring side.

While Kerry O'Keeffe and Ashley Mallett were preferred for the last Test in Adelaide, I still had high expectations for New Zealand. The 14-man squad was due to be named at the conclusion of the Test.

I knew with my previous history in NZ and the fact that O'Keeffe wasn't overly successful there previously, that I should be ahead of him. Even a comment by Benaud that the selectors may take a finger spinner for experience in view of the following year's trip to England didn't unduly bother me. Ray Bright, the Victorian left-arm spinner had taken 32 wickets but in his last start before the team was released, he didn't bat, bowled just 10 overs and failed to take a wicket.

I should have realised, however, when someone of Richie's standing had spoken that something was up. They took Bright. It seemed I was never going to get ahead – even at a time when I considered myself to be at my absolute peak. To say I was disappointed was an under-statement. It wasn't even a year since I'd been Australia's No.1 spinner and taken a 5-for at Port-of-Spain. Granted I wasn't a Richie Benaud and didn't have the confidence to even attempt a flipper. But I had developed a slider, a round-arm leggie and a round arm wrong-un. I also used the crease to create different angles.

Writing in the Sydney *Sun*, Benaud said:

"Frankly I would have preferred to see Jenner in the 14 and challenging for a Test place. I am not discarding Jenner, even though he is left out of this team, for I believe he will challenge strongly against the England team, when the Tests begin here in December. Englishmen have a habit of being more fallible against the over-the-wrist spin in Australia than against their county, run-of-the-mill finger spinners."

Richie had always been very constructive and encouraging when it came to my bowling. In a Shield game in Sydney before Christmas, I took three wickets, bowling a lengthy spell in tandem with Rowdy. I kept the cutting:

"The highlight was the way Jenner has improved since the tour of the West Indies. There is no better player of spin bowling than Doug Walters and Jenner sorely troubled him in the first half-hour of play, then picked up three good wickets during his splendid effort."

My ex-WA teammate Keith Slater named me in his team of the year in the Perth *Sunday Times*, saying I was the leading leggie in the country.

"Jenner has developed magnificently not only as a bowler but as a cricketer. His bowling, however, is what should be of paramount interest to the selectors as a specialist leg-spinner is essential in any well-balanced Australian side."

I appreciated their support, but it didn't lessen my anger. At times like this, you back-track and wonder if the selectors have got it in for you. After Sir Donald Bradman's resignation, Phil Ridings, Neil Harvey and Sam Loxton were responsible for picking the sides. They were all guys you could talk to and have a beer with. But they never communicated to me what I needed to know and where I had to improve to get the regular game I craved. Considering the number of times I was in and out of the side, I thought my relationship with them was okay. I enjoyed Phil's company on many occasions but never was there a time which I considered truly right to have a heart-to-heart. Years later, when "Harv" found out in the locker room of the Australian Golf Club that he'd been dumped as a selector, I shared his disappointment. But now he knew how the players felt. When we were dropped, that's how we found out.

I'm pleased to say that all three became close friends of mine and that is what makes cricket such a great game. During our Australia-wide tribute dinners to the Invincibles in 1998, there was never anything but pleasantries exchanged between Harvey, Loxton and myself. Time does heal wounds.

But I still live with the innuendos; that there were reasons other than cricket for my non selections. Okay, I was provocative on the field, said too much at times and rubbed a few people the wrong way. But I'd back myself against any of the slowies, even Rowdy Mallett, to get the big wicket when it counted – if only they'd given me the chance. I did line Phil Ridings up one day and asked why I'd been left out and he repeated what everyone else had said, "I'm only one vote".

At the end of the 1973-74 season, we had a farewell party for Ken Cunningham at the Ambassador Hotel and a silly action of mine was to rebound. Our young left-arm paceman Jeff Barnes from West Torrens was having a lengthy conversation with Geff Noblet, one of the selectors, a vice-president of the SACA and a lovely bloke with a great cricket record. "Nobby" was almost 60 and when he poured a beer, his hand would often tremble, causing the bottle to clink the glass. Unfairly we'd mimic him and clang our glasses, too, as we poured a beer. It was all in good fun and never meant to be personal or to cause any hurt.

We were sorry to see "K.G" go as he had a lot of good cricket left in him.

Everyone was having a good time and after I thought Nobby had gone, I said to "Barnesy", "How was that, mate?". He just nodded and not realising Nobby was standing directly behind me, I said, with my hand shaking, "Did he show you how to bowl the wobbly one?".

Nobby turned me around and said, "Very funny, Terry Jenner. I rue the day you came to South Australia".

I was immediately embarrassed and didn't know what to say. I should have said sorry but, instead, took up the attack as we often do when caught out.

I returned his volley with one of my own: "&%#@ off".

Next day Les Favell spoke to me and I agreed I should apologise. I waited for Nobby where he worked at the Bank of Adelaide and said, "I want to apologise for what I said yesterday."

I didn't mean him any disrespect. In fact, I'd always admired him for what he had done in the game and the service he'd given since his retirement.

He said it was okay, we shook hands but the incident overall caused me a lot of damage. When I needed their support for the captaincy just 18 months later, memories were long. We have spoken many times since without a problem. I just wish at the time I hadn't been such a smart-arse.

I try to control myself now and not say the first thing that comes into my head. I still make mistakes but I am now prepared to immediately say sorry if I'm wrong. It took me years to realise that people aren't necessarily at ease with the truth.

***

AROUND THIS time my employer, Coca-Cola, went on a rationalisation campaign and I was transferred to Mt Gambier. My choice was simple: stay there as an area manager and forget first-class cricket, or leave and seek other employment.

Feeling unwanted by the national selectors, I threw myself into my work. I intended to play cricket, should the opportunity present itself, but at local level they trained and played only on concrete wickets. It wasn't ideal.

In South Australia like virtually everywhere else, the only way you can be picked for State cricket is via senior club cricket and by rights they shouldn't have even considered me. But Les Favell, who was now a selector, felt I should be allowed to play the opening Shield game in Adelaide while I considered my options. It was a precedent, but he considered my service and experience too invaluable to ignore.

While I was mulling over my decision, I found a strong ally in Coca-Cola's Mt Gambier manager Tony O'Shea who reckoned to retire without saying goodbye would be wrong. I'd been disallowed leave but he volunteered to do my area for me whilst I came to town to play a farewell game.

We had a young team, with four newcomers and Ian Chappell gave me every chance, batting me at No.5, and allowing me almost 25 overs. We were beaten first-up by Western Australia, but only just and with four wickets for the game, they were coming out well. I rang Tony and said what about if I play just one more? He understood and covered for me again.

The following weekend we played the MCC and I took eight wickets, including John Edrich lbw in both innings. He was beaten by the angle on both occasions. Like a Ken Barrington, for years he'd been a thorn in Australia's side. The tougher the going the better he liked it. He even had a triple century at Test level to his credit. To get him twice in the space of 72 hours was really something. My confidence was up again and I made the first Test squad, just as Richie Benaud had predicted the previous February. And, incredibly, given my topsy-turvy track record at national level, I was to remain in the Australian XII all summer. It didn't do much for my sales reports for Coca-Cola, but as a cricketer it was incredibly satisfying being involved with the team which was thrashing the Poms. This was a world championship team and I was privileged to be a part of it.

There was a Shield match to play in Perth before the Test, but in mid-match I strained my side and could bowl only six overs. Ian and

Greg Chappell and I were all on the plane back into Adelaide, before we took off again for Brisbane. As soon as we landed, I was met by Phil Ridings, one of the selectors. Beside him was Don "Doc" Beard, the SACA's medical man. "How are you?" Ridings said.

"No problem at all Pancho'."

"Do you mind if Doc takes a look?"

"Sure, no worries."

Doc and I both knew how important it was for me to play in Brisbane. Doc also knew he had his reputation to consider. He did these tests and made me bend. Some of the pain was excruciating.

I felt if I didn't play, I'd never be heard of again.

He looked me in the eye at the end of it all. "You won't let me down will you Terry?"

"No, I won't Doc."

I didn't bowl the first day at practice. I told Ian I was struggling a little and he kept me away from bowling when Neil Harvey, another of the selectors, was watching. I just batted and did a bit of leisurely fielding. Come matchday I was feeling much better and they named Kerry O'Keeffe 12th.

We batted all day on the first day and I was required to bowl only six overs in England's first innings. I got a lot more work, however, in the second dig when Ian used me at second change. I had Keith Fletcher caught by Greg Chappell in the gully, as well as picking Derek Underwood up at the end. The Poms batted for more than a day in the first innings but lasted less than 60 overs the second time, Jeff Thomson taking nine wickets in an extraordinary Ashes debut. As good as Dennis Lillee was in his comeback Test, "Thommo" was clearly faster. He'd just amble up to the wicket and go pow!

My employment was sorted out. Ross Hall, Coca-Cola's general manager in Adelaide, sensed my predicament and transferred me back to town.

I was 12th man in Perth – "Rowdy" Mallett being the solitary spinner chosen – and remained "twelfthie" in Melbourne and

Sydney, before playing a Shield game for South Australia and being re-included in the fifth Test in Adelaide where I had just 20 overs in two innings, despite "Thommo" breaking down playing tennis up at Yalumba on the rest day! My match figures were 1-67, but they could have been better. Tom Brooks was umpiring and I deceived Tony Greig with my slider. He nicked it and it was caught behind. Rodney Marsh, the whole crowd, the press box, everybody was up, but Tom said, "No, not out".

I couldn't believe it. "F&#@ ," I said.

Tom was a policeman. "Don't use that word on my oval," he said.

"With all due respect Tom, this is my f#4@ing oval."

I lost my cool and my line and was hit for a few runs.

Dougie Walters, with that whimsical dry wit of his, claims Tom actually did Australia a favor that day.

"You realise T.J. that Tom actually won that Test for Australia," Dougie loves to say.

"How do you work that out Doug?"

"Well, when Tom gave Tony Greig not out, it changed the game. If he had given it out, the captain would have had to keep you on!"

***

WHILE I was 12th man so often in that series, I always felt it was preferable to be 12th, rather than 13th and not involved at all.

I became the most expert cordial mixer and tea-maker in Australian sport! Whereas most players would drink whatever came out, as long as it was wet, others like Dennis Lillee, for example, would insist on having fortified Sustagen. And it had to be just right. I didn't fancy it but unless I tasted it, Dennis would complain that it was too weak. It became a test within a Test to get it right!

I always wore my Australian jacket as 12th man. There were no trolleys or carts in the early 70s. I'd fill the big outside pockets with different flavored chewing gum or small bottles of Dougie's favorite ginger beer.

Drinks were only admissible at these breaks. Standing on the boundary at fine-leg and giving your fast bowler drinks in-between overs was a no no.

All the guys understood that being "twelfthie" wasn't much fun. Several years earlier, Paul Sheahan, or "Timbers" as he was known, finished his drink and threw his glass on the ground for the 12th man, me, to pick up. I wasn't too impressed but I didn't have the confidence to say anything so retrieved it. The 12th man would always look after the two not out batsmen or the two bowlers who were operating at the time. We'd bring them something to eat and drink; the rest of the team looked after themselves. Timbers said at one tea break: "Can you get me a cup of tea?".

"No," I said, "you can get it yourself," and walked off.

Having been 12th man in the previous three Test matches in 1974-75, I was expecting to be 12th man again for Adelaide. Dougie Walters was my room mate. Wet weather was predicted and we both thought we could gamble on some rain and have a late one.

It was a Saturday start and the night before, I met up with some people I hadn't seen for awhile and we burnt the midnight oil. Doug had a reasonably late night, too. Sure enough it pelted down overnight, washing out the entire first day. In those days nobody even questioned your right to have a drink. In fact it was almost expected that you be at The Lion or the Arkaba having a beer. The problem was if you were seen talking to someone, you were supposedly sleeping with them. If you were having a drink you were apparently drunk.

I tried to live up to my reputation. I feel I have a good sense of humour and was always having a joke or two, often at someone else's expense. It wasn't necessarily diplomatic, but it was only meant as a little fun. Unfortunately it wasn't treated like that by some and I made some enemies along the way.

In the dressing room I was the same. And I took it upon myself to teach the younger fellows all the roles and duties of being 12th man.

The usual procedure on getting to the ground was to have a cup of tea, head to the nets, have a bit of a bowl and in my case, as the likely 12th man, make sure there was enough Staminade and Sustagen to go around. After the Saturday washout, Rowdy Mallett and I were bowling to Ross Edwards and as usual, we had fieldsmen everywhere he hit it and of course, all were razor sharp! We called "last six" as the ground announcer, Neil Blundell from the SACA, made an announcement: "Ladies and gentlemen," he said. "Mike Denness of England has won the toss and sent Australia in to bat. 12th man for England is Chris Old. 12th man for Australia is Ross Edwards."

I stopped in my run-up and said to Rowdy, "Did you hear that?".

"Come on," said Rosco, oblivious to the announcement. "Throw it up." He drove one at full bore and I said, "Bad luck Rosco".

"Why? Have you got a fieldsman there too?"

Rowdy bowled one, he belted it and Rowdy also said bad luck.

"Surely you couldn't have anyone there," he said. "No," said Rowdy. "Bad luck, you're 12th man."

"Jeepers," he said, rushing out of the nets. "I'd better get up there and do my job."

I was batting at No. 7, which was huge for me. "Marshy" was at six. The series was over. We were already leading 3-0. Maybe they just wanted to take a look at me, with the English tour approaching.

Normally in Adelaide, captains went by the old Len Hutton adage. Bat first at all times and if in doubt, still bat. But there was a damp patch on the pitch from all the previous morning's rain just made for Derek Underwood. In these sorts of conditions he truly was "Deadly Derek". He took all four before lunch and added a fifth wicket, Marshy soon afterwards. He'd made great players look ordinary. Ian Chappell was out third ball to one which reared. Greg Chappell was also out quickly.

I sat in the viewing area with my pads and gloves on, my hands sweating like they were in an oven. It was my first match since

Brisbane at the start of the summer. With the '75 tour of England fast approaching, I felt this was all or nothing. When Marshy skied one to Tony Greig on the legside fence, I was in. We were 5-84 with Underwood having taken all five.

It was a full house, with more than 30,000 in and they gave me a huge cheer. Walking onto the ground, my pads were slipping; I'd obviously done them up when I was tense and on arrival at the crease, I had to re-buckle them.

Luckily they had crossed when Marshy was dismissed.

Underwood's first one to Dougie pitched leg stump before jagging like it had hit a stone and being taken by Alan Knott, the 'keeper, head height in front of first slip! I thought to myself: What's going on here?

Dougie cut one for three and I'm on strike, but only after again having to re-adjust my pads. The field was close, the atmosphere tense. I dead-batted a couple of balls and then went for a sweep, which probably wasn't on given the up-and-down nature of the wicket. Luckily for me it didn't kick, I got a bottom edge to it and it went straight through Colin Cowdrey's legs at leg gully. I was off the mark. I charged to the other end, truly relieved and re-adjusted my pads for the third time. Only now were they starting to feel comfortable.

The sun came out and we both started to play some shots, the pitch having settled. We added 80 in under an hour, even Underwood cracking and forcing Denness to make some changes. At no stage did Dougie or I plan the onslaught. It just happened.

After Doug was out, Maxie Walker thrashed it around. We brought up the 200 and started heading for 300 with me having reached my first-ever Test half century. Geoff Arnold, who'd opened with Bob Willis, came back, and tried to bounce me but I was seeing the ball pretty well and hooked him twice to the fence. Suddenly I was 70, but really starting to feel it and was cramping badly. It was ages since I'd batted more than a couple of hours.

I felt there was a 100 there for the taking. I was in full control, but with my cramps, I felt I needed to change my tactics a little, take a few ones, bring in the field and then hit out again. Underwood who was bowling again, brought an extra man in close and the very next ball, I went for it, only to under-edge it into my stumps.

I'd made 74, my highest Test score and in front of my own home crowd, who gave me a tremendous ovation.

The boys all congratulated me and I went straight into the showers, getting ready to go out to field.

We didn't get a wicket that night, but it was unforgettable just being out there. As England's opener Dennis Amiss was taking guard, it seemed the whole crowd, even the members, were on their feet, chanting "Lill-ee, Lill-ee, Lill-ee". It was awesome. He made a pair in that game and another duck in the next. Few were able to withstand Dennis. Or Thommo for that matter.

We dismissed them cheaply and come Day Four, with a 400-run lead, we struck early again, Amiss going fourth ball. David Lloyd and Colin Cowdrey were also quickly in and out.

Dennis had Denness in all sorts and Ian Chappell carefully positioned me at a fly slip, two thirds of the way to the boundary, in case Denness went for an upper cut. Fly slip is a frightening position, as the ball really whooshes hard and at an unusual height. It was eerie being in the middle of the Adelaide Oval all by myself in such an unusual position. I was down in the north-west corner and felt very alone. Two balls later, Dennis pitched in short, Denness went for it and it sped straight for me. I took it and cradled it into my stomach. It was an absolutely inspired piece of captaincy from Ian. At 4-33, the Poms were cracking. Come lunch-time on the last day, they were 6-for, but fighting with all their worth. Alan Knott seemed immovable, as did the veteran Freddie Titmus, who was using his pads at every opportunity against Rowdy and myself.

I suggested to Ian that I go around the wicket and bring in a gully, suggesting I was to bowl leg breaks from wide out, looking to catch the edge with one. Instead, as we discussed, I'd bowl nothing but wrong-uns and see if I could get Titmus lbw padding up.

The first ball spun back sharply and hit his pad. "Not out," said the umpire.

There was a big shout the next one, too. Again not out.

I mixed it up with a leggie and then going as wide as I could on the return crease, bowled another wrong-un, which pitched in line, shorter than the others, spun back and this time Robin Bailhache upheld my appeal. It was a working day in Adelaide and only 6000-7000 were in, but they were all up with me. It was a huge roar and Titmus was on his way. Ian immediately brought Lillee back on and he did the rest.

On top of my 74, which had helped us get to 300, I had done something else which was pretty important. After three straight Tests as 12th man again, I felt I was close to belonging.

***

WE WENT to Melbourne and for the first time in my life I was sure I'd get a game. We practised Wednesday and Thursday and come Friday morning, had our picture taken as a group in front of the MCC's famous old "cigar" stand.

Geoff Dymock had been brought into the 12, as a replacement for Thommo. Rowdy and I had heard on the grapevine that a bowler was in the gun, but we were sure it wouldn't be either of us. It was 10.40am. We felt we would have been told by now. But as we gathered for our photo, Ian approached me and said, "You've got it, T.J.".

"&%#@ing what?"

"I don't make the decisions," Ian said. "I just have to &%#@ing pass 'em on."

I was so sure I was going to play and have another chance to prove myself. Now I was back to mixing the cordial.

I was pretty upset but you wouldn't have known it looking at that photo. Inside the rooms, I was burning. Ian came up to me around lunchtime and said he didn't know what I was carrying on about.

"What do you mean?" I said. "This is the straw that breaks the camel's back."

"That's rubbish T.J."

"Seriously, this is the one."

"How do you read that?"

"Because there is absolutely no way I can play myself into the tour of England."

"I look at it this way," he said. "There's no way you can play yourself out of it. You've made 74 and got the important wicket (Titmus) in Adelaide."

"I know what they're up to. They don't want me to go to England. They're shutting me down right now."

"T.J.," said Ian. "If that's right, for the first time in your life, you have my permission to open your mouth."

What made it even more painful for me was that Dennis Lillee broke down very early on Day One and I fielded as Denness and Keith Fletcher both made big 100s. Ian had to fill in as the second spinner, a role he'd never liked. Replacement paceman Dymock took 1-130.

Just a few weeks later my worst fears were confirmed. We'd just finished playing New South Wales in a rain-ruined game in Adelaide. As soon as I saw my ex-teammate and cricket writer buddy Alan Shiell I knew the worst. He was crying. He knew how much it meant to me.

"Mate," he said, "I can't believe they have done this to you. They're taking Jim Higgs."

"How in the &%#@ing hell can this happen? How can Higgs not be in the best 12 and then make a touring team?"

I never got any explanation. No phone call. Nothing.

The Adelaide press were pretty keen to speak to me. I gave them what they wanted. "Obviously the selectors don't think I can bowl," I said, "which means that 280 batsmen can't bat.

"I expected to be in the team. I've never let Australia down when I've played. I was selected in six Tests this season ahead of Higgs and now I can't get in a party of 16 ahead of him.

"Higgs has been selected because he had a good year. I have been performing for 13 years. I'm tired of being used. Obviously the selectors underrate my ability."

It was a fair pay, which, incidentally, had nothing to do with Higgs. With the World Cup tucked onto the series, it was obvious that Jim wasn't going to feature. He couldn't bat and was a poor field even though he was an up-and-coming leggie. He wasn't to play a Test, or make even one run for the whole tour.

One consolation for me was that I was one of three Australians, along with Max Walker and Malcolm Francke to be chosen to join Derrick Robin's side to South Africa. We played only a couple of matches but they were very competitive, especially when opposed to guys like feisty South African Eddie Barlow. He padded up to a wrong-un at Newlands but the local umpire wouldn't give him. "No wonder you get so many runs," I said, "The umps here have eliminated one way of getting you out." Next morning, Barlow, all smiles, gave me a T-shirt with the words MICKEY MOUTH inscribed on the chest!

While we were in Cape Town, a letter arrived from the Australian Board of Control. My first reaction was that maybe I'd been put on standby. But on opening it, it was a far different message:

> *"You have been asked to respond to the question of whether you have breached the player-writer rule with your comments following your non-selection in the 1975 touring team to England."*

I had no intention of responding. As far as I was concerned, they could all go to hell.

I returned home in early April to a message at work: please ring Don Bradman. And there was a phone number.

I thought someone was taking the mickey out of me. I rang the number and Sir Donald himself answered and asked if I could take the time to come and see him. There was something he wanted to discuss.

Over the years just seeing him around the dressing rooms was always very uplifting. If he ever put his hand on your shoulder and said, "Well done" it was one of the best feelings that you could ever have. I always felt it was a bonus playing in South Australia when he walked in the room.

I went to his office in the Da Costa building. We shook hands and he ushered me to a seat.

"My understanding, Terry, is that you have received a letter from the Australian Board of Control concerning your comments in the paper and are yet to respond."

"Yes, that's right Sir Donald."

"You do have to respond you know."

"I don't think it is fair that I have to."

"Well," said Sir Donald, handing me a note. "I've taken the liberty of typing this letter for you to read."

The text of the note was that I had received the letter about breaching the player-writer rule. I felt it was unjust based on the fact that twice during the summer other players were quoted in similar fashion. For example, Ashley Mallett said, "I have been kicked in the guts before" on being left out of the first Test side. Ian Chappell had also made comments which could be seen to be provocative. Both are going to England, yet as I understand it, they did not receive any "please explain" letters. I wasn't, yet I did.

He said, "now put that in your own words Terry and I think that would appease everyone".

"Thank you very much Sir Donald," I said. "I will be delighted to do that."

"May I also give you one more piece of advice?" he said.

I nodded.

"Can I suggest that you don't send your letter to the Board to arrive until *after* June 4. At that time Tim Caldwell (the ACB chairman) will be in London at an ICC meeting. I will be acting chairman in his absence. I will receive your letter."

I duly wrote and it was dealt with, just as Sir Donald had said.

Over the years, especially since his retirement from active public life, Sir Donald has had to endure some barbs from people for not granting interviews. But he'd been involved in the game for more than 50 years as a player and an administrator. Surely he's paid his dues. I'll always be in his corner because I've seen up close how he was prepared to help me. And going back to my very first Test series, he was the only selector to tell me that I wouldn't be selected. At the time it didn't matter whether I agreed with it or not; it gave me something to hang my hat on.

Sir Donald's interest in me at the end of that 1974-75 season made me feel vindicated. It was soothing to know that the greatest cricketer of all time seemed to share my feelings that my breach of the player-writer rule was no more serious than others.

Jenner is bitter

ADELAIDE: Terry Jenner is angry at his omission from the Australian cricket team to tour England.

Jenner (30), who these days is considered more of an all-rounder than purely a leg-break bowler, said last night that he was unlikely to stay in first-class cricket for more than one more season.

"Obviously the selectors don't think I can bowl," he said. "Well, if I can't bowl there must be about 280 batsmen who can't bat.

"I expected to be in the team. I've never let Australia down when I've played.

"I'm extremely bitter. I was selected in six Tests this season ahead of Higgs and now I can't get in a party of 16 in front of him.

"Higgs has been selected because he has had a good year. I have been performing for 13 years. I'm tired of being used. Obviously the selectors under-rate my ability."

CHAPTER NINE

The Last Hurrah

*Turning around, Ian started to call them
wankers and returned their insults. They left
me alone and went for him.*

Summer's arrival never failed to bring with it all of my old
expectations, proof that I still loved the game, even if I didn't
enjoy the everlasting insecurity of it all.

Invariably I'd be up and in-form early, only to be experiencing a
sinking feeling by December that my season was going to be a
struggle again

I was keen to become Kensington's captain, but had competition
from Ashley Woodcock, who was a product of Prince Alfred College,
the same school which produced the Chappells. When a count was
called for, I lost by a single vote. It was an important decision as the
Kensington officials felt if "Splinter" was elected club captain he'd
also assume the inside running for the State captaincy when Ian
Chappell was away with the Test team. Not only would it be an
honour for him, but the club itself.

I was experiencing increasing problems with my back and knee
and had worked out what I could and couldn't bowl. As limiting as
that was, I managed to maintain my spot.

One of the problems was when I was picked for Australia, I didn't
bowl the same as I did in Sheffield Shield cricket, but rather the way
I thought the selectors wanted me to. I'd heard the criticism that I
bowled too flat, so I'd try and toss them up. They had this idea that
I was a flighty leggie. But I was a much quicker leggie when I started,
especially back in Western Australia.

Approaching the 1975-76 series with the West Indies, I had no idea that Brisbane was to be my last Test. Ian had again given me some long stints for South Australia and a 5-for from 40-odd overs in the tour game against the West Indies and eight wickets against the Queenslanders, including Greg Chappell, saw me named for the first Test. However, when Alan McGilvray's player profiles in the *ABC Cricket Book* came out, I wasn't amongst them. And when a team poster selling through service stations was released, guess who wasn't pictured! Given what had been before, it was gut-wrenching.

Rowdy and I took 15 wickets in the game against Queensland. He got Greg in the first innings and I got him in the second. He was on 99 and there was no way I wanted him to get his 100 off me. I bowled a slider which he simply patted back to me. He looked at me with that ring of confidence of his and smiled. Next ball, another slider and another defensive shot. "Haven't you got the guts to bowl a leggie, T.J.?" he said. It's not often a batsman sledges you, but Greg was and he was right!

"Bugger you," I thought, "I'll bowl the leg break." It was a full toss! Delighted that he'd sucked me in, Greg tried to hit it too hard and only crunched it straight to cover. He must have been really irked by that. I reeled around the top of my mark and came in again quickly and let him have another leggie. This time it landed and in trying to go wide of cover, towards his grandfather's gates, he got an outside edge and Ian caught it at slip. G. Chappell, c I. Chappell, b Jenner 99. I was pumped and followed him out to mid wicket as he was walking off and said: *"That* was a leg break Greg!"*.

In retrospect I probably played him into form! Come the Test match a fortnight later, his first as Australia's captain, he made a century in each innings. That was the match in which I was booed by sections of the crowd at the Gabba just because the selectors had picked me ahead of Malcolm Francke, the Sri Lankan-born Queensland leggie who had fulfilled his residential qualifications and was available for Australia.

I'd taken eight wickets against Francke's one a fortnight previously. And the week before in Queensland's tour game against the Windies, his figures were 1-100. I couldn't see what the fuss was all about. The crowds around Australia generally appreciate good cricket, but the interstate bias is alive and well. I don't think they realise at times how hurtful they can be. Fancy walking out onto the ground representing your country on home soil and being booed! If they knew how it did affect me, I'm sure they wouldn't have done it.

I was particularly keen to make an impression, but bowled only four overs in the first innings. Maybe that was why I went for an early hook shot against Andy Roberts, only for it to graze my head. Boy was it close! Andy could bowl at near express pace, especially when there was a chance to knock over a tailender.

Bowling wise, I thought I did okay in the second innings, with 2-70 from 20 overs. I got Lawrence Rowe, after he'd made a ton and Clive Lloyd, without scoring. I also had Alvin Kallicharran caught behind only for my nemesis Tom Brooks to spoil the party.

We had set him up for the sweep and my wrong-un did enough to hit the back of his bat and balloon from Rod Marsh's shoulder into the air and he ran around, dived full length and took a brilliant catch. It was such an obvious out that I was already down the other end celebrating with "Marshy".

"Not out," said Brooks.

"&%#@ me," I said.

"Don't use that language on my oval," he said. Seems I'd heard that one before.

Ian ordered me to get back and bowl.

At the end of the over I grabbed my cap back off Tom. "Hey Terry," he said, "Don't snatch your cap."

I walked with him to backward square leg and said, "Tom, it's not like I didn't need that wicket".

"The reason I didn't give it out was not because I didn't want you to have the wicket. In my opinion he didn't hit it."

"Well how the hell do you think it got from a foot outside leg stump to hit Marsh in the shoulder?"

It wouldn't have looked too good, a bowler arguing with an umpire in-between overs. Soon afterwards, Brooks warned me for running on the pitch which only added to my frustration.

Brooks was a reasonable bloke, if bordering, at times, on being overly serious. He didn't like swear words – even if you were chastising yourself. Unfortunately for me, I was a big swearer.

What happened in this match in a way pictured my whole career. I always saw myself as playing catch up.

I know it wasn't Brooks' fault, but he'd been involved in some big decisions crucial in my career.

Deep down, I knew this was my last chance. One of the Sydney journos, Dick Tucker, said to me, "Even you can't come back from this one T.J.". Another wrote I was as good as dead and buried.

Even though there wasn't anyone a whole lot better floating around, I firmly believed them. It seemed a foregone conclusion that I was to be written out of the script. Sure enough, after being made 12th man in Perth, when the selectors went in with four specialist pacemen for the only time I could remember, I was omitted from the squad and this time, there were no comebacks.

I failed to get a wicket in SA's return game with the Windies and "Rowdy" Mallett played in the Christmas-New Year Tests in Melbourne and Sydney. The pace combination of Dennis Lillee, Jeff Thomson and Gary "Gus" Gilmour was cleaning up the Windies more often than not. When he was required, Rowdy was doing his job, so it was back to full time Shield cricket for me.

I didn't enjoy the rest of the year as much as I should have, despite us winning the Sheffield Shield. Little things were upsetting me. In one of our important wins of the season, against New South Wales in Adelaide, in which we got home by 21 runs, a whole heap of us, including Ian and myself, went on report. Ian bowled a series of head high full tosses and swore at Kerry O'Keeffe, who was doing his best to save the match. I took my frustrations out on Rick McCosker, who wasn't batting particularly well, but was hanging in, showing marvellous concentration. Nothing was going our way and we were having a fair bit to say. I went up and stood beside Rick to set my field, trying to break his concentration. I shaped to do a big cover drive then looked to fine leg and placed a man there. Throughout it all, Rick just stood there, not even acknowledging my presence. The longer he stood expressionless, the angrier I got. Rowdy finally got him out and we were into the middle order, Wayne Prior taking his second 5-for for the match. It was a huge win for us, but there was some explaining to do to the South Australian Cricket Association. Four of us ended up with a reprimand and Ian later said that a part of his love for cricket had been killed that night. His immediate reaction was to retire there and then.

During the winter months Ian moved on to Victoria and I knew I was going to miss him greatly. My initial thought was that I should go, too. That's the sort of captain and person Ian was. He bred loyalty. Just like with Rowdy, he'd always been very supportive and helped us both throughout our careers. Even when Les was captain, Ian was in the side and advising. I was going to miss him more than anybody.

When I got into trouble a couple of times and the crowd was getting into me, Ian had the knack of shifting the emphasis. He'd give them a rocket and in turn, they'd leave me alone and get stuck into him. We were playing the Vics in Adelaide and there was only about 200 people there. A small group was heckling me and I'd fallen for it and even at the start of my run-up was answering back. Ian marched up and told me to leave the crowd to him. Turning around, Ian started to call them wankers and returned their insults. They left me alone and went for him. I again started concentrating on bowling and took three or four wickets.

"See what I do for you!" said Ian, tongue-in-cheek.

***

WHEN IAN Chappell played well, so did South Australia. If he was off the boil, so were we. Ian remains one of the most decorated of all Sheffield Shield cricketers and in all, he played in four winning Shield sides. I was lucky enough to be in three of those teams.

We could have all played in another in 1972-73. We only had to win one of our last three games outright to clinch the Shield, but the West Indies tour selection changed everything. Without the batting brilliance of Ian and Greg and the bowling strength of "Bomber" Hammond and myself, we couldn't do it. West Australia beat us by an innings in the last game to win the Shield.

Our last and most eventful victory was in 1975-76, Ian's last season with SA. He'd made an arrangement with the South Australian selectors the previous year that he'd be consulted before they made their final selection.

It was late in the season and he was batting against the Victorians when our team to go interstate was released. We only needed a few bonus points to win the Sheffield Shield and had two games to do it, one in Sydney and the last in Brisbane. The selectors decided to drop Rick Drewer from the 12 in favour of Bob Blewett, Greg's Dad. Bob was going to be the spare man in the squad, given that Prior, who had missed the Victorian game, was expected to be fit for both the NSW and Queensland games. For years the SACA had been bitching about meeting our laundry payments and other incidentals. All of a sudden, they were now saying they *could* afford to send an extra player that the team probably didn't even need.

Ian had had his run-ins with authority and was becoming increasingly intolerant and impatient in his dealings with administrators. He was ropeable at not being consulted. The pressures of first-class cricket and years of captaining SA and Australia had drained him mentally and physically. If that's what they wanted to do and ignore the standing agreement, they could do it without him. He was out.

Drewer had been in the side all year. He had made three ducks and a 5 in consecutive games against Lillee and Western Australia, but plenty of blokes failed against Dennis. Bob Blewett had done well at club level, but he was 32 and had never even played for South Australia before.

Phil Ridings and the selectors went into damage control. "How could we consult you? You were out there batting," they said.

"Isn't that my &%#@ job?" said Ian.

While this great hullabaloo was happening around him, Ian produced one of the great innings seen at the Adelaide Oval, making 171 and lifting us to a two wicket victory and a big 15 bonus points. It was a huge effort. We'd chased 364 in the fourth innings. It was the crucial day of the season.

At that stage no-one knew if "Fang", our nickname for Prior, would come up, at least for the first game starting in four days time at the SCG. Ian was adamant that he wanted him with us. He was always big on people who gave a lot for him. Before chipping his ankle in the game against Western Australia, Fang had taken 35 wickets including a rare hat-trick which finished off New South Wales in a stormy game in Adelaide before Christmas. If it hadn't have been for the hot competition at the time, he could easily have been opening the bowling for Australia.

Ian wasn't against taking a 13th player. But why take an extra, who probably wouldn't be needed, at the expense of Drewer? He had struggled since January, but earlier in the year he'd been terrific. We needed only 7 or 8 points to guarantee the Shield. Why not keep him in the squad, as 12th man, ahead of someone who had never even played before?

Ian addressed the players afterwards and said, "This is my decision. I'm not going on tour".

That morning, without the knowledge of most of the team, Rowdy Mallett had also told the selectors that he, too, wouldn't tour, unless they rescinded their decision to send 13 players.

We were all shocked. We'd just won one of the greatest matches in memory and two of the people most responsible were saying they wouldn't be with us for the climax in Sydney and Brisbane. It seemed to me, as one of the senior players, that we should show some solidarity for Ian and Rowdy and have a vote. If they were out, so should we all be.

"You bastards," said first-game fast bowler Rodney Hogg, with a grin. "I've waited 10 years to go on a Shield cricket tour and you've just blown it for me."

As an employee of Coca-Cola, one of key SACA sponsors, I was in a ticklish position. It was important that I abstain from voting. Ian, Rowdy and Drewer did, too. Six supported Ian and Rowdy and said they, too, wouldn't tour. Two said that they wanted to go. I felt it should be an all-in or none-in situation and while it was everybody's democratic right to say no, if Ian lost this battle, it could mean that we might not win the Shield. I asked if the two guys who voted "no" would like to speak. They didn't have to, but both did. One was Gary "Jaffa" Cosier and the other, Rick Darling. Jaffa said he'd transferred to South Australia from Victoria the previous year to further his Australian team ambitions and this may terminate his career. Rick said that he was just making his way in the side. He, too, didn't want to do anything which would complicate higher selection.

We talked through it again and highlighted Ian's 171 and Rowdy's eight wickets and important runs at the death. I asked for another vote. This time it was 9-nil.

I went down and told the selectors, Phil Ridings, Geff Noblet and Les Favell that all the players were supporting Ian and Rowdy. If they were out, so were we.

The selectors met and came up with their own ultimatum. They announced that we had until midday the next day to agree to go, otherwise an entire new team would be selected. By then, we were at The Lion celebrating the big win – and I was having enough beer to get myself pinched for drink driving that night.*

On hearing the ultimatum, Ian said to us that we should all go.

"You, too?" I asked.

"No."

"Ian, we have agreed as one, if you don't go, we don't go."

---

* He was fined $60 and disqualified from driving for six weeks.

That night football great Neil Kerley rang Ian to try to encourage him for the sake of the players not to go ahead with the strike. He also received a phone call from Blewett who, until that afternoon, had no idea of the storm and said he'd gladly withdraw from the team if it meant a resolution. Ian explained it was the pettiness of it all; nothing personal against Bob.

One minute we were being denied a laundry allowance increase and the next, the SACA was ratifying an extra player for a two week tour.

Ultimately, Ian decided to play, in the interests of the team. Typically he didn't hold back. "I have lost all feeling for the SACA. I have no respect for the association. I am going for the players," he said.

Rowdy also pulled back into line. Maybe the no-win situations facing Cosier, Darling and a young David Hookes, then in his first year with us, had been influential. They'd been willing to follow Ian and Rowdy through a brick wall even at the risk of their own careers. Ian said later that Blewett's phone call and offer to stand down to avert the crisis had also been important.

We all ended up going, except for Drewer who announced his retirement. Prior played in both games and Blewett made his debut in Brisbane, when only one day's play was possible. By taking first innings points in Sydney, thanks to another Chappell century, we clinched the Shield with a game to go. Ian and I added 50-odd for the seventh wicket at an important time in a low-scoring game to get us past NSW's score, making the last game inconsequential. Boy, did we party that night!

CHAPTER TEN

An All-Time Great

*We all reckoned Doug must have an indoor
net underneath his home in Sydney. How
could he get to be that good, without seeming
to work at it!*

I was in one of the all-time great eras and in a side recognised as one of the best ever. And for that I'll always be very proud. It was a privilege playing with guys like Dennis Lillee, Jeff Thomson, the Chappells, Rodney Marsh and Doug Walters. All were champions on and off the field. So were two of the Victorians, Ian Redpath and Keith Stackpole.

Because I was so much in and out of the team in those early '70s, I never really felt totally part of it. One who did make me feel at ease was one of the all-time best knockabout blokes, Dougie Walters. We liked a drink and a smoke and were always laughing.

Doug was a batting genius. He could switch on and off in a twinkling of the eye. We all reckoned he must have an indoor net underneath his home in Sydney. How could he get to be that good, without seeming to work at it!

I roomed with Dougie on the '73 tour of the West Indies and can't remember him beating me to bed too often! When he did, he'd sit up and write to his wife, Caroline. He was always armed with information about local history and would always be asking the driver about buildings and important landmarks. He'd write the information down on a cigarette packet and at night, line up his packets and relay all the info to Caroline. More often than not, he'd be sitting up in bed writing and I'd have to go and take the pen out of his hand because he would have fallen asleep.

One morning in Kingston I opted to go to town with Bob Massie to buy some LPs. Cat Stevens was recording on the island at the time. We even got a glimpse of him and bought our records before heading to Sabina Park and arriving not long before play.

Greg Chappell came up to me, looking pretty worried. "T.J.," he said. "If I was you, I'd give your mate a quick call."

"Why?"

"Because he's not here. He missed the bus."

Finding a phone wasn't the easiest task. I ended up making the call from the secretary's office. Eventually they put me through. Doug answered. He'd had a big night and had slept in.

"Geez, T.J. what's the time? Why didn't you wake me? I'll be right there."

Dougie reckons I'd forgotten all about him, hadn't booked a wake-up call or bothered about his breakfast. In reality, he'd slept through the phone reminder and in his haste to get out of the room, tripped over the breakfast tray sending everything I *had* ordered flying!

His taxi driver exclaimed, "Mr Walters, you are running very late".

"Don't worry about that. Just get me to the ground. Quick."

There are no highways or by-pass roads on the islands. They're all narrow lanes and as they got closer to the ground, their progress slowed to a crawl. In his panic, Doug even ordered the guy to drive up the footpath! Finally he arrived, thanked his man, threw him some Jamaican dollars and headed for the rooms without waiting for his change. Already he was 15 minutes late.

He hurriedly dressed before dashing down to the gate, catching the attention of 12th man John Benaud, who was sub-fielding. He also waved towards Ian Chappell, who was ignoring him totally. Several overs went by and still he hadn't had the call to come on.

"Bugger this," said Doug. "I'm going to come on anyway."

He ran on and John Benaud ran off.

"Fine leg. You," said Ian.

At the end of the over, he slowly trotted up to mid-on, before Ian called again, "Third man. You."

And for the rest of the first hour, Dougie had to run from one end of the ground to the other, from fine leg to third man and back again, over after over.

At drinks, Ian waited for Doug to join the group. "It won't happen again will it Doug?" he said.

"Actually, Ian, I can't guarantee that."

Only Doug could have said something like that. It was never mentioned again.

***

IT WASN'T the first time Dougie had gone "missing" in mid-match.

He made a 100 against the Rest of the World XI on the first day of the game in Perth and afterwards met up with a couple of old mates and they ended up going to someone's place for a late dinner. I was rooming with him and he wasn't there upon my return – or when I got up!

I'd been out to Mum's place and didn't have any idea where Doug might be.

I knew Brian Taber was in town and on the off-chance, I rang him and asked if he'd seen Dougie.

"Why?"

"He hasn't made it back."

"Leave it with me."

"Tabsy" tracked him down. He'd stayed with friends in Cottesloe and had retired latish, about the time the sun comes up!

Had Tabsy not made the call, Dougie mightn't have got to the cricket that day until 4 p.m! Wonder what Ian would have said then!

***

DOUG TAUGHT me how to play cards during the West Indies trip in '73. He also taught me to play crib, as he needed someone to play with. No matter how good a hand you had, he always seemed to come up with something better. I could count my wins against him on the fingers of one hand.

Doug was also the world champion of a game called "switch" where you had to be the first to 1000 points. Games would often go long into the night. He spent a lot of time on tour teaching Johnny Watkins how to play and proceeded to knock him, me and Kerry O'Keeffe off on consecutive nights.

In Bridgetown, I actually had a rare win and straight away declared my unavailability to be immediately challenged. Knowing that "Wock" (Watkins) was still a learner, I finally agreed to a game with him, but deliberately spread it out over two or three nights, much to Doug's frustration. He was forever pestering us for the score so he could challenge. I kept my title for about a week, before having to put it on the line and in one night it was gone.

We also used to play Five Hundred. I'd partner Doug but rarely got to win even one trick. He always liked me to call something, just to give him an indication of who held what. We used to tag up against Dick Tucker and Ronny McKenzie, two of the media boys from Sydney.

They could play a bit, but they never got the wood on Dougie. If there was such a thing as a cricketer who counted cards, Doug was it. He was uncanny.

One match-day in Melbourne, we were playing switch and it was getting closer to lunchtime.

Doug was padded up, ready to go in. Whoever was in, was going alright.

"Do you want to have one more hand so we can finish this off, Doug?" I asked.

"Okay, let's finish it. You deal."

Just as he was studying his hand and had thrown out his discards, we heard a roar. A wicket had fallen. He put the cards down, went out and played out the over before lunch was called.

As he walked through the door he said, "T.J., it's your lead. Hearts are trumps!".

CHAPTER ELEVEN

A Decision Made in Haste

I was white-hot with anger and felt I had to do something.

Everyone would love a second opportunity at life, be it for a day, a week or a year. Terry Jenner Mk II would have been less talkative, less provocative and more dedicated. Maybe I would have played more Test cricket, but then again if my personality was different and I hadn't been as openly aggressive, I probably would have been content to stay in Perth and focus on helping Mt Lawley to a grade premiership. I mightn't have played even one Test match.

Dad had taught me to "call it as it is". I did and paid for it, many times. I was garrulous, naive and maybe not as street smart as some – one ex-West Australian captain even suggested I was thick.

But without being super competitive, I don't know whether I could have made it. Given my time again, no doubt I'd temper my aggression. On many occasions I was my own worst enemy. I had the skill. I just had to believe it. One day playing for Mt Lawley against Perth, I played a square drive for four off the bowling of Dennis Lillee. Barry Shepherd, my captain, later told me that only Norman O'Neill could have played that shot. Yet I was so insecure and would always be doubting myself.

Maybe the answers lie in the way I led my life as a kid. It was a topsy-turvey existence. Dad barely acknowledged any of my sporting achievements and from the time I was 11 or 12, the constant arguments with Mum had an effect.

Dad called a spade a spade and I followed suit. Maybe I should have been a fast bowler because I could really get fired up. Dennis

Lillee once said I should have been a 60 or 70 Test match cricketer. Coming from Dennis, a real legend of the game, that was quite a compliment. I didn't know that one of my peers thought of me that way. I figured that because I was in and out of the side all the time, that is how my teammates automatically perceived me, too. I'm only now finding out that they truly did rate me.

Unfortunately, the officials didn't. Maybe they were scared by the maverick in me. It certainly cost me any chance of captaining South Australia. That walk-off in Perth years back wasn't a one-off. There were all sorts of flare-ups and confrontations, which today make me wince.

Les Favell did tell me that he would have trusted me with the SA leadership, but he didn't know if the others would have. Les knew I had the knowledge but I had obviously offended a couple of the blokes with my aggression and mannerisms on the ground and they weren't going to give me that chance. These were the same ones, incidentally, who initially thought Ian Chappell may be unsuited to leadership!

With Ian's transfer to club cricket ranks in Melbourne, come the start of 1976-77, "Rowdy" Mallett and I were the most experienced members of the team and there was increasing debate on who would be Ian's successor.

I had support from many people in the press. David Capel wrote in the *Sunday Mail* that I'd greatly matured and should be Ian's successor:

> *Jenner is articulate, popular among the SA players, a top class allrounder and a fighter. He has had his share of criticism over the years. His flamboyance on the field irks many. But he would still make an excellent leader."*

Ashley "Splinter" Woodcock had the inside running for the captaincy as he'd led in one game the previous year against the West Indies when Ian withdrew with an injured ankle.

In that game, Splinter predicted that Rowdy and I would spin us to victory, yet we didn't even get a bowl in the first session on Day Four when the Windies were batting a second time, almost 250 behind! He bowled the pacemen Wayne Prior and Geoff Attenborough and followed with Gary Cosier's seam-up stuff. By the time we got on, we couldn't win. In his frustration, Rowdy sent down a few leg breaks and I bowled bouncers, all in the name of getting our message across to our first-time captain.

With that in mind I wasn't sure that Splinter was going to be the captain for me. When he was named ahead of me, I was bitter and don't mind admitting it. I was 32 and he was 29. We worked out that I'd played something like 130 games and he'd played just 78.

We played the first game, in Adelaide and I was the sixth bowler used. Under Ian, I was invariably first or second change.

I'd had a couple of approaches from the Kilburn cricket club about playing Adelaide Turf cricket and I was tossing it over. While I'd taken four wickets against Western Australia in that first game and felt good in the body, my head wasn't right. I was definitely contemplating life after cricket. The only plus for me, as I saw it out of the game, was that my Dad had come to see me play for the first, and as it proved, for the last time.

I went and saw Alan Shiell and told him how hurt I was over the captaincy issue. I'd lost an ally at the selection table with Les Favell retiring. He'd always provided a necessary balance to the panel. He had faith in my ability and knowledge and knew me better than most. I told "Sheff" I was seriously considering pulling the pin.

I also spoke with Ernie Clifton, the South Australian Cricket Association's coach. "Would it help," Ern said, "if you knew that Ashley Woodcock has a university exam and isn't available to go on tour (to Brisbane and Sydney)?"

"Yes, it does," I said.

Cosier was Woodcock's vice-captain, but I thought him unlikely to get the job so soon, because of his inexperience. I genuinely thought that I'd be the man. But not only did they make Cosier captain, they promoted Rowdy to vice captain, which was fair enough, but then made Dennis Yagmich, who'd had only one full season in the side, the third touring selector. I'd been effectively shut out. It was the final straw in a career of many disappointments.

I was named in the side, but within days had withdrawn, saying I'd lost my enthusiasm to play. I'm sure those who didn't want me in the side saw it as their revenge. My replacement was a teenager from Prospect by the name of John Frick. He was to play only four games.

I have a lot of regrets in my life and this one is right up there. I wish now I had the courage to ignore what I felt was a deliberate rebuff and go on tour anyway.

World Series Cricket was in its planning stage and within months was to be announced to the world. The best Australian players of the time were about to sign to play rebel cricket and it so stretched State reserves that some players who weren't even Shield regulars in 1976-77, were representing Australia 12 months later.

Surely, given my experience, I had to be in the second best XII in Australia. It would have meant a full series against the touring Indians, another trip to the West Indies and if my form had held, another Ashes battle with England the following summer. But I was playing out of the mainstream, in Adelaide Turf ranks while guys who weren't regulars, like Tony Mann and Sam Gannon from Western Australia, got games out of virtually nowhere.

It was a huge mistake of mine. The opportunities were there to be in either the Kerry Packer camp on good money, or in the Australian Test team. I can't ever forgive myself for being so stupid. At the time I said I didn't regret going into retirement – no matter how premature some said it was – and I was glad that it had happened. But I was white-hot with anger and felt I had to do something.

Richie Benaud wrote in his column:

> *Frustrated he might be, temperamental at times, but he is also a good cricketer and has given splendid service. He was very much part of South Australia's Sheffield Shield win last summer. This is not the age*

Cleaned up by John Snow in the historic seventh Test in Sydney in 1970-71. I started to duck but the ball just followed me.

I might have fallen over but it still went for 4! A hook shot against "Beetle" Watson and the Sandgropers in 1973-74, when I enjoyed my best-ever Shield game, scoring 59 and 47 and taking 4-43 and 7-127.

The most memorable tour of all, to the West Indies in 1972-73. It took Australia more than 20 years to defeat the Windies again in the Caribbean. Back row, left to right: Yours truly, Ross Edwards, Jeff Hammond, Dennis Lillee, Maxie Walker, John Benaud, Bob Massie, Kerry O'Keeffe and John Watkins; Front: Doug Walters, Ian Redpath, Ian Chappell (capt.), Bill Jacobs (manager), Keith Stackpole, Rod Marsh and Greg Chappell.

Christmas in Adelaide, 1972-73. We beat the Pakistanis by an innings. Guess who we 12th! Back row: Kerry O'Keeffe, John Benaud, yours truly, Rod Marsh, Greg Chappell, Dennis Lillee and Ashley Mallett; Front: Bob Massie, Ian Redpath, Darb Munn (SACA), Ian Chappell (capt.), Paul Sheahan and Ross Edwards.

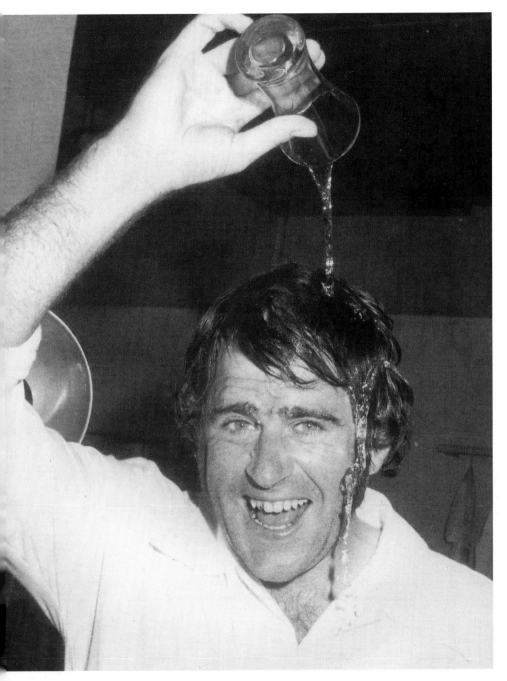

*Top score (74) for Australia, Adelaide, 1974-75. We were 5-84, got to 300
and won by mid-afternoon on day 5.*

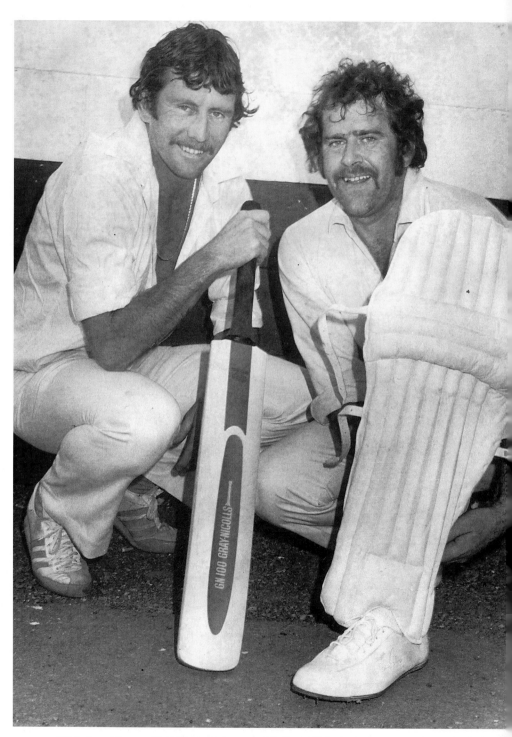

With Ian Chappell, Kilburn versus Pultney Old Scholars, 1977-78. I should have asked "Chappelli" about joining World Series!

h Jacky on our
lding day in 1984.

Dark days: in prison at
Mobilong, 1989. It may
look like a motel suite
but I can assure you,
it wasn't.

With my beloved Trudianne, easter-time 1990, soon after my release on home detention.

It was only a dream but a friend turned it into reality. The start of my house at Wynn Vale in Adelaide.

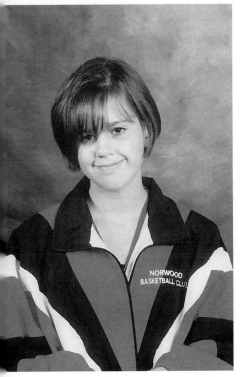

dianne in her Norwood basketball gear.

With my partner, Ann, at the Grant Burge winery at the Barossa Valley during the 1998 Invincibles tour.

Talking cricket with HRH Prince Philip, the Duke of Edinburgh at Windsor Castle in 1997.

The Invincibles, an important part of my life, at Government House in Adelaide in 19
Back row: The Governor Sir Eric Neal, Bill Brown, Ian Johnson, Neil Harvey, Ernie Toshack, Sam Loxton, Bill Johnston, Ron Hamence, Arthur Morris, Doug Ring and Lady Neal;
Front: Barbara Brown, Ali Johnson, Joanna Loxton, Kathleen Toshack, Lesley Ring Sir Donald Bradman, Nora Hamence, Judy Johnston, Judy Morris and Barbara Harv

*of players remaining mute and bowing and scraping to
administrators who often have difficulty in recognising
them without their Australian blazers it shouldn't be
the age when poor decisions like Jenner's omission
from the tour committee should happen."*

I joined Kilburn and that was the beginning of my demise. I ran away from everybody and everything from that day onwards.

In hindsight I should have waited it out and realised that opportunities would surely have come. In the next few months, Woodcock, Cosier and Bob Blewett all captained South Australia. Woodcock's career was winding down. He'd stood down from the leadership even before the end of the year.

My timing was shocking. I wasn't finished as a bowler and whilst my enthusiasm had waned and I wasn't practising as much, new challenges would have provided the immediate lift I needed. It was the beginning of a nightmarish period of my life when everything started to go wrong and the wheels literally fell off.

***

THE MONEY at Kilburn was important, but my competitive nature seemed to spark trouble. I was reported more times than I care to remember and it cost me, even things like Association awards, which while an incidental, would have been nice to have won.

One season in Adelaide Turf, I took 73 wickets and made 300 runs, but was beaten in the Association's Cricketer of the Year award by a bloke who took 20 wickets and made 200 runs. And not only did he win it, he won by a long way.

I asked to see some of the votes and they showed me. In one game I took 9-for in the first innings and 6-for in the second and also made 30. Yet I only got three votes from the possible six! One of the umpires, Doug French, considered I'd been the outstanding player in the game, but the other guy ignored me completely! I wouldn't have minded if he'd said I'd mouthed off too much and he'd deducted a point.

I used to get so incensed when some of the players received votes even for their smart dress! I never thought a player's kit should outweigh performance. One Bradman Medallist many years ago used to wear red and white socks, yet no-one ever docked any points from him.

Right from the time I arrived in South Australia, the awards seemed to be personality-based, rather than decided strictly on a player's contribution.

I may have blued with a few umpires, but others were among my best friends. Norm Townsend, for example, who umpired in Western Australia and was good enough to see Test action, was a great mate. He died much too young. French from Adelaide Turf ranks was another. Likewise Wayne Singh. Most of these guys would let me go and if they saw me getting out of hand, would say, "Come on T.J. Let's get on with it". They didn't try and take control.

I'd always gambled from a young age on horses and Norm and I and a couple of other blokes would be down at the Inglewood hotel after a game for darts and a bet. While it was nothing serious, there were enough times that I lost all the money in my pockets.

***

THERE WAS no doubt that I missed the profile that automatically goes with playing cricket for your State or country. After I quit South Australia, I also had to find a new job. Coca-Cola no longer had any need for my services, but kindly allowed me continuing access to one of their company utes for almost six months.

By rights I should have been taking advantage of the contacts I'd made, both through Coke and cricket and really set myself up. I was selling insurance and could have done very well at it, but instead, wasted virtually two full years, just frittering away my time. If I sold a policy on Monday, I wouldn't work from Tuesday to Friday. Instead I'd wake up and go and play darts with a few blokes down the pub for five cents a game. I needed the discipline of a job where I had to clock on and clock off. Increasingly I was becoming incapable of disciplining my own life.

I'd been punting for a long time and had some terrible moments. I was playing Sheffield Shield cricket at Adelaide one day. I was next in and was sitting in the viewing area with my pads on, when a guy wandered up and said, "Got a minute, Terry? I'm here to repossess your car!".

I got out of my seat and went around to the side and told the bloke I didn't get paid until the Thursday.

"Okay," he said. "I can't find you today but I will definitely find you on Thursday."

I had the money for him, on the Thursday, but it was a narrow squeeze. The money from Kilburn should have paid more bills than it did. But I was irresponsible with it, always living for the moment.

Dad gave me $10,000 for a sports shop and I decided because I was playing cricket in Kilburn I should open a sports shop there. Premises were available and they seemed pretty cheap. But I didn't think it through sufficiently. There was no carpet or shelving and I had no vehicle. Dad's $10,000 very quickly became $5000.

I took time off to attend the Centenary Test in Melbourne, which was not inexpensive, even though our fares and accomodation were paid for. I had a fantastic time catching up with old friends like Frank O'Driscoll, my old captain at Mt Lawley. I probably acted the role that I was doing better than I was and so wasted some more of Dad's gift.

Three of us put some money into a quadrella but what we didn't realise in Melbourne was that each ticket had to be done individually and we had about 180 combinations which cost a total of $90. It cost us $30 each and took us forever to fill out the tickets. Frank put the money on and returned to the cricket, only to accidentally leave the tickets in the back seat of a cab. We madly tried to chase them but ended up going out in the first leg of the quaddy anyway. Theoretically I was spending money that wasn't mine.

I had to stock the shop and was very aware that I didn't have enough money to do it properly. It was then that I started to get out of control with my gambling. I bought stock on consignment and was constantly chasing my tail. I opened on April 1 as that was the day I'd originally arrived in South Australia 10 years previously. David Hookes and Gary Cosier were among my ex-teammates to attend the launch. I had everything on special and grossed just under $800 for the entire week, which was okay, but only enough to meet expenses.

You can't have a sale every week, and when the prices reverted to normal, my custom plunged. The location was poor with little through traffic and I was fast becoming desperate.

By June, Dad told me to shut the doors. Whatever I sold seemed to just cover the rent. He was right. I should have just walked away. It would have at least saved some credibility. Quite a few people supported me, but I let a lot of them down. One guy came in, brought $600 worth of gear, said he'd be back the next day to fix me up and he never came.

By the end of September, I couldn't meet the rent and the landlord changed the locks with all my stock inside, along with many personal belongings like my Australian blazer and scrapbooks. Eventually I became bankrupt, all over $9000.

I was on a complete downer. And soon it was to get worse.

CHAPTER TWELVE

Calling a Spade a Shovel

"Mate, you have two choices here. Either you report me, or shut up. But don't keep going."

I admit I wasn't the easiest cricketer to handle. I still can't explain the day I walked off the ground at Mt Lawley, I can't believe I did that. I was only a young bloke so there was obviously something that was in me that I was totally oblivious to and that no one could explain to me.

As a bowler I became more and more aggressive and I thought in the end that was me and so I kept being me. If I was guilty of saying a few words at times, it was because I thought I had to justify myself and stick up for myself. No-one else seemed to do it for me.

If a bloke played a french cut or a lucky shot, I'd have a word. The opposition knew that they could "get" to me and quite often they did.

In a Shield match in Adelaide, I was bowling to Phil Carlson and Greg Chappell was talking to me as I was coming in to bowl and I was giving it back to him! He got me in nicely.

When I was on the Test arena, I was less aggressive. I felt less at home.

At club level it was different. I was always calling a spade a shovel:

Don "Doc" Beard says they didn't have a tribunal in Adelaide until I got there.

We were playing for bonus points and it was the last over of our match against my old club Prospect. Kensington was just one wicket short of a further bonus point and I was bowling to Rob O'Shannassy, who was to play a couple of games with the State. Rob couldn't read my wrong-uns and having bowled just leg breaks to him, I saved my googly for the very last ball. He played back, it hit him plumb in front and as I pirouetted around to appeal to the umpire, John Wilson, I slipped over and landed on the pitch. He looked down at me, looked up at O'Shannassy and looked down at me again and said, "No, not out".

"That's bullshit," I said, "You're incompetent."

We nicknamed Wilson "One Short". He loved being in the game. If nothing was happening we reckoned he'd call one short just to remind everyone he was out there.

I knew I was gone because my captain Brian Hurn said so. What I didn't expect was the other umpire, George Thomas, to also come into the rooms and say that he was reporting me, too.

"Just a minute, George. Where do you fit into this? You had nothing to do with it."

"I'm reporting you for using abusive language to the fieldsmen last week."

I had in fact said something that I shouldn't have said while batting to a lad called Paul Craig. His father, Reg, had been my coach at Prospect and helped "Rowdy" Mallett and myself to get jobs. I hadn't seen anything of him since I'd moved clubs.

Up I went to face the tribunal – which was closed to the press – and there were three people, "Doc" Beard, Rex Sellers and Reg Craig. I wasn't too sure how it was going to go. I felt that Reg shouldn't have been sitting on it since it was his son who was involved.

The one that I was least in trouble for in the end was the incompetence bit. The umpire testified that he was always in fear of me when he was umpiring because of my aggressiveness. But at that time I didn't have a track record of being abusive to umpires so that worked in my favour.

They took the second charge more seriously and it was pretty touch and go. Doc Beard said there had been good reason to suspend me, but in the end I was let off with a reprimand. He asked me at the end of the hearing why I was so aggressive on the field, but I couldn't tell him. I still can't.

***

WALKERVILLE WAS playing St. Peters Old Collegians one day, and an umpire, who had obviously been preparing himself for any confrontations, took objection to an appeal.

Even our fast bowler Harvey Dawes, who normally wouldn't say boo, got angry. "Don't worry Harvey," I said, from slip. "Just get back and bowl and *hit* the stumps." The umpire immediately went on the attack. "Are you questioning my decision?"

"Sorry," I said, which was unlike me.

"Any more from you Jenner and..."

"Slow down mate," I said.

At the end of the over, drinks were taken and I said to Harvey, "Obviously this bloke is not much of an umpire mate, but if you hit the stumps he'll give it out."

He suddenly appeared from around the back of the group. "I heard that Jenner. If you say any more like that I am going to report you." He was very uptight and said something else back at me and this time it was my turn to walk over. "Mate, you have two choices here. Either you report me, or shut up. But don't keep going."

"I am not staying out here with you," he said and promptly walked off the ground, got his gear, into his car and off he went. We just kept playing with one umpire!

I fronted the tribunal, but when the other umpire couldn't support his mate, I was found not guilty.

***

SOMETIMES EVEN my own club members didn't appreciate the aggressive way I played.

At Walkerville a few thought I was over the top and would come out onto the balcony and heckle, invariably urging me to give someone else a bowl.

We were playing Weapons Research and were doing quite well. One bloke played and missed at me six times in a row and I had a go at him.

"That's enough," said the umpire.

"Come on mate. You're only watching this. It's worse for me. I'm actually bowling it."

An over was bowled at the other end, I began my next and again the bloke played and missed. "Mate," I said beginning to walk down the wicket, "this is no good to you and is sure no good to me."

"That'll be enough," said the umpire and the guy at square-leg started to converge thinking there was going to be an altercation.

"No, no. George," I said, "Just stay out of this. This young man is extremely embarrassed, aren't you mate?"

"Yep."

"Because he doesn't know which way they are going, do you mate?"

"Nope."

Both umpires were now telling me to get on with it. But I wanted to make my point.

"When they go that way, they are called leg breaks and when they go the other way they're called wrong-uns," I said.

He was a nice young lad and I was making a prick of myself.

"Which one would you like?" I asked him. "Which way would you like the next way to spin?"

"This way," he said, indicating the one coming back from off to leg.

"Okay, that's the wrong-un," I said. "And here it comes."

I duly bowled it. He hit it right in the centre of the bat and it disappeared over mid-wicket and into the Walkerville Bowling Club next door!

The hecklers were ecstatic, "How do ya' like that Jenner, you big mouth?".

I walked down to the lad and said, "Well played. Now we're both in the game!".

***

A YOUNG lad called Adrian Gordon from Elizabeth was playing well against Grange one day and took a single to land himself at my end. I'd been giving him a gobful and when his mate at the other end patted away my next delivery, which was a pretty harmless one, Adam replied in kind, "That's the way to handle that shit," he said.

I turned around and glared at Adrian, who was standing back leaning on his bat and as I walked back on the on-side of the pitch, I stabbed the bottom of his bat, causing him to over balance. Silly but pretty harmless stuff really.

Little did I realise that I'd been reported for attempting to kick him. Nothing could have been further from the truth.

We were sitting in the rooms afterwards when the umpires marched in straight towards me and told me I was under report.

"That's silly," I said, "don't go on with that report mate. You'll only embarrass yourself."

"That's it," said one. "You are reported."

One of the other blokes said something as the umpires were walking out and the bloke doing all the talking said, "Right, got you again. Abusive language". It wasn't even me.

It was on the eve of the finals and Grange was well-positioned. I rang Adrian and asked him if he could come into the tribunal as a witness. He did, even though his wife was due to have a baby on the very same day. He said I'd kicked his bat and no way could that be misconstrued as attempting to kick him as he was leaning on his bat which was well clear of his pads.

I beat that charge. Now for the abusive language one. Neville Thiele, the guy who had said it, was waiting in the foyer.

"I have a witness," I said, "who'll tell you that he said it." That stopped the room dead.

"What's to stop you from getting someone else to say they did it when in fact it was you?"

"Because this guy is as important to the team as I am. He is one of our best players."

Neville got into trouble but they couldn't charge him because they had already charged me with the offence. Again the charges were dismissed.

***

VERY EARLY during my time in Adelaide Turf, Kilburn was playing Flinders Park and it was absolutely bucketing down. It was so wet that the crease lines were being washed away, but still the umpires were insisting we play on.

"You can't appeal," they said, "only the batsmen can."

But I knew I could. Years earlier, playing in my first final in Adelaide, we were caught in the rain at the Adelaide Oval, Colin Egar was at square leg and said to me: "Doesn't your captain know he can appeal against the weather".

That day we went off, but this day we didn't.

Neither the umpire standing at the bowler's end nor his mate at square-leg knew the rule. A bloke called Lyall Green was smashing us. We couldn't hold the ball. I held up play and told the umpire that the blokes without jumpers were going off. Five did, but still we had to play on. It was farcical. Green hit the next ball clean out of the ground and I was livid. The umpire bent down and sheets of water poured off his hat. "Look mate," I said. "You are putting yourself in an incredible position here because you don't know the rules."

If anything the rain was getting heavier but still he wanted us to play on.

"Okay, that's it," I said, "We're going. Come on fellas. We're off." Everybody went, bar our wicketkeeper, who I don't think particularly liked me.

That evening I was having a few drinks at the bar and one of the opposition supporters, Malcolm Whitford said to me that we'd forfeited the points by walking off. We had a $5 wager.

We went to the tribunal that week, for walking off without permission, and took some photographs with us, plus the ball which even then was damp. The case was dismissed.

"Okay," I said, "what about my team? We can't possibly lose that game because the umpires didn't know the rules. They were wrong, players could have been hurt. One guy nearly got hit because he tried to take a catch and with the rain in his eyes had to turn his head away."

They deliberated again. The game was declared a draw and I'd won my fiver!

***

PLAYING FOR Kilburn for the first time against a particular side and this old bloke was sending down darts, literally! I was on strike and I'd call him as he threw them: "Double 30, double 20, double 16, oh double 10"

At the end of the over I got up the other end and I said to the umpire, "I can't believe that you could let that stuff go!".

He looked at me with a smile. "Terry," he said, "he's been bowling like that for 30 years. I'm not going to be the first to call him now."

CHAPTER THIRTEEN

The Merry-Go-Round

The bottom line is that I started failing at 14.

Until my involvement with Shane Warne and the kids at the Australian Cricket Academy, I've only had one job that I've been truly proud of and that was with Coca-Cola for five years. Think of a job and I've probably done it. In all, I must have had 40 jobs and that's no exaggeration.

Generally, there was an instability about my employment – not that I'm one out there. There are a lot of people just like me.

Dad enrolled me in an accountancy course when I was just 14. Dad figured if I learnt about accountancy it'd help me later if I took over the shop. It was a correspondence course and there wasn't anybody in town who could help me with it. The fact that I couldn't do it was a major disappointment to him. But profit and loss statements were just too hard to understand at that age. The bottom line is that I started failing at 14. In fact, my decision to opt out of school was really because it was the easy option.

Mum encouraged me to sit for an exam for the West Australian Railways when I was approaching my 17th birthday. She discovered I didn't need to have my junior certificate to join the Railways and that I only had to pass the test to qualify as a clerk. "You're smart enough to do that, Terry," she said.

Mum saw this job as security for me and I got in, just before the cut-off date.

Later, I worked at John Martin's and was ordering some food at the canteen when the lady serving said, "You're too smart to be working here".

Apparently she liked the way I spoke. "You're real educated," she said.

There are a lot of people who thought I was well-educated. Off the cricket field, I could talk alright. But there was always a feeling of embarrassment and hurt when I couldn't go for a certain job because I didn't have the necessary schooling.

I was a pots and pans salesman, sold insurance, and worked as a labourer. Until Hall's and Coca-Cola, I never really had any job security. I considered myself too young to sell insurance. I did the training school and knew what I was about. I suppose it gets back to a self confidence thing. I didn't have any.

After my sport's shop failed, I ran away from people, living on dole money and playing darts to while away the time. One of the guys at the pub I went to was a plasterer. He knew I needed cash and asked me if I wanted to do some work with him up at Moonta.

I'd never done manual labor before and this work was horrendous. The house was up a hill and it was wet. We had to mix the cement down below and then cart it 40 yards, mainly over rough, uneven ground and then I'd have to shovel it up to him, all from an old barrow with its steel tyre which tended to get bogged!

Before we got a place to stay, we even had to sleep in my mate's old Valiant! I appreciated the opportunity but it was demeaning work. At least I was earning cash money, even if it was just four dollars an hour!

The only good thing about this period for me was that I met Jacky. She was young and vibrant and fun to be with. She also helped my self esteem.

***

SOMEONE IN the Moonta Hotel spoke to me about playing cricket up in the town. Apparently it wasn't a unanimous decision to hire me. I signed a contract but I knew they were dubious of me honouring it. Being a declared bankrupt, I was feeling very much like a low citizen, not liking myself much at all.

However, my relationship with Jacky was growing and I went to her 21st birthday party and stayed.

I was going up to Moonta at weekends and hoping that Jacky's little Torana would get me home again. A couple of times it cooked itself. And I slept where it stood. It was just an existence.

I began coaching some of the promising Yorke Peninsula schoolkids at one dollar a child. There was 10 in one group and 11 in the other. It was pocket money for me and the kids were as keen as mustard, but some of the parents weren't impressed. They reckoned I shouldn't have been taking money off kids. Despite the reservations, I did develop one or two good friendships and Moonta cricket club, a perennial loser, did start to improve. I made 100 in my first game at Paskeville, which gave me some immediate credibility. But teaching the team to win was a nightmare. I asked them to practise in whites and the wives reckoned I was only doing it to give them extra washing! Invariably we'd start matches well, only to fall off the rails after the tea interval. The clubrooms were air conditioned and a few of the boys liked to have an early beer. I soon stopped that.

One particularly hot afternoon we were coming off the ground. The blokes were heading, as usual, for the cool of the main rooms when I stopped them and said we were all to have nothing stronger than lemon cordial. What's more we'd have our drinks in the player change rooms, which were tin and like a sauna. There was plenty of complaints, but they were ready to play again in the heat afterwards!

One of the side's characters was a local bank manager Graham Alexander, who, when he had a drink, loved to drive his little Volkswagen up footpaths and around front lawns of the blokes he knew. I was running for a three with him at Moonta one day. We went for the first and crossed back for the second when there was a loud noise. After completing the three I met Graham in mid-pitch. "Did you fart then?" I asked.

"Bloody hell," he said, "We can't have a drink. Now you're telling us we can't even fart!"

We made the semis before running into a champion country player, Rod Davies, who made 70 after he'd been dropped off my bowling early. It gave them a reasonable score and we failed to reach it. I was immediately judged as being unsuccessful.

There were plenty of down times but some up times, too and during that period Jacky was there giving me confidence. I went for a job selling oil additives, got it and things started to lift. It was steady work but if I happened to sell my quota I'd drop off again, especially when I discovering the more I sold, the more they reduced my commission! I became friendly with another of the salesmen and while we were in competition with each other, at the same time we helped each other. We found good new markets and outlets and markedly increased the turnover, so much so that instead of earning $200 a week, I was getting closer to $400, mainly through selling one particular, in-demand product. The bosses must have reckoned it was too easy, reduced the commissions payable and eventually both my mate and I quit.

***

CRICKET WAS one constant for me and after Moonta, I played for Para Hills, Walkerville and Grange in the Adelaide Turf competition before having one final season with an old mate of mine, Trevor "Buddha" Jarman, on the hard wickets at Salisbury North.

By now I wasn't enjoying training and after we won the flag, I'd intended to stop completely before the lure of some cash money with another old mate, Barnie Arnfield at Rostrevor Old Collegians, got me back again. Always when there was money involved, I was vulnerable.

In the first game, I bowled into a howling gale and had numerous stumpings and a couple of catches dropped. I didn't try and hide my disappointment and at the end of the day, after we'd finally dismissed the opposition, I was sitting down, resting my legs which had cramped when Barnie came up and asked me to say something nice to the 'keeper, who was upset at having missed all the stumpings. He knew I was disappointed but I did it anyway.

"I don't want you to feel too bad about today," I said to the 'keeper, "in fact I take full responsibility because I have not had a game for ages but as I get better I'll find your gloves more readily!" Sure I was sarcastic, but I was also dog tired. It didn't win me any brownie points.

By now I was selling tow bars for a living. I was having a bet but nothing too dramatic. Jacky and I were surviving. I got on pretty well with the guy who ran the business. As part of my role, I'd call on car yards to drum up new business. One day someone stopped me and asked, "What's Terry Jenner doing selling tow bars?".

"Everyone's got to make a living mate."

He asked me how much I was earning a week and when I told him, he said that would be my weekly retainer and I'd get commission on top of that for every car I sold.

I was 38 and while it was unusual to be starting in the car trade at that age, Jacky thought it would be a good idea, too, so I went with it.

I had no mechanical knowledge about cars, but in many ways that was an advantage. I wouldn't try and kid the clients. If they asked me something I didn't know, I'd say so and take them out the back to see the mechanics. I learned from probably the best car salesman in Adelaide, Ken Mucklow, and soon I was selling as many as most and making money I hadn't seen before. The down side was that punting was rife in car-yards. One of the managers was really keen and even had his own phone account. Once I realised you could have a bet without money changing hands until Fridays, I was into it. I'd doubled my tow-bar wages from $200 to $400 a week and sometimes if I'd had a good day or two, could pick up an additional $150 to $200 in bonuses. Even if my bets didn't come off, I'd console myself with the thought that I'd make it up the following pay day. I was working long hours and studying the form guide. Making bets was a good way of filling in time in-between clients. I told myself that it was a release from my immediate responsibilities. Wrong again.

I wasn't smart enough to put anything away for the future. The only shares I'd ever bought was when I was with the South Australian cricket team. Ian Chappell, at one time, had worked at the Adelaide stock exchange and done well when Poseidon shares took off. He got another tip and the whole team put their game fee of $25 each in. The shares were only 16 cents each. We were all going to make a fortune, except the company disappeared, never to be heard of again! I didn't understand how a company could be there today and gone tomorrow. Unfortunately I did understand that if you put something on and it won at 15/1, you were going well.

In the old days, the TAB would close on Sundays and you wouldn't be able to pick up your Saturday winnings until the Monday. I was playing at Kensington and on one day took a daily double in Melbourne, Sydney and Adelaide. I also had some single bets and won the lot. It didn't amount to a fortune as I was only betting five dollars at a time, but winning was exciting.

I started to bet over and above my regular pay again and again. Instead of having $10 each way, I'd have $25 each way thinking to myself that it's only Thursday and even if the horse doesn't get up, I'd sell a couple of cars and make up the money through bonuses. I was a good salesman, but once again my own worst enemy. I wasted such a huge opportunity. The people there were generous and supportive, but once I was caught in a web, it became a tangle of lies and deceit. I was on a merry-go-round and couldn't get off.

***

WHEN IT comes to purchasing or selling a motor car, people believe they have permission to play with the truth. A Church of England minister I dealt with once was a tough old nut. He told me he'd been instructed by his ministry that he had to get several quotes on the trade-in value of his car. I was the first off the rank. We talked, an offer was made, which obviously wasn't enough and he said so-and-so had offered him more and was prepared to pay cash.

"But Father," I said, "I thought you said I was the first person you'd been to" and said how shocked I was at him telling a fib.

"God gives us a license to lie when we are buying a car and forgiveness when we have got the best deal!" he said.

CHAPTER FOURTEEN

Running Away

I was now running away, a bankrupt and a
down-and-out gambler who didn't want to see
his old mates or even be recognised in public.

One Saturday afternoon I sold a car and received a $5000 cash deposit, wrote the receipt and put it in the glove box of my car before going off to the trots at Globe Derby Park

Halfway through the meeting, I'd lost what I had in my pocket so left the course and was hopping into my car when the thought hit me: "What if that horse I like comes up in the next race?"

Next minute I'd talked myself into borrowing a couple of hundred of the deposit money which was in the glove box. I knew it wasn't my money, but it was available. I took another couple of hundred just in case.

By the last race I'd lost $500, leaving only $4500 of the deposit monies. The receipt had been written for $5000. Come Monday, I took the money in, said I only had got $4500 of it, but the rest was coming. I had to wait until pay day to make up the money, but the round-robin had started. Because I'd done it once and been able to make up the balance later, I thought I could do it all the time. One day I lost more than I could replace. It became a web where I had to get a deposit from one car and put it against another. I was going around and around in an ever-deepening circle of debt.

I was living off my wits and trying to sell enough cars to cover everything. In the end, the very receipts I wrote were damning.

I had a feeling it was all about to break apart about the time Jacky and I went to America as part of an incentive program provided for all new car managers. Being away from the dealership meant I was unable to answer any questions that arose. I knew the risk I was taking, but didn't want Jacky to miss the trip. Sure enough in my absence, the accountants studied the receipts, found abnormalities and when we returned, I was put on the spot.

A lot of people thought Jacky knew what was going on and turned a blind eye. But that wasn't true. She had no idea of the monies being wasted. I'd reached manager status, was selling a lot of cars and driving around in a Nissan 300ZX. It wasn't as if I wasn't bringing any money home. Unfortunately none was being banked.

I was ashamed of my deceit and hated living a lie. I didn't want to tell Jacky in case I'd lose her.

I told them what I had been doing and, of course, was asked to leave. They told me there would be a full audit and I'd hear more later.

Telling Jacky the truth was terrible. First I had to ask her to give back the company car and it got harder after that. We'd married in 1984. I was 40 and she was 27. After living together for six years marriage was a big step for both of us as neither admitted wanting children.

I had been approached by another car-yard previously and wasted no time in going to them and telling them I was looking for a job. I said I'd had a fall-out with management which was true and I started immediately.

At that stage, I hadn't been charged with anything. I started to do really well at the new dealership ever though there were rumours I could be in trouble.

A few months later, a couple of detectives came to the dealership and asked me to come with them and have a chat. They asked lots of questions and then left a folder with me while they went outside. "Look at it and make your own mind up," they said.

I looked over it and everything was familiar. I knew about the deals they'd left me to see.

They returned to the room. "I know where you're coming from," I said.

One of the detectives said I'd be charged. Did I want a solicitor? The phone call was made and I was formally charged.

It had been suggested that I owned boats and had all these hidden-away assets, which of course wasn't true. I'd gambled the lot.

I had to tell my new boss at the car-yard what was going on. My name was suppressed when I went to court, but everybody in town knew who it was. I was described as a former international sports person, living in the northern suburbs. They did everything bar spell my name out. It was a very difficult time. I went to court and sat there with my solicitor while people acting for the newspapers were calling for the suppression order to be lifted. Some of the statements were very hurtful. One solicitor said the newspaper he represented should have a right to use my name to protect society against people such as myself.

There were some terrible things said. It wasn't as if I'd be going around knocking people out. I had done the wrong thing. I'd been touching money which wasn't mine. But they were all for comparatively small amounts. No-one lost their vehicle or anything like that.

The audit didn't uncover any extras, but at the new dealership, my boss said if the suppression order was lifted and I got any publicity, I'd have to go.

Eventually, after about six months, I was made aware that the order was going to be lifted. I'd been under enormous pressure and this was a real cruncher. I told my boss and he said, "Let's wait and see what happens".

I went and bought the paper and there it was, all over the front page in huge headlines. I'd made a lot of friends in the media over the years but there was nothing they could do about this one. My employer was sorry. By now I was one of his top salesmen. But I had to go. I was again unemployed and now I was unemployable.

It had been 12 years since I'd retired from cricket. From being a high profile player in the news and in the national cricket magazines, I was now running away, a discharged bankrupt and a down-and-out gambler who didn't want to see his old mates or even be recognised in public.

I was enormously depressed and when you're like that, what do you do to take your mind off things? You gamble. Again. And again.

One weekend, there was a knock on my door. I was unshaven and this guy told me he didn't really know why, but he'd come to offer me a job. I couldn't believe what he was saying. Nobody could truly know what impact those words had on me.

I invited him in and we sat down and drank a bottle of scotch while we talked. I told him everything.

He took me up to his car-yard which was close to where we were living. He had a lot of old stock which he hadn't been able to move. He said he was going to put one salesman off and put me on. Given the adverse publicity I'd had, you could have knocked me down with a feather.

Within days I was working for him, by myself most of the time and turning over the old stock and starting to produce really good figures.

Despite my unexpected good fortune with this job, however, I was getting more stressed at my impending court appearance. I needed an outlet, went to the casino one night with $5000 belonging to the yard and lost the lot. I knew I was doing wrong, but literally I'd lost control. I had no self esteem and was insecure. I didn't know how to tell Jacky, so didn't say a word. I was on the slippery dip a second time. The harder I tried to wheel and deal, the deeper into trouble I plunged.

I was scared I was going to jail. I had these silly fantasies about how to make a lot of money so that I could pay all the bills. The reality was harsher. We had to sell our house and rent another.

Jacky was pregnant and our baby was due on September 10. My court appearance had been set down for September 8, my birthday.

We had to work to the worst – and most likely – scenario. If I was remanded in custody, permission would have to be obtained for me to come out for the birth of the baby. I was told they could time it within the hour to get me to the hospital. I'd be allowed two hours there. However, it was unnecessary because Trudianne, my pride and joy, was ultimately 11 days late.

She was born on September 21, 1986 at 7.04am. Jacky was in labor for 25 hours. It was unbelievable. There's nothing quite like experiencing a birth. Trudianne was really struggling and they came in with these huge forceps.

"You've got to go again," I said to Jacky.

She gave a final push and Trudianne was born.

I went home and wrote a poem.

> *I opened my eyes the moment I was born,*
> *Saw a clock on the wall. Twas 7.04 in the morn,*
>
> *Looked around and saw a woman and man,*
> *A doctor named Peter and a midwife named Jan,*
>
> *I looked even further and my heart felt glad,*
> *Because that's when I saw my Mum and my Dad,*
>
> *A message to Mum I want to make clear,*
> *The reason I'm here is that God answered your prayer.*

There was a lot of significance in Trudianne's birth. Initially there was never going to be a baby. Jacky used to say she didn't want any kids. When she first became pregnant, she was nervous about telling me, but I was thrilled. We got to about six months and the baby died in her tummy which was quite traumatic. She said she'd never want to go through that sort of experience again. But she did fall pregnant again. The doctors couldn't tell us if it was a boy or a girl because there was a complication with the umbilical cord. But we had a wardrobe full of pink clothes, so we were hopeful!

Jacky started to have some problems again at about six months and was in hospital for a time. It made Trudianne's arrival truly miraculous.

***

BEFORE GOING to Court for sentencing, I left a confession with my latest employer, telling him about the $5000 I'd frittered away, in a little over two hours at the casino. I knew I'd done wrong.

I was remanded in custody in the Adelaide jail where I spent five anxious days not knowing about Jacky or when the baby was going to come.

The day before sentencing, the bloke from the yard came into see me posing as my lawyer. It was the only way he could get into see me.

"You are a stupid bastard," he said.

I didn't have to be reminded.

The next thing he said amazed me. "I'm going to promote you to manager. We'll work out what's owing. You'll be out of here soon."

It was a huge uplifting feeling. He was also a referee for me.

Everything, of course, revolved around my Court hearing and the ruling of Judge Burnett.

As a first time offender, my counsel was hopeful I'd get a good hearing. It was nerve wracking waiting for his verdict.

The Judge said I'd abused a position of trust and he'd thought long and hard about sending me to prison. But, he'd decided to suspend the sentence. He gave me three years with 18 months non-parole and a two-year good behaviour bond. Restitution was considered to be made because there was money owing to me from the yard which more than covered the amounts I'd stolen.

There was no direction for me to do anything else. I had to wait on a signed release and then was free to go.

I went back to work and tried to repay the money I owed so I could get back my confession which he held. But the more I tried, the deeper I got into trouble.

Jacky walked me up to Gambler's Anonymous one night but neither of us felt comfortable. There was only four people there and I did not find the stories believable.

To work off the money I owed, a complicated repayments system was arranged, which was to come out of the old bombs which were sold for cash. He'd use that cash to deposit against the money I'd "borrowed".

It never seemed to me that the balance owing was ever going down.

We'd spend many nights drinking together and almost every time it could come up in discussion.

I needed to get rid of that debt.

I wish I'd been able to borrow the money somehow but when you get in my position you're not going to ask family or friends – you've already done that.

And, of course, a bank loan is out of the question.

My torment led me into the same mistakes. The boss was away and I "borrowed" to try and win back the $5000 I owed. I got within a thousand, only to lose the lot.

I drove home without a red cent and knew I was going to have to explain myself all over again.

I was now a desperate man. He was away interstate and not returning for two weeks. Each day was more difficult than the day before as it got closer to his return. I tried a couple more times, each time with the same result. I was only going backwards.

On his return I told him what I'd done and he was totally disgusted and understandably so. He told me he wanted to see Jacky to tell her. I told her first. God it was hard. She then went to see him and he said he'd never have me charged, but he expected me to pay it back at some time.

I thought I'd just have to find another job and pay him back when I could, but as it turned out, that was foolhardy. I'd done the wrong thing and if he was irked one day he could easily do something about it. He did, the police were called in and I was arrested. I knew I was in huge trouble.

From then on it was just a case of working through court and trying to plan how we were all going to survive, Jacky, Trudianne and me.

I sought out a friend, Creagh O'Connor, who I felt I could trust and told him my plight. I needed a job and would do anything, but cleaning out toilets. That would have finished me. He gave me a job.

With Jacky working during the day, I needed to look after Trudianne, so worked nights as a welder's laborer. I was dog tired from lack of sleep, but it gave me all-important time with Trudianne, time which would have been impossible had I still been selling cars.

I was getting home at 3am and just seemed to have closed my eyes when Jacky would wake me up and give me Trudianne to look after.

A couple of the blue collar blokes I worked with had been to prison and I listened and learned. In the tea room there were seats for about 100 and the first night I went to sit down in a seat and one of the guys came up and said, "That's my seat mate".

My initial thought was to point him in the direction of dozens of spare seats. We only had 15 on night shift. Instead I apologised and moved.

People were initially wary. The boss had put me on and they didn't know why. When they found out I was waiting to go to court and needed the work to help my wife and just-born daughter, the mood immediately changed and I was accepted as part of the night shift team. It was an experience which held me in good stead later.

Soon afterwards the night shift finished and I started to do days. But it was no good from Trudianne's point of view. We moved closer to the city and to Jacky's work, adjacent to a Day Care Centre. I was able to get some more laboring work and slowly I was building myself up and feeling fitter and stronger.

By now I was seeing a psychiatrist, Milton Bowman, who was fantastic. It took me a long time to tell him everything, especially that I'd been out and had another bet while I was seeing him. But I needed to be totally up front with him. He wanted to understand more about gamblers. He had other patients he consulted and because I was so open it helped him advise them.

My fears about losing Jacky and Trudianne were constant discussion points. It had been so tough for Jacky. I knew I'd put her in an invidious position. Losing her could mean also losing Trudianne.

I hit absolute rock bottom one night at a pub, not far from where we were living. I used to go in there occasionally and have a game of darts before I had to go home or pick Trudianne up. I had very little money. I was getting one day's work a week and giving it all, bar five dollars, to Jacky. A guy befriended me. I was playing darts this night with him when he asked me if I was having a drink. I said no, because I didn't have any money. He said he'd lend me $20. I thought you beauty and paid him back the next time I saw him.

I gradually started to get a bit more work, three or four days a week, but I still needed to borrow some money to have another bet. I went and waited for him at the pub, feeling sick about what I was doing. I would have been there at least 45 minutes waiting for a bloke who I really didn't know to borrow $20. Finally he arrived. We sat down and had a drink. Eventually I asked him if there was any chance of borrowing $20. He said, "No" and just picked his drink up and walked off.

I cried all the way home thinking to myself how low I'd sunk.

I'd played cricket against a Q.C. by the name of Michael David. I went and saw him and told him I was in big trouble. He asked me about the representation I had and agreed to act for me if I pleaded guilty.

I transferred my case to another solicitor who worked more directly with Michael and soon afterwards he called me in to tell me that I was going to court on such-and-such a date and to prepare myself psychologically to go to jail.

"How do you do that?"

"I don't know, but that's where you're going."

I asked him for how long and he didn't hold his punches. The first sentence I'd got was a heavy one, even though it had been suspended. I'd re-offended during the parole period. I was likely to get the original three years plus another similar stretch. And this time there would be no restitution.

Even if I was a model prisoner and had my sentence halved, I was looking at at least two years, if not more, before parole.

My worst fears were being realised.

I felt I needed to see what it was like in prison before I went in and went to visit a 50-year-old long term prisoner. His hair was pure white.

"Ask me anything you like," he said. "I've been in here for quite a while."

If I was naïve when I first played cricket for Australia I was more naïve entering the prison system.

I asked him: "Was your hair white before you came in?"

"What are you?" he said, "A &%#@ing smart arse."

I said I was scared my hair would go white from the worry. We chatted a bit more and he said whatever I do, don't ask people what they were in prison for.

I visited him again but the second time, I asked smarter questions and avoided the abuse.

By this time, Jacky and I had no relationship at all. I'd hurt her a lot and I couldn't face her. There was a delay in proceedings and at least I was able to spend Trudianne's second birthday with her.

I arranged to meet Doug French, Phil Hodges and Creagh, who'd got me the job in the factory and a couple of other blokes for a farewell drink and to thank them for their support. I wasn't going to see them again, not for a few years anyway.

CHAPTER FIFTEEN

The Gambling Bug

*I hated what I was doing, but in the end I
couldn't help myself. The couple of times I did
win big, I should have stopped there and
then, but was never strong enough to do it.*

People wonder when my gambling habit started. But there wasn't
any one day. It built up over many years. And unfortunately for
me, it was to become an addiction, impossible to ignore.

Many people, even those close to me like Ian Chappell, never
knew I had a gambling problem. There was hardly any gambling at
all among the Australian teams I played with. Until Ken Eastwood
was picked for a Test at the end of the 1970-71 summer, I'd never
seen another Test cricketer with a form guide in his back pocket.

When we went to the West Indies in 1973 only Ross Edwards was
interested in the Roulette. Dougie Walters, for all his brilliance with
cards, was not a punter then. We'd go to the trots after a day's play
and while most of the boys would have just one or two bets and leave
it at that, I'd have to bet on every race. Later if I was to have a big
bet, say $200, I'd try and disguise the amount of money I was betting,
I'd wager $200 on different horses and place the bets on at three or
four different windows.

Our tour allowance was far more menial with the South Australian
team. I'd go to the manager, get some money, hop into a cab, go to
the casino, lose and have to go quiet for the rest of the trip.

One night at the Adelaide casino, I was playing Roulette and No.
8 came up in three times in four spins. I smothered it with more and
more chips. My money doubled once, twice and then three times. I

should have picked the chips up, cashed them in and walked out, but no. This was going to be my big night. I stayed and lost the lot.

One day, at Victoria Park, I got a fourtrella which paid $5500. Luckily for me, it was the last race and I walked out of the track with it all.

Another day I had a terrific day only to leave the gallops and head straight for the Saturday night trots and lose the lot.

One night at Darlinghurst at one of those illegal gambling places, I took $40 with me and soon lost it. Another Australian cricketer also lost his money playing roulette. Next minute he was cashing in his Test match payment cheque. I couldn't believe it. In my wildest times I wouldn't have done that. It was sacrilege. He bought $230 worth of chips, backed evens and it came up. He collected his money and left. I stayed, watched a little more and cashed my cheque too. I lost the lot.

I remember collecting my cricket payment from Kensington and was unable to get the cheque cashed. A mate and I went to the races at Morphettville and it wasn't long before my surplus cash was gone.

I anguished over going to a bookie and asking if he could cash it. Ultimately I did. He said, "Leave it in the bag and we'll divvy up at the end of the day. If you win I'll give you the cheque back. If not, I'll give you the change." I felt compelled to have a bigger bet than normal because of the size of the cheque. I can still remember the horse. It was Surround and the meeting was at Sandown. My most vivid memory is of Bill Collins announcing as they came around the corner into the home straight: "Surround can't win."

It was another hollow, very empty feeling in my stomach. I did manage to take some money home at the end of the day, but the cheque was left in the bag.

I hated what I was doing, but in the end I couldn't help myself. The couple of times I did win big and cleared my immediate debts, I should have stopped there and then, but was never strong enough to do it. I knew right from wrong, I always have, but it didn't stop me from gambling.

Having access to extra money in the car game from the early '80s was fatal. I went from earning around $150 to almost $1000 in a good week. I'd only dreamt of handling that sort of money before. All it did was fuel my gambling.

Milton Bowman asked me at one of our first sessions if I gambled to win, or to take my mind off other things? I certainly didn't gamble to win because when I did, I gambled until I'd lost it all again.

I told Milton that once I got stuck into the gambling bug, I could never walk away. Whatever I had in my pocket and whatever I won, I'd fritter away; time and time again. It was a constant torment and I seemed powerless to stop it.

I listened to some tapes by an American, a Dr Custer, during my first weeks in prison. He had worked with compulsive gamblers and was considered an authority in his field. He fought for and finally won recognition in USA medical books that compulsive gambling be recorded as an illness.

Listening to him, I realised that I wasn't a freak and that psychiatric help for understanding is as important as going to organisations like Gambler's Anonymous.

Dr Custer said Governments gain massive incomes from gambling revenues and turn away from the problem.

Even today, almost a decade after I said goodbye once and for all to prison, people still say to me, "you wouldn't be able to have a bet would you?"

I say, "it's 10 years ago now. Life goes on."

I felt a little guilty the first time I went to a casino after my parole finished. But I had made a decision that I was going to be master of my own destiny. I was not going to try to live to other peoples standards or expectations. It was my current partner Ann's son, Damian, 18th birthday and the celebration was at the Adelaide Casino. We played Keno and won and roulette and won before walking away. We weren't there to gamble. We were there for Damian.

In a perfect world a person who has a drinking problem will never drink again. A cancer patient will have a growth removed and it'll never return.

But the reality is far different. Drinkers do drink again. Cancers re-emerge. You need to be aware of the danger.

In a perfect world a person that got into trouble the way I did would never have another bet as long as they live. I got food poisoning from eating fish one day. But I still eat fish. It's just that I'm more selective.

If you have had a huge interest in horse racing and see a horse flashing down the outside and getting up on the line, it's something you can't ignore. You want to go again and see that horse repeat the win.

Just because I may have got a bad lbw decision one day playing cricket doesn't mean that I'm not going to come back for more.

If you haven't gambled, you will never know what it's like. I didn't only steal because I gambled. There were other anxieties. Gambling was one way of taking my mind off them.

Milton said at any time when I may think about putting a bet on a horse, I should substitute the word "bet" for the word "risk". Ann's attitude is that whatever I do with any surplus money I may have is my own business.

I've been to the races with Doug Walters in Hobart and it was a great fun day. Dougie laid the bets. While in England with a tour group, we went to Royal Ascot.

I have a different lifestyle now. I'm so involved in my coaching and rarely even have time to think about going to the races. I just do my job.

Mind you, I'll never live to anybody else's expectations. If I want to have a bet I will. If I don't, I won't. But there is no way I will ever hurt myself or those closest to me.

I still do have a flutter at the TAB when the mood takes me there. But having endured what I have been through, it's always with my money. I have my life back again. I'll never live somebody else's. I have my house at Wynn Vale and I have my respect. If I was the old T.J., the house would be gone, Ann would be gone, I wouldn't be seeing my daughter and I wouldn't be doing the things I do now.

Ann doesn't have a gambling bone in her body, nor does Jacky. My wish is for Damian and Trudianne to follow in their mothers' footsteps, as far as gambling is concerned.

CHAPTER SIXTEEN

Welcome to Hell

*I burst into tears. I later discovered that crying
was a no-no and a sign of weakness in jail,
but it wasn't so bad if you cried for your
daughter.*

Deep down, I knew I had to go to jail. Six-and-a-half years was a big stretch. I'd been weak and let a lot of people down. I'd embezzled more than $10,000 to fuel my gambling habit. It was traumatic enough knowing I'd put my marriage in jeopardy and didn't know if I'd ever be able to see my daughter again. Now I was behind bars with the Judge's sentencing words echoing: "JENNER, YOU'RE A PARASITE."

The prison officer walking me around to the cells at the Adelaide Remand Centre offered me some advice: "If you're going to survive this system, Jenner, you are going to have to lift your self esteem."

"How do you lift something that you haven't got?" I said.

I was taken through to a wing where there were 28 cells, 14 on the bottom level and 14 on top. I'd been given instructions to walk down one side, virtually hugging the wall and wait while each security door was opened. I could see the other prisoners through the thin strips of perspex. Many of them had beards. They all seemed angry and aggressive.

It was lunch time and just like at O'Connor Engineering, you had to line up for food and not sit in the wrong spot. I got my food and stood and waited until there was an empty seat. Only then did I go over and ask if I could sit down. This tough guy looked at me and said, "Yep". I sat down. There was no conversation.

After the meal I was told I had a visitor. I had just gone through the angst of would I or wouldn't I see my daughter again and concluded that probably I wouldn't because I left an AVCO debt unpaid.

I didn't want my marriage to be over. Jacky hadn't said it was, but there wasn't much for her to hang on to. If Jacky was going to disappear from my life, Trudianne would too. She'd been my little girl. To lose her would have been unbearable.

I was taken out to the visiting section, which was a very small area, with the prison officer not more than three feet from me. Next minute there was Trudianne running around the corner. I burst into tears. I later discovered that crying was a no-no and a sign of weakness in jail, but it wasn't so bad if you cried for your daughter.

Jacky followed Trudianne around and we were given close to 20 minutes. A close mate, Doug French, also came. I was very emotional. It was the first sign of light at the end of the tunnel.

"Time's up, Jenner," said the "screw" and I was led away. Jacky told Trudianne I was going back to work. When the cell door closed behind me for the first time, I immediately felt terribly ill and claustrophobic.

Unlike the Adelaide jail with its old-fashioned cells and bars on the windows which at least let in some fresh air, this cell was inside a wing. With its cold concrete walls, you were totally cut off from the outside world. It was like being in a mine shaft, completely closed in. I didn't think there was any air in the room and started to panic, lying face down trying to breathe. I was in a bad way and in my desperation pressed the alarm button. A screw arrived. "What's your problem?" he said, speaking to me through the perspex.

"I can't breathe in here."

"You may as well get used to it."

The other prisoners hadn't known who I was when I first came in. That night I was all over the TV news. The upside of that publicity was that the other prisoners knew I wasn't a child molester or a granny grabber. They also knew I didn't have any money.

I was told I had to give a blood sample as part of an AIDS check, but was too distressed so they left it for the following day. Coming in, I'd been issued with a toothbrush, paste, soap, comb, small bubble of shampoo, shaving stick and pocket tissues, plus a pack of cigarettes and some potato chips. They temporarily withheld a plastic razor in case I was suicidal.

The rules were rigid. There was no room for negotiation. Prisoners were allowed to have up to 10 letters and six photographs in their possession. Any more either had to be destroyed or kept in storage. I was allowed one free phone call on the first day and two after that, which had to be paid for. One free stamped envelope was also issued each week.

I was to be given a wage, 10 cents per day, plus an additional $1.90 per day if my cell was clean and I obeyed orders.

A key to the cell was issued to each prisoner. You'd lock yourself in and out. If anything was lost, it was your own fault.

Remand Centre prisoners were allowed an hour in the gymnasium, an hour playing pool and an hour in the yard. Other than for lunch or dinner breaks, the rest of the time was spent locked up.

No wonder most of them were angry. Some had been waiting 18 months for trial or a court appearance. All the talk naturally was about lawyers, trial dates and sentences. The young guys were the most abrasive and inclined to stay in their cell rather than go out for an hour's fresh air. The older blokes always went outside.

Our options during recreation hour was suddenly limited when someone wrote in chalk all over the pool table: ALL SCREWS ARE DOGS. The table was immediately confiscated.

To fill in time, guys played cards or looked at the racing form. Early on I was asked if I wanted to go into tipping competition for horses but declined.

I was waiting in the queue to use the phone when one of the inmates asked me: "Do you mind if I skip in? I'll only be a minute. I just want to put a bet on."

I had to smile at that one.

When you enter prison for the first time, you start from scratch. There are a lot of "inside" rules which apply – but no-one tells you which you have to find out for yourself.

There is "hard" time or "easy" time. You can't just sit anywhere you want, you don't ask what people are in for and you avoid eye contact. Any of these three can get you a hiding.

You also can't afford to be nice to the screws or you become a "screw lover". That creed also applies in reverse for the prison officers.

I found it incredible but everyone except me seemed to be innocent and had been set up by the cops!! Some of them are still in prison today. Once they go to trial, it is probably like a breath of fresh air for them to be able to admit that yes, they had done it. I learnt very early not to ask questions. It makes me shudder even now thinking about some of their crimes.

One day I was sitting down and an older chap came in and started talking. He was very uptight and said he'd just come in from Ceduna. I told him what I knew of the rules and out of the blue he said to me, "Do you miss your wife?".

"Yes," I said. "I hope it'll work itself out."

"Gosh I miss mine. I know I'll never see her again." He started to get pretty emotional, saying how they were going to throw the key away with him. He'd never again be able to hold his wife, feel her breasts or make love to her.

I told him that nothing was that bad and that he shouldn't give up hope. "My wife said she wouldn't come to see me but then she did. You never know, your wife may come too."

"No," he said, starting to sob. "She can't do that. I killed her." Next day it was all over the papers. He'd stabbed her with a kitchen knife and then virtually cut off her head.

The reality of the viciousness that was surrounding me was never far from the surface. The tension in prison was unbelievable.

Every day was identical, with the same routines applying, over and over again. All some of the prisoners thought about was how to put one over on the screws. There was a big kerfuffle during my first week when the screws thought they'd found some heroin. All a few guys had done was shave some soap and set it all up for fun.

During that week, a decision was made where I would be taken for further assessment. In prison, you just don't go anywhere. You have to be placed.

I decided that I should try and clear the loan I'd left behind and rang my old South Australian teammate Ken Cunningham, whose radio show in Adelaide has always been a top-rater. I told "K.G." that if a fee could be arranged for my story, it could see the loan paid off and give me a chance of Jacky and I surviving together. I didn't want that debt to be the one thing to break the camel's back with Jacky.

K.G. said he'd ask management and since he couldn't ring me, could I ring him back tomorrow?

Later that day, my old cricket teammate Neil Hawke, who was working for the Adelaide *News* paid a visit. I never related Neil's visit to his job as a journalist. I only saw him visiting me as a friend. We talked and it was good, caring stuff. I knew what he'd been through in his own life. Now he was supporting me.

The next day I went and saw the head screw and asked if I could make an extra phone call. Sometimes they could be generous and sometimes they could be difficult. He allowed me to make the call, so I rang K.G. and asked how things had gone.

"I don't suppose you've seen the afternoon paper?" he said.

"No."

"Well Hawkey' has done an exclusive interview with you. And now my people aren't interested."

I wasn't sorry that Neil had got a story. But I was sorry that it had effectively blocked me getting the money to pay off the loan. Neil hadn't done it intentionally and several months later when he became aware of the debt which was causing me all sorts of worry, he organised a function at the Italian Club, with Alan Jones as the speaker and helped raise enough money to not only clear the debt but buy a second-hand car for Jacky.

**

THE PRISON system is designed break your spirit. The only way to survive it all is to keep in touch with reality. People don't understand that prison isn't about the bars and the razor wire. It is about people and surviving with people you have nothing in common with. It is also about being separated from people that you care about. That's the real punishment.

I was transferred from the Remand Centre to Yatala, the big house. Just driving through the gates was threatening enough. I was to be there for assessment before being designated a prison program. After a period in the holding cells we were issued with new clothing. Well, different clothing anyway. Everything was second-hand including the jocks and socks. My trousers were half masters, but complaining wasn't an option. They certainly didn't give you much chance of feeling good about yourself.

We lined up in single file and marched to "E" Division, manacled. On the way we passed some of the heavyweight criminals having their recreation. I recognised a few of them. Most were in for vicious crimes, some of which I'd seen publicised on the news. They were in "B" Division: maximum security.

Once in "E" Division, we were taken two at a time to our cells. I was paired with a young bloke, a nice type of kid who hadn't done anything terribly dramatic. He'd been in there before and knew what went on. It was a relief not to have someone who was a real rotten egg who could make life tougher for me than it already was. He even let me take the bottom bunk. At this assessment stage, everyone is trying like hell to stay out of trouble.

My immediate options, as I soon was to learn, were strictly limited. Either I was to go to Yatala's "B" division or to Mobilong, a medium security prison. One thing was for sure, I wasn't going to a low security prison like the Cadell Prison Farm because mine was too long a sentence. You work your way through the system and earn your rights. The Assessment Board told me I was a high-profile prisoner and couldn't be seen to be getting privileges.

The social worker explained how the system worked and how I was to serve my time. Everyone, he said, started at a maximum security prison like Yatala before earning medium status (Mobilong) and then minimum status (Cadell), before finishing at The Cottages prior to release. While my term was for six and a half years, including a three year non-parole period, I could slash the non-parole period by a third with good behaviour. The last six months could be served under what was known as home detention. It meant that if things went right for me, I could be released as early as mid-March, 1990. If I said it fast, it didn't sound too long.

I wrote to Ian Chappell to thank him for his support. He'd appeared on K.G. Cunningham's radio show saying I wasn't a criminal and that everyone should give me a chance. He was one of the first to visit me. He also wrote a story in the *Sun Herald* which I really appreciated. In part, it said:

> The sombre voice at the other end of the phone said simply: "T.J. got six-and-a-half years with a non-parole period of three years."

> I had known for some time my former South Australian and Australian teammate was in a bit of strife. Already on a suspended sentence, he'd been convicted a second time for embezzlement. But until that phone call, I hadn't realised just how much trouble.

> I was shattered when I heard the severity of the sentence, especially with the amount of money involved.

> You see I don't consider Terry Jenner to be a criminal. Never have, never will. In fact, I've always classed T.J. as a very honest cricketer, so honest at times he made life difficult for the captain.

There never was anything behind the back with T.J.. If he was cranky with me for not making more use of his leg-spinners, or for not bowling him into the wind, I soon knew I had incurred his wrath.

At the close of play T.J. would plonk himself down next to me at the long wooden table that used to dominate that home dressing room at the Adelaide Oval. He'd bang his glass firmly on the table and then pour a beer for both of us from the bottle of Southwark he was carrying .

The formalities out of the way, Terry would look at me straight in the eye and say, "What's wrong with my bowling?".

I would then have to explain my captaincy for the day, particularly as it affected T.J.. He'd hear me out, then proffer his own thoughts on how it could have been done better.

That done the matter was closed – until the next time I erred in his eyes.

Importantly though the next time was always a separate incident. T.J. didn't hold a grudge. As a captain it was difficult to be annoyed with a bowler who was complaining because he wanted more work!

Given where I was and how I was feeling, support like that was like gold. In the months ahead, many of my ex-cricket mates followed Ian's lead and visited. Ross Edwards and Bob Massie saw me. So did Peter Sleep and Trevor "Buddha" Jarman. Max O'Connell, the Test umpire and Alan Jones the Sydney radio icon also came in.

Jacky and Trudianne continued to visit, too, at weekends. Trudianne kept telling everybody that Daddy was at work. She'd pass a red brick building and automatically say, "That's where Daddy is working".

***

YATALA WAS a hell of a place, the real McCoy. The difference between the Adelaide Remand Centre and Yatala's "E" Division was like comparing the front bar of a plush hotel to a front bar at a workingman's club.

All prisoners came to Yatala for assessment. In "E" Division, most were either serving time for assault or break and entering or were credit card type criminals.

The extra discipline at Yatala hit you in the eye. At meal times, unless actually using your knife, fork or spoon, they had to be laid out on the table in full view of the screws. The food revolved around stewed meats, packet mash, canned peas and carrots, with an orange later. Even Coke seemed to taste different in jail.

I couldn't even draw my sister a layout of the cell as it could be considered a potential escape plan. Screws opened and read your mail. They even watched you having a crap. It was all part of the philosophy to break your spirit. The only way I felt I could survive the prison system was to dare to be normal. By succumbing to institutionalisation, life on the outside could never be the way it was.

The cells weren't large and had solid steel doors interrupted only by an opening about 15 inch long and six inch wide which was used mainly as a peep hole by the screws. Cells had to be kept immaculate. Each morning they had to be mopped and polished, ready for a daily inspection when prisoners were required to stand outside the door at attention. They would then go in and inspect and call you in if a knife or fork was out of place or your bed was improperly made. If the chrome was dirty they made you clean it with a toothbrush.

Only when inspection was completed were we allowed to eat.

You even had to sleep a certain way around, so the screws could do their night-time head count!

If you wanted anything special, like a loan of a radio or a television for a night, you had to apply in writing to the head screw and hope that it would be approved. You also had to have a ready supply of smokes, the prison currency. A radio could be traded with a fellow prisoner for four or five cigarettes and a newspaper bought for one or two, but few were prepared to part with their TV's, which were, after-all, one of the few links to the outside world.

One night my cell mate, Peter, wanted to play cards. I suggested I could teach him Switch, the game Dougie Walters had taught me in the West Indies, seemingly a lifetime before. The only problem was that we didn't have any cards, but the guys directly adjacent to us did. The distance between our cell and their cell was about 12 feet. It was against the rules to pass things between cells. But we thought what the heck. "Woody" in Cell 15 unravelled threads from his cotton blanket and joined them all together. He attached one end to a toothbrush and using it as an anchor, put his hand out of the slot and whizzed it around, casting the brush in Peter's direction. Peter had his arm out ready for the catch. The whole cell block was alerted to what was happening, with the guys at the end looking out for any sudden appearance by the screws. If our situations hadn't been so serious, it would have been hilarious. Seeing Woody cast his toothbrush was like watching Grandad fishing and after two or three goes, Peter finally caught it and waited while the box of cards was attached to the thread and slowly lowered to the outside floor. When the all-clear came, Peter pulled the pack in up through our slot like it was a flounder!

When Dougie Walters and I needed a pack of cards to play, we could ring room service! Hadn't times changed!

My morale at this early stage in "E" Division was not too bad. We had an approach from *Woman's Day* and I spoke to a lovely lady called Liz Johnswood who assured me she'd write the story with great care and with the knowledge that I wanted to get back with Jacky and Trudianne after I'd done my time. Originally we were going to do the interview face to face. But the prison management knocked it back, citing preferential treatment. The screws, especially a few bad tempered ones, enjoyed that. Some didn't like me getting publicity. Some preferred to treat me like a child and belittle me at every opportunity.

Dealing with Liz was uplifting and humanising. I looked forward to the story appearing.

As much as I hated the rules and all the conditions and didn't want to be in prison, I did feel an enormous load was lifting off my shoulders. No longer was I on the run. And no longer was I having to lie. Milton Bowman, my psychiatrist, was continuing to come and see me, too; even though he didn't have to.

***

ONE OF the screws at Yatala fancied himself as the ultimate Gestapo man and treated us like pigs. He was young and overweight, walked like a penguin with his hands on hips and played with his walkie talkie as if it was a gun.

Our unit, all 34 of us, were sent to the tennis courts while the sniffer dogs, which were trained to detect drugs, went to work. We had a football, three or four tennis balls and a cricket bat. The tennis courts were locked behind us and the football kicked across the 2 courts so as to avoid kicking it over The Wall. When it did go out of our immediate area, usually we were allowed to go and pick it up. But not with this bloke. He incited everyone and loved it. In the end another officer came along and we asked him to get the football and Jo Cool, with his dark sunnies, told him not to get involved and that he'd go and get the ball when he was good and ready. This sort of behaviour happened regularly.

A Mr White was about the only screw I found helpful. He gave me some phone tokens and later was to help break the red tape, when I tried to get a TV. I'd been told I couldn't survive my sentence without one.

I rang Jacky and while she understood, said we didn't have any money. She suggested I ask my sister. I rang Laraine. "You must be joking," she said. "You're in there to be punished; not for a good time!"

I know she didn't say it to hurt me. Being in jail, as I explained, wasn't fun. It was bloody frightening and it was going to be tough for me.

She ultimately loaned me the money, $391, and after some initial hassles, I finally got my colour TV. Her support throughout my time in prison was enormous. In all reality, we grew closer than we had ever been before. Sis reckons me going to prison aged her by 10 years.

***

AFTER I had been at Yatala for about two weeks I attended another meeting with the Assessment committee where I was asked what type of work I'd prefer to do. The boys had wised me up. "Tell them you'd like to grow oranges or plant crops," they said. "That way you may end up at Cadell."

My response was just that. There were a couple of smiles among the board members.

Cadell was a low-security prison near Waikerie. There they grew their own fruit and vegetables and even had their own cricket team!

I'd heard the superintendent at Cadell had asked to get me up there immediately because the cricket season was just starting. But maybe he didn't have enough pull. The people at Yatala said it would have to be the following season because I was going to Mobilong for a year. Then, if all went to plan, I'd have six months at Cadell and six at The Cottages. That brought things into perspective.

Just days before being transferred, we'd all been locked up for almost a day after some sort of hassle.

I desperately wanted to get outside and away from the confinement of my cell. Trying to take my mind off things, I started reading a story about Ricky May and how he'd died young after a heart attack. It triggered an immediate and giant attack of claustrophobia and I was finding it almost impossible to breathe. I had pains in my chest and was sweating like I was in a sauna. I called for help and began knocking on the cell door to attract attention. Finally a screw came and said it was normal stress. If I hadn't recovered in 15 minutes, he'd get me off to the doctor. When I finally got into the medical room I was so light headed I almost fainted.

CHAPTER SEVENTEEN

The Bongolong Hilton

*I was always fascinated by the prisoners
who'd yell, "I'm not eating this shit!". What
were they expecting? Sirloin of beef, cooked
rare with peppercorn sauce washed down by
a nice red?*

In jail, there are always prisoners you won't agree with. We all understood the code, even though we didn't like it. Child sex offenders do it the hardest. The bush telegraph is very much alive in prisons. When someone new appears, inmates are immediately suspicious. If they haven't seen him somewhere in the system they feel he may be a protectee. If he is, he rarely lasts long in his new surrounds.

My way of dealing with it was to keep as much as possible to myself. But it was just so claustrophobic in jail. And it led to some frightening situations, including one life-threatening one for me while waiting to be transferred to Mobilong.

Along with three other blokes, I was in one of the oldest prison cells in the jail, solid concrete with only one tiny hole in the roof. It had a steel bars, plus a forbidding steel door I'd only ever seen before in old movies. At least you could see through the bars and feel the air coming in, but not when the steel door was closed. The beds were solid concrete, not that anyone was doing any sleeping.

Suddenly the steel door which had been ajar was pushed shut without warning. I felt entombed. A couple of the blokes were smoking and I had this overwhelming panic attack. I remembered where I was and told myself that I didn't know who these guys were or what they were in for. Two looked harmless enough but the other guy who was smoking was an aggressive type. I wasn't about to tell him that smoking kills.

I was gasping for air. It was just like when I was first locked up in the Remand Centre, only worse because this time there was only two metres between the back wall and the front wall with its steel door. I banged, rattled and kicked the door to attract attention and the aggressive looking guy with the cigarette told me to knock it off.

"I can't breathe," I said.

"Don't be so &%#@ing stupid. Knock it off."

Finally a screw opened the door slowly. I said, "Excuse me, can you leave the door ajar for me please?"

"Why? What's your problem?"

"I can't breathe."

He pointed to the pinprick hole in the roof and said, "that's air" and shut the door again.

I tried to control myself, taking deep breaths but I couldn't settle down. I was starting to sweat like mad. Another of the blokes told me to calm down, but I kept on rattling the door. By now, I was panicking so much I didn't care what anyone said to me, even though I knew I might get hurt. The door opened again and it was a different face.

"Excuse me sir," I said. "I am absolutely paranoid and claustrophobic and with that door shut like it was I can't breathe. Can you just leave it slightly ajar so I can see out?"

"Sure," he said. "That's not a problem." I was then able to relax, breathe normally and settle down, albeit with one hell of a headache.

I later found out that the door was shut because a corrupt, high-profile police detective in on drug charges was being taken to court. One of the guys in the cell with me had been part of the corruption and the prison superintendent didn't want any eye contact.

As far as I was concerned, it was a life threatening experience and people who don't suffer from panic attacks or are perfectly comfortable in confined spaces wouldn't know that it's just the worst possible feeling.

We were then put in a van, manacled and taken to Mobilong where we were met, the procedure outlined and each of us issued with a new set of prison clothes. They were upmarket compared to the ones we'd been wearing at Yatala.

Mobilong was known to the prisoners as the "Bongolong Hilton" – "Bong" as in marijuana and "Hilton" because it was the first modern prison with a toilet and a shower in every cell.

As the clothes were being issued, one screw said to me: "You think you're better than the rest Jenner, don't you?"

"No."

"Well you're not."

He then allocated me to my unit and I was escorted to my new home: cell six.

Later, I was given options of where I wanted to work and requested the kitchen. They only employed long-term people there and as I was to be there for 12 months, it was considered long enough to get into a routine.

As in most institutions, meal times were the highlight of a day and it was important for overall harmony that most liked what they got.

Not only did it allow me to work seven days a week – at four dollars per day – it also put me much closer to food. I ate quite a bit and stacked on the weight.

One of the popular tricks around meal times was for the prisoners to get to see the medical staff and be granted permission to eat salads because they needed it. It provided an option to the staple stew with mash, or over-cooked steak or fish.

It meant us having to have enough additional salad to make special meals for special cases. I'd combine the celery and carrot and whatever else I could muster to try to make it look reasonable on a plate and then wrap them, name them and arrange for their distribution.

When you're cooking for 160 people and steak is on the menu, the cooked meat is placed on aluminum trays and kept warm in ovens before being served. I was always fascinated by the prisoners who'd yell, "I'm not eating this shit!". What were they expecting? Sirloin of beef, cooked rare with peppercorn sauce washed down by a nice red?

Both the No.1 and No.2 cooks were lifers. They'd both committed atrocious crimes. One of them had murdered his homosexual lover and the other, older one had returned to prison after murdering for a second time. My chores when I first went to the kitchen included hosing the benches and mopping the floors. These guys had big carving knives and the moment wasn't lost on them.

I was cleaning the big benches, above which was the shelf with all the big tins of condiments. I sensed someone coming up from behind and as a reaction threw my hands out. "Touchy, aren't we," said the cook, the bloke who'd done in his boyfriend. All he was trying to do was reach for the flagon of tomato sauce!

Soon I graduated to the salads and took great pride in them. I learnt how to shape a tomato and by cutting them ever so fine as if I'd used a razor blade, became expert at making them go around. Sometimes 10 lettuces would have to feed 160.

The orders would arrive on Monday morning and everything would need to be sorted and planned so the supplies lasted into the following weekend.

With up to 40 special salads on order, it meant I had to become very adept at coleslaw, even if it meant the prisoners went without cabbage on roast day!

***

DAYS WEREN'T so difficult as my job took up most of my time. But the evenings were something else.

After lock-up, the sound of the warder's keys is consistent as they parade up and down. At first you can't imagine being able to go to sleep with that sound and in the end you can't go to sleep without it.

Some nights you are awakened by the rattling of the keys in a door. That usually means bad news. It's either an illness or a death in the family.

When you heard those keys in the early hours of the morning, you prayed the screw wouldn't stop outside your cell.

One Saturday afternoon, after a visit by Jacky and Trudianne, they returned to Adelaide in torrential rain. The drive from Murray Bridge at the best of times can be slippery. This night the conditions were horrendous.

I was so anxious for their safety this night, I talked myself into a lather of sweat. I was always worried about them, but this time it was over the top and there was nothing I could do. I looked up and saw the cigarettes on a shelf. I'd given up smoking for more than two years but boy did I want one now! I did everything in my power to distract myself, including deep breathing, the lot. Fortunately I remembered I'd hidden a boiled egg under my bed. I ate it and it helped me overcome the desire to smoke. Eventually I went off to sleep.

When I woke up the next morning, I made a phone call and was reassured that Jacky and Trudianne had arrived home safely. Talk about relief. For the first time I knew the meaning of "taking one day at a time". Lots of people had advised me that was the way to go, but up until then I didn't know what it truly meant.

I found out that if I could survive that one day, it meant that it would be longer before the next panic attack and I'd be stronger for the experience of not giving in. By not having a cigarette, I'd at last given myself some self esteem. I'd done something I was proud of. It was a turning point. I felt good about myself and knew if I could keep strong, I was heading in the right direction.

Milton Bowman continued to visit me. He did this on his own time. His visits meant a lot to me and I looked forward to them. Our topics of conversation would invariably revolve around Jacky and

Letters from jail
(from Terry to his sister, Laraine, in Perth)

Mobilong, November 20, 1988: *I have the feeling that a giant load has been lifted off my shoulders but my problems are very much the same, minus gambling anxieties. My debts haven't been reduced, my future isn't any rosier and I haven't changed. I am T.J., minus gambling.*

Trudianne and how I was frightened of losing them. My gambling had moved one pace left. No longer was it important, not compared with my family.

Jacky visited every Saturday with Trudianne. Jacky would always look smart and extremely well groomed. Trudianne, too, was always dressed to please her Dad. She'd run towards me, her eyes sparkling. "Daddy, Daddy, *my* Daddy." I'd cuddle her for almost the full 40 minutes.

Jacky and I would discuss some things but mostly it was pretty tense. I didn't initially know how difficult it was for them in the visit area waiting to come through. It wasn't until much later that I realised just how much Jacky was sharing the whole thing with me. I'd see them arrive from my cell window and I'd immediately become excited. I couldn't wait to see them.

After the publicity generated by "Hawkey" in the Adelaide *News*, other media organisations also showed interest in my story.

People from *A Current Affair* contacted Jacky seeking an interview. They said they wanted to do a sympathetic story. I was dubious at first as to their true motive, but I'm glad I agreed. Once prison management agreed to have the reporter, Martin King, and his film crew at the prison, it meant I was going to be on show for all the inmates – which probably was my major concern. When the day came and Martin and his crew arrived, they were terrific. Jacky and Trudianne came up especially to be filmed. It meant an extra visit.

The filming went on for five or six hours. A couple of inmates agreed to go on camera and talk about me.

One approached me later and said, "You must be getting some money out of this. I think I should have some of it, too".

"No," I said, "I am doing this because I think I should help people understand what jail is all about." He was okay after that.

Part of the filming involved me saying goodbye and even though we did it more than once, every time there was a tear in my eye. But it wasn't for the cameras. I cried every time they left.

I was pretty tense the night I knew it was going to air. One of the guys saw a promo and they showed me wiping a tear from my eye. "I hope you don't cry in this, mate," he said.

"I was saying goodbye to my daughter."

"That's okay then," he said. "As long as you're not crying because you're in jail."

It duly went to air. Channel 9 didn't let us down. It was the talk of the prison for days.

Jacky and Trudianne were treated as giants. Martin King was at pains not to jeopardise my position, not only with Jacky, but with the other inmates. I couldn't thank him enough.

***

IN PRISON, everything is done at a measured pace. You learn not to rush, as any surprise can cause problems. But when you're ranked as a "straight head" like me, not a lot tends to happen in front of you.

I was fortunate that Reg Spiers, the former Commonwealth Games javelin thrower was in my unit. He was serving time for conspiracy to smuggle drugs.

Reg was a great character and having also spent time in prison in Indonesia knew the ropes. He thought Mobilong was paradise.

An enormously powerful man, Reg worked out in the gymnasium every day. Nothing seemed to bother him. As I was becoming accustomed to prison life and its daily dose of anxieties, Reg was on hand to save my bacon on more than one occasion. He'd explain to any prisoner I'd accidentally offended that it was purely my naivity and that seemed to fix it. However, I'm sure his size helped.

In his super-confident way, Reg once said to me: "Terry, we don't belong in here. Why are we here? So you knock off a couple of bob from your boss. He's got plenty and I'm in here for making people happy."

I couldn't help but laugh.

Reg noticed Jacky's body language at visits. His advice to me was to get rid of her and go and stand at the bus stop at peak hour because there was a busload of sheilas, as he called them, coming past every 10 minutes!

"But what about love?" I said to him.

"Love 'em all, Terry. Love 'em all!"

I got tonsillitis and was so ill I was semi-bedridden for a time. But this was prison and I still had to keep my cell neat and tidy. Not only did Reg clean up my cell, he organised my laundry so my wages wouldn't be docked. Prisoners normally didn't do this sort of thing for other prisoners.

I enrolled in a computer course and the prisoner in charge was the ex-policeman Colin Creed, who was known as a "rogue" cop. A Christian organisation had brought in a show for us to watch and after computers, I walked to the gymnasium with Colin and naturally enough sat with him. After the show, on the way back to the unit, Reg sidled up to me and said on the quiet, "You're not fussy who you sit with, are you?"

"What do you mean?"

"He's a dirty cop."

"Aren't we all equal in here?"

"Yes, it's just that some are more equal than others."

Later, it was explained just by sitting with him, the other prisoners would automatically classify me with Creed. Once a cop, always a cop.

I appreciated Reggie's help throughout, but he wasn't going to become a lifelong buddy. Not so another of the guys I met.

I received a message telling me a prisoner from another unit wanted to see me. I was immediately suspicious but went anyway. I met Frank, a man close to my own age. He was in, I discovered, for the same crime as me. We hit it off straight away.

Apparently he was playing tennis each day with Colin Creed. I was able to advise him very quickly that it wasn't the thing to do and their games stopped. We'd walk around the oval most nights and talk. Like me, he'd been a gambler and had told his wife he was in trouble only on the very morning he went to court. As we walked, we talked family and freedom. Frank served his time by full moons. I did mine daily and we decided that one day we should all go to see *Phantom of the Opera* in Melbourne.

I began to look after him from the kitchen with extra big salad sandwiches all nicely wrapped up. One day he complained that I was sending him too much, so the next day his package arrived and it was all the skins from the spuds and peelings from the carrots. He got the point.

Frank's sentence was half of mine, so it wasn't long before he moved on and eventually was free. He wrote me a letter as I was nearing the end of my sentence and these words have always remained in my mind.

"I didn't realise how long your sentence was," he said. "I've been out as long as I was in and you're still there."

We went to "Phantom" the day Frank's parole expired. It was great and very gratifying that we had completed something we'd started in prison. Frank is the only true friend I made in prison.

***

Letters from jail
(from Terry to his sister, Laraine, in Perth)

January 15, 1989: *From now on when you write to me, remember where I am and stay off the morbid news and give me uplifting stuff. I need encouragement and have been getting it of late. Everything is going well. Mum has been terrific, despite what you say because she knows where I am. Good news is easy to live with. Bad news I have too much time to think about.*

Believe me when I tell you I have come a long way in recent times and provided things follow on from here, the gambling won't be too big a danger later on. It will always be waiting for me to drop my guard but I am very confident that my head is coming right.

HOMOSEXUALITY IS part-and-parcel of prison life and everybody knows it. But I didn't see it. Most of the time I was in a cell by myself. Anyway, people reckoned I was too big, too old and too ugly! The youngies were always the targets. You know things are happening. You see the results.

Fighting was also rife. I stayed away from the gymnasium, because if you're going to get hurt, that's one place it would happen. I kept to myself as much as possible, especially after Frank moved on.

I was a prolific letter writer. I wrote to Laraine weekly, explaining what was happening, how I was feeling and telling her about my visits and asking about how she and her family were going. I also kept in touch with Mum and Dad, who had both taken my imprisonment pretty hard.

I received heaps of mail, too, many with enclosures quoting messages of inspiration.

On occasions I was quite melancholy. One Sunday afternoon I was inspired to write a poem, trying in my own words to explain what prison is.

I called it Hard Labour:

The sound of a truck
Or a car on a road

The sound of a bird
Even a croak from a toad

The sound of laughter
A smile on my face

The casual stroll
Not a measured pace

The right to vote
Or to trust a friend

The freedom to think
Beyond an "inside" trend

The feeling of peace
Not anger or rage

The tranquil surrounds
Instead of this cage

The chance to begin
And live life again

The hope in my heart
Replacing the stress and strain

The chance to be free
Not treated with contempt

The "system" is degrading
And no person's exempt

The world outside
I'm impatient to please

The return to society
A gradual ease

The lesson is learned
I'm not coming back

The punishment is torment
It's the mind they attack

***

GOING TO the visits and coming back again was really tough. You often had to take your clothes off and squat over the mirror so that they could check to make sure you weren't concealing anything. I can still hear them saying now: "Squat and cough."

They'd also check your mouth for drugs. Only then could you dress and go and say hello to your wife and little girl. After the visit, the same routine often applied.

There was always a lot of vomiting after visits. Drugs had been smuggled in and passed over to prisoners who'd swallow them and then bring them up again. After visits you could see inmates hovering to see if anyone scored. It was times like this that I was glad that gambling was my problem and not drugs.

I couldn't believe it one lunchtime when the screws played an R-rated movie, complete with lots of boobs and hanky-panky. There were lots of smiling faces after lunch.

I always found the prisoners, rather than the prison officers, were the most supportive. Several of the screws seemed to delight in breaching the fair conduct code.

To one visit, I brought a full pack of unopened cigarettes because I'd been told an old mate, Peter Wearing-Smith, who was a smoker, might be coming with Jacky and Trudianne. He didn't make it on this particular day and returning from my visit, still with the brand new packet of cigarettes, I was chosen at random for a full strip search.

"What are you hoping to find?" I said, "A TAB ticket stuck up my arse!"

"Don't get smart, Jenner. Just get on with it."

Seeing my cigarettes, the screw said, "Are they yours?".

"No," I said. "They're for visitors."

He then tore the cellophane off them, opened them up and started to take them out, clearly trying to get me angry.

"It's a brand new packet."

"It's not now," he said, fumbling with them and bending a few as he tried returning them to the box.

He gave them back, 15 in the packet and five in my hand. I was fuming but didn't respond any further. I knew the game he was playing.

Visits were supposed to be a maximum of 20 minutes but often went longer. Sometimes the screws, for no particular reason, would step in shortly after the start of a visit and say, "Conclude your visit." If you kicked up about it, you could be charged for questioning authority and have "privileges" withdrawn.

Ian Chappell came to see me one day and was made to wait and wait. No-one came to tell me I had a visitor until Ian had been there for more than half an hour. He had applied for a visit through management and was granted a long visit which was usually at least 40 minutes.

Letters from jail
(from Terry to his sister, Laraine, in Perth)

Thursday February 23: *Very depressed today. Feel so sorry for a mate who's going to face what he's facing.*

It really saddens me Sis, as I do not want anyone I know to experience what I have. Remember like me, his life apart from this, is straight. No drugs etc. Prison is even harder for people like us because we don't fit in. For some arse-holes who regularly rape and spent 75 per cent of their life in prison it may be paradise, but it's not for the rest of us.

Eventually I was called to the visiting area and asked Ian how long he had been waiting. "Quite awhile, mate. But that's no problem."

I was furious. Ian tried to calm me down, assuring me he'd sooner be kept waiting than have me get into trouble. Ten minutes in, a screw came over and said, "Finish Jenner".

Again I got angry. It was humiliating. Ian again attempted to calm me down. "No, Ian," I said firmly. "They can't do this."

The screw turned and said, "Are you asking for an extension of your time Jenner? Is that what you are doing?".

I took a deep breath. "Yes sir."

"Then ask," he said.

Again, I had to play the game. "Please sir, may I have an extension of my time?"

"You can have 10 more minutes and that's it."

Unfortunately, I think Ian was probably more upset in the end than me. He felt I was going to be in trouble.

I lodged a complaint with management, the upshot being that the officers who played ducks and drakes with me got into trouble. I'd had a win, but they'd have the last say. On another occasion, I asked permission to receive some cassettes. They duly arrived, only for me to be denied access to them. My approved request had been changed by one of the screws. He'd simply added "Not" (approved) to the front of it. Again I complained. And again I won. I'd found someone in the system who believed in fair play to a degree.

Fridays were "Buy Day". It meant you had an opportunity to purchase items of need from the canteen. You were able to spend your wages and an amount equal to your wages from your personal account (monies left in trust by visitors).

I bought a card wanting to tell Jacky and Trudianne how much I loved and missed them. I sought permission to give them the card at visits. Permission denied. I complained and saw another officer. It was the same one who'd given me the problem with Ian.

"I am seeking permission to give this card to my wife and daughter at visits tomorrow sir."

"You know the rules, Jenner. Your request has to go in the week before."

"I understand, sir. But I feel there is an urgency to tell my wife and daughter how much I care."

"You know the rules Jenner, post it."

What he wanted me to do was to try and smuggle it through in my shirt to the visit. On the way through to visits they check what you have got but you are not at that stage asked to take your clothes off and squat over the mirror unless you are randomly called.

I thought about taking the card but I knew if I was caught, it would be an offence and that I could lose remissions or get early lock-up. These were the little mind games that went on regularly.

If you wanted to keep your one-third good behaviour remission, the trick was to stay out of trouble. Any misdemeanor that found its way to the magistrate could in fact see you lose some of that time. You also had to keep your emotions in check otherwise you could be picked on.

I wanted to keep my sheet clean so there could not possibly be an excuse for them to keep me locked up one extra day.

***

PRISONERS DID lots of things to earn more money, or in most cases, cigarettes. Some worked on clocks. Others did leatherwork or ceramics.

I wanted to get a leather bag for Laraine's daughter, Angela, for her birthday. Frank also wanted something made. We paid this guy upfront but he kept running us around. The trouble was that he was 18 stone and in for murder. Neither Frank nor I were fighters, so we had to tread carefully. Any accusations almost certainly would lead to the need to fight. We would have lost, both the fight and the goods!

One young chap we played darts with in our unit boasted he'd started to collect a supply of redback spiders. This was scary stuff.

But he disappeared pretty quickly when he was recognised at visits one day by a mother whose child he'd offended against. Now I know why he had the redbacks!

Two prisoners in my unit told their girlfriends one day not to come back unless they bought drugs with them. No drugs, no visits.

The guy in Cell five next to me, had spent a lot of his life in prison mostly because of drugs. Bungled robberies were his speciality, like the time he stole an antique blunderbuss, sawed it off, went into a chemist and said, "This is a hold-up!", only to be over-powered by the young woman behind the counter. It was never his plan to hurt anyone. He had a drug problem and he used to tell us that he had more than a million dollars up his arm. He needed money to feed his own habit. When John wasn't playing awfully mournful songs on his borrowed saxophone, he was forever botting my cigarettes I kept for visitors.

At Mobilong each prisoner had his own key and at any time would lock themselves in their cells. The prison officers had main keys and they could always get in but for safety, once you locked your door, other prisoners couldn't enter.

But the prisoners had a way of overcoming the key situation. They'd take the blades from the plastic razors, break them up and feed them into the lock. This rendered it useless. It's probably what would have happened to the young man with the redback spiders had he stayed.

There were 20 cells in my wing, 10 each side. It was a long, gloomy passage. You had to be careful as you made your way towards your cell. One day I grabbed my key from the prison officer's board – trustees were often afforded that privilege – and headed to cell six. I put the key in the lock and it didn't work. Immediately I broke out into a cold sweat, thinking of the shavings. I turned and saw John the saxophonist heading towards me. Surely it couldn't be him trying to get me. He'd been knocked over by a sheila. He put his key in the door and it wouldn't work either. At that moment we looked at each other. John was first to speak. "Oh," he said, "I've got your key by mistake. Have you got mine?" Sure enough I did. We'd accidentally picked up each other's keys!

To the outsider it may have seemed unimportant and just a silly mistake, but it's hard not to become paranoid in jail.

I got into my cell, locked the door and expressing a great sigh, imagined what could have been. This is prison.

Passing the time of day was the difficult thing. I was told not to mark the days off on the calendar as it'd take too long that way. But that's how I did my time: one day at a time.

As well as looking forward to my visits, I also enjoyed giving gifts. I started buying some ceramics from a young fellow called Tony who was in for robbing a couple of banks. He was working a kiln, making vases and lamp shades and either selling them to inmates or giving them away as presents. He suggested to me one day that rather than fork out $20 a week plus cigarettes, I could make them myself. Little did he know that other than spinning a cricket ball, I was useless with my hands. I bought some ceramic wear and each day did a little bit until I became quite proficient. It was then that I began to plan my week around my ceramics. I'd start Saturday night after visits and finish on Friday before the next day's visit and give them to Jacky and Trudianne. It was exciting handing them over, knowing I'd done everything myself. Of course I was different and instead of a skull and crossbones or a serpent wrapped around a pole, my vases had soft decals such as a rose or bunny rabbits. I tried to do something different every week. It created a little bit of discussion on visiting

---

Letters from jail
(from Terry to his sister, Laraine, in Perth)

Saturday April 22: *My appreciation for money is certainly greater than before. Earning $30 a week surely does that for you. When I am back out there and useful again, I will honor my debts, Sis. All of them.*

days as other ladies would ask why they didn't get pottery pieces like mine! But it wasn't seen as being manly to make them with any softness.

***

AT ONE stage at Mobilong a decision was made to put a team in the local rugby league competition. The prison had been getting occasional visits from the rugby league teams and decided to take full affiliation, the only proviso that all our games had to be played at home!

The team used to get thrashed but it seemed to be a good way to let off a bit of steam. I was too old and not in any shape to play, so I became the team's reporter, covering games and contributing stories to the Murray Valley *Standard*, a bi-weekly newspaper.

The first four stories were published with very little alteration, but the next was changed and had me in trouble with inmates due to the heavy sensitivity towards criticism. Mobilong was beaten 52-16 which is a hiding, but so I'd stay in one piece, I referred to the game as "a tough encounter" and praised the skillful opposition. However, the editor scribbled that out and instead wrote, MOBILONG THRASHED as the headline and repeated it on the first line of the story. For a week, I had to tip-toe around the prison, copping flak from all and sundry, none of whom understood that I didn't write the headline, or the opening line. But the heat soon died. Somehow we won the next two games and became an even better side when our ranks were bolstered by several Sydney bank robbers who'd just been sentenced. The newcomers had a rugby league background, so instead of our team consisting mainly of unathletic former Aussie Rules blokes trying to play a foreign code, the team had some guys who knew what they were doing. Accordingly, we started to win.

We were doing so well that it seemed we'd finish high enough to make the finals, the only problem being that finals were played on the "outside" and it would mean we'd have to automatically forfeit. No prisoner could leave Mobilong without being manacled.

There was a lot of enthusiasm for the team and it received a good deal of publicity, thanks to K.G. Cunningham on his sports show.

Unless there had been a lock-in, the prisoners would generally be allowed out to watch the games. Often they'd walk up and down the sidelines following play. We called it the mobile grandstand. Inevitably there'd be some trouble on the pitch and the spectators occasionally wanted to join in which would have meant the prison side would no longer be.

One day, very close to finals, a fight broke out during a game and three or four went to rush onto the ground. For some unknown reason, I jumped out in front of them, saying, "Don't be so stupid. Stay off the ground".

All but one walked straight off. The odd-man-out walked up to me and started poking me with his finger. "No-one talks to me like that. You and I are going to party."

This guy had been in and out of prison, in fact more "in" than "out". He was serving seven years this time for aggravated rape. I tried to explain myself to him and the reasons for my actions, but it fell on deaf ears. I was in trouble.

I went back to my unit and did my story. On the way to the kitchen the next day, he stepped out in front of me and repeated his threat. "You and I are going to party. I'm getting transferred to your unit."

I tried to explain again that what I did was for the rugby team, but he didn't understand.

I spoke to an inmate in my unit who knew him and said, "Can't you explain to him that this had nothing to do with him." But he refused. "This is just between you and him," he said.

I spent 48 hours virtually alone, not going anywhere near where a fight could happen, such as the gymnasium or the oval. I'd go straight to the kitchen to work and then back to my cell. I couldn't spend the next six months doing that.

Next day at work, someone said there'd been a disturbance in another unit. Apparently somebody standing in the food queue had been pushed. The bloke had turned around and punched the other one and immediately been sent back to Yatala. They called it being shanghai-ed.

"Oh yeah," I said. "Who was it?"

My luck was in. It was my problem man!

About that time I had a visit from a man named Harry Phipps. He was from Sydney and had read the story Neil Hawke had written. He was a genuine, caring character and didn't think that people like me should be where I was. He said he knew there was a need for punishment for breaking the law, but didn't think prison would solve the problems.

We talked for some time and at one point he said to me, "You'll have to overcome your anger. You're a very angry man".

"Wouldn't you be angry with yourself if you were sitting where I am?"

"You need to be more at peace with yourself," he said. "I'll be back to see you in six months and if you're not angry, I promise I will give you a new start in life."

He was talking about giving me a job. It was just the lift I needed and something to hang my hat on. I hung out for the six months to go by.

Harry didn't turn up exactly then, as he'd first said, but when he did he immediately noticed that I *had* improved and yes, his promise stood. He told me I was able to be helped now as I wasn't so angry. He'd see to it that I got the start he'd promised.

Chapter Eighteen

Paying the Price

It's doubtful if any cricket team has had a better record than ours. We had a murderer, a drug pusher, two embezzlers, a couple of bank robbers and a few blokes who'd tried to diddle Social Security.

It was hard for Mum, Dad and Laraine to realise their son and brother was a criminal and that I was in there trying to survive with real criminals. Dad, in particular, couldn't understand. All he could think about was that I'd disgraced them all.

We were talking on the phone one day and he hung up on me. I had to get to my cell very quickly because of the tears and emotion I was feeling. My mind went back to the time in New Zealand when I thought he was dead. I didn't want to part enemies with Dad. I know I was in prison because I did stuff up. But it doesn't make you a person without normal feelings, even if in jail you have to hide them. I immediately sat down and wrote to him:

Mobilong, February 10, 1989

Dear Dad,

Having just spoken to you on the phone I felt it important to write this letter. The telephone conversation wasn't the most enjoyable I've had but then it wouldn't be you if you weren't being aggressive.

When I said that I felt glad that I'd been imprisoned because it took the monkey off my back, it was a very truthful statement.

However, (being) in prison alongside murderers and rapists isn't a comfortable feeling.

But each day I have to face it, forever alert that someone may not like the way I look, or talk and decide to do something about it.

Being in prison has nothing to do with bars. It's to do with people, both inmates and prison officers and the in-games which are played. The prison system is designed to break your spirit with all its rules and amendments to rules. And childish adaptation by some officers.

But do the crime, do the time, as is said.

Here I am explaining prison to you and the fact that it isn't bars or high fences, it's a state of mind. But I really do think you know that Dad. Because I think you have been in prison in your own way for at least 35 years. My memory only goes back that far.

I am not writing to be a smart-arse or a nasty little boy. If that was the case, I'd be itemising issues for you.

I am writing, however, in the hope that you might just recognise, even for a short time, that your lectures to both of your children are not easy to cop because we can remember back when you were making mistakes and plenty of them.

I have been and am being punished albeit 20 years too late, as you say, for my stupidity. I'm not blaming the devil; the demons didn't make me do it. It was all my own doing and I will serve two years in prison and a further four and a half on parole for it. Yes I am paying the price. Isn't that enough for you?

Shame is a funny word. One doesn't have to become a criminal to create shame. One only has to behave below another person's moral standards to create *shame. Dad I am ashamed of myself. I'll admit that to you and to myself and to the rest of the world if necessary. I'll also tell you that I've faced up to my sickness and character defects.*

I've stopped running away. With me, it all ends here. Aren't I the lucky one!

When my sentence gets towards the end, I hope to be on home detention. That, in blunt terms, is being imprisoned in your own home. You don't have to be behind bars to be in prison. You can serve time in your own home. For me, however, at the end of time, 14 September 1990, the sentence is over. I'll have paid that price. The next stage won't be easy either but now I know I have the guts to face it. Really I'm quite lucky.

Love Terry.

***

LARAINE EVENTUALLY brought Mum and Dad around by explaining to them that I was not really a bad person and that, no matter what, I was their son. She brought Mum to Mobilong when I was in there and it broke the ground between us. Mum used to say when I was little that Laraine used to fuss over me like a second Mum. Now she was helping keep the family together as one.

In September after a year at Mobilong, I was transferred to the Cadell Prison Farm, near Waikerie. I tried to stay at Mobilong as I'd got into a routine and every weekend, rain, hail or shine, Jacky would be there with Trudianne.

Cadell was a low security prison, one which was used as the final major stopping-off spot before your last weeks in jail, which normally saw you at The Cottages.

Rapists can't go there as it is an open jail; no fences.

Letters from jail
(from Terry to his sister, Laraine, in Perth)

Mobilong, April 6, 1989: *My mate Frank has been moved onto Cadell. It came very suddenly. Only 24 hours notice. He wasn't very pleased with only three weeks to go before his release. Today is his 48th birthday which is even more disappointing as I'd organised a cake for him. Anyway I sent him a card which should get to him on Monday.*

We've been playing tennis and walking and talking for five-and-a-half months so it has left a gap for me

Cadell grew all its fruit and produce. It also fielded its own cricket team. I was going to be the first Australian Test player to represent the prison!

Unbeknown to management I'd slipped in the kitchen and so badly wrenched my knee that I'd been forced onto crutches. I was even considering an operation, until being told that would almost certainly see me back at Yatala. A transfer back to Mobilong would have been okay, but I definitely didn't want to return to Yatala. If it meant staying at Cadell, I'd play cricket, even if it was on only one leg.

They allocated me to the garage which was about a 500 metre walk and I was in no condition to walk. They also put me in Dormitory One with its 48 beds all very close together. The short-term guys tended to be placed there. The long-term ones would go to Dormitory Two, which had just 24 beds and much more room. There was also the cell block, *the* place to get into if you were going to stay a long time. It housed some of the lifers.

I couldn't move my leg in the cramped space and was soon moved from Dorm One to Dorm Two.

Instead of the garage work I was allocated to sweeping the Dorm and monitoring the sugar, tea and coffee. What was normally a simple task could become complicated, especially if the inmates had an alcoholic brew on the go. All of a sudden there'd be no excess fruit, all the juice from the tinned fruit supplies would have disappeared, along with Vegemite and sugar! It was always difficult requesting more sugar when they'd just got in a weekly supply only a day or two previously! I'm sure the officers would have known there was a brew being bedded somewhere. I can't begin to imagine what a brew mixed with Vegemite with some fruit juice would taste like, but it obviously had a kick. It beat me where they hid the stuff, but I didn't want to know either.

Letters from jail
(from Terry to his sister, Laraine, in Perth)

Thursday April 29: *In other words, Sis, when you write down your bad side in self inventory style, it's very depress-ing, like being sentenced. However, once it is done and accepted, then you can only improve because you have accepted what you cannot change.*

Saturday, May 20: *Dad told me that he didn't like any of the songs on the tape I sent him. His tape of his favourite songs arrived on Friday. The flip side is Suzanne Prentice and includes titles such as "There's Dust on Mother's Old Bible", "When God Comes to Gather his Jewels", "Why Me Lord?" and "The Old Rugged Cross". No wonder he found "The Living Years" out of his depth!*

Mobilong won the rugby today. It's the first win for the season after three games. However, more important to the inmates is the fact that it's the first ever win in rugby. They played an entire season in 1988 without a victory. Talk about losers.

Cadell was a long way from Adelaide and I never expected any visits from Jacky and Trudianne but they did come twice. I'd been there for seven or eight weeks before their first visit. The second was special and raised my hopes that we could all get back together again. The visitors on that day were permitted to bring exactly what you wanted – within reason, of course. Jacky brought an Esky containing all the stuff I loved: crabs, prawns, kabana, asparagus and bananas, plus a huge pavlova. We couldn't eat all the food, so I kept the Esky, loaded it up with all the excess food, stored it under my bed and feasted for days! I hadn't tasted food like that for at least a year.

While I was resting my knee, I was on the princely unemployment benefit of $11 per week. Later the money improved, slightly, when I took a job as a server worker, dishing out meals, cleaning the dishes and keeping the dining room clean.

Regular physiotherapy in nearby Waikerie saw my knee gradually improve – just in time for the start of the cricket season, in early October.

I was told that I'd be captain of the cricket side, but when you looked at the available talent, that wasn't much of an honour. Athleticism doesn't tend to be a strength amongst criminals! But a few of the white collar crims at least did show a little bit of ball-sense at a couple of our practices.

One hassle was that we had only 11 t-shirts to go around and the team was picked according to shirt size as much as anything else. Whoever could fit the shirts played! I'd gone from 92 kg to 106 kg, so immediate took the largest one, a XX. My extra beef tended to protect me in jail. But it also meant the exclusion of a big red-headed guy who was very keen and actually bowled fair left-arm slows. We simply didn't have a shirt to fit him! He was pretty unimpressed when we announced the first team and he wasn't in. As we got onto the bus to go into Waikerie for the first time, he yelled, "If you lose, Jenner, don't come back!".

Getting off the prison bus at Waikerie, a local smart-arse started on me. It's doubtful if any cricket team has had a better record than ours. We had a murderer, a drug pusher, two embezzlers, a couple

---

Letters from jail
(from Terry to his sister, Laraine, in Perth)

Monday, May 29: I think I told you about the Disneyland poster I was having framed for Trudianne. It was finally completed and I gave it to her as a big surprise on Saturday. She really loves her Disney characters so I knew she'd really flip. We said for her to close her eyes while I got it for her (Jacky didn't know what it was either). And then, "Da Da. Open your eyes!"

Trudianne's exact words were: "I've got two now."

I said, "shit" and Jacky burst out laughing and told me she'd also saved it from the newspaper and stuck it in Trudianne's bedroom. For more than six weeks I'd been sitting on my surprise.

---

of bank robbers and a few blokes who'd tried to diddle Social Security.

This little plump guy who wasn't fit to play volunteered to umpire. "Who's captain?" he said, knowing full well that I was.

"I am."

"Have you got a scorer?" he said.

"Yes, Mum's here. She's brought the afternoon tea, too!"

I told him I'd score and he said, "What? You're in for embezzlement, aren't you?".

"Mate I can add up," I said. "I just forgot to bank it."

We wanted to do okay, so there'd be more games. I thought our best bet was to bat first, try and set some sort of target and then defend for all our worth. It was an 80 over match, 40 a side, with each bowler allowed a maximum of 10 overs. We made less than 150, of which I would have got about 25. Considering I was in my 40s and totally out of practice, it was a fair effort. I used my overs when and where I felt they were needed, but we were struggling to contain them. I thought the only way we could win the game was to keep them out until dark so I slowed things down and watched it get darker and darker. A few of the opposition, especially the little, loud fat bloke were jumping up and down and complaining, telling us to get on with it. They were eight-down and needed only six to win from the last over. I gave the ball to Ronnie, our quickie, who was in for drug smuggling. Short of cash, he'd got away with it first, only to be caught the second time. I told him whatever happened, he must pitch it up.

He came charging in, bowled a half tracker and the guy whacked it over mid wicket for four! It was a pretty fair shot considering you just about needed the headlights on to see. One to tie, two to win.

Letters from jail
(from Terry to his sister, Laraine, in Perth)

Tuesday, June 13: *I'm expecting Milton tomorrow. Should be a pretty casual visit this one, as my problems are all the same ones that I had in the beginning, except that I know now what they are.*

I have nine months from Thursday to be eligible for home detention. You could say it isn't that long, until you know that it is a repeat of the time I have just done.

Friday, June 30: *Looking out my window across the lawns onto the hill, filled with trees in the background, it is almost possible to forget where I am. Almost. I'm luckier than some, though, because all of this mental torture that I'm experiencing can be pushed into the background if I con-centrate on Trudianne.*

Had I kept going my totally selfish way, it's doubtful that I would have appreciated her, become as close, or cared as much about her future.

Next ball that batsman was clean bowled. Enter No.11. Still one to tie and two to win. First ball he swung from his bootlaces and skied it high on the off-side where our mid-off, an Aboriginal boy, took it like a chest mark. We were rapt. A win is a win is a win, as the legendary Ron Barassi once said.

But there was no time for a victory drink or anything like that. The screws immediately ushered us back onto the bus, but not before the little fat bloke rushed up and snarled, "You're going to be reported for your conduct, Jenner!".

"What are you going to do?" I said. "Lock me up?"

There was a real buzz on the bus coming back.

We were very late returning and when we got off the bus sure enough, the big red-head was waiting. All the blokes were yelling, "we won, we won". As I came past him, I made sure I was with someone and he said, "You'd better not lose next week, Jenner". But my luck was in again because the guy got into an altercation and was sent back to Yatala.

I did have to front the tribunal in Waikerie and was exonerated. I think they were pretty relieved. It would have been a tough one handing out a penalty to a bloke already serving six-and-a-half years!

In all I played three matches. I tried to play the games seriously but we didn't have any talent so our chances were remote. One ageing leg-spinner wasn't going to make the difference.

In my last weeks at Cadell, Harry, my benefactor came to see me. He'd bought a blinds business in Golden Grove. It was showing a healthy return and by the time I was released not only would I have a job to go to, but a little nest egg as well.

That news was so uplifting. I couldn't wait to tell Jacky. I wondered if this would give her fresh hope, too.

***

I SPENT my last four or five months of non-parole at The Cottages, which are back in town, right next to the women's prison and just up the road from Yatala. The Cottages are a pre-release

Letters from jail
(from Terry to his sister, Laraine, in Perth)

Saturday, July 29: *The old saying is you can root, shoot and electrocute – but don't steal. The injustice of sentences never fails to amaze. A bloke who pumped four shots into his wife has served just two years and five months and is out again. I saw it on Hinch. I certainly deserved to be imprisoned for stealing someone else's money, but when you hear of those arse-holes receiving those light sentences it makes your stomach turn.*

Wednesday, September 13: *My knee is so bad today I can hardly walk. It came about because they told me I had to leave this morning and I hadn't said "Seeya" to a couple of people (the kitchen education bosses). I had to run and in doing so I really hurt the thing again. Not sure if I'll have to have it operated on.*

centre, much tougher than Cadell. It was a return to the razor wire and a place for long term prisoners to be re-introduced into society. At The Cottages you looked after yourself, including cooking your own meals as well as carrying out duties, in my case, looking after the food supplies and some gardening.

I was in a unit with three others. On each side was a toilet and shower which were shared between two. The rules were if any drugs were found in the toilet they belong to you both. Being so close to qualifying for home detention, it was a huge worry. Two of my "flat mates" were murderers, including one just coming to the end of an 18-year stint. The third was a sicko who had been involved in child pornography.

I wanted to move but you had to be very careful because it could be seen as being offensive to those you moved from. Unit eight was vacant and no inmates would go there. It seems a long-serving prisoner, on being prepared for release, had a day in Rundle Mall to look around, couldn't cope and on return to unit eight, hung himself.

Suddenly I wasn't superstitious and unit eight became my final home in the prison system.

There seemed to be more drugs and other things going on than at Cadell. You were nearly back in the mainstream. I watched the visits and it would become something of a frenzy to see who scored. The prisoners would hang out for it and immediately start planning for the next visit because they had that need. I always counted myself fortunate not to be involved in that scene. Having gambling as an addiction is a damn sight better than being involved in drugs.

I had a problem with one of the screws at The Cottages. Initially I thought he liked me, only for him to have my wages docked when he claimed I wasn't doing my job. I appealed and won but he didn't like that and made my life pretty uncomfortable. Throughout my time in prison, I had to be so careful in my dealings with people, who didn't necessarily speak as well as I did. Mind you, I never put myself on a pedestal. I left school at 14, but talked okay. Sometimes that put others off. You couldn't be seen to be treating them like dummies.

In fairness to the prison officers, they are just doing a job like anyone else on the outside. They may not have qualified from school to any high level, but it isn't an easy job. Just like at Yatala and Mobilong, some seemed to enjoy the bullying.

There were some special moments, especially when people like Tony Mann came to visit. "Rocket" was managing the West Aussies on tour, in Adelaide. That was the game that Joe Scuderi took six-for hardly anything. It was great to see an old mate from so many years back. New Zealand's coach Bob Cunis also turned up for a visit.

I was on my hands and knees doing the garden one day when the gates opened to allow a taxi in. The guy looked at me and said, "Have you got a Mr Capone here?". I couldn't help chuckling at that one. There *was* a Mr Capone. He was in charge of recreation!

For a time, until his release, my gardening colleague was a guy called Ted, who had served close to 20 years. During the later stages of his sentence, he had met, courted and married a devout Christian lady. While we worked together, we talked about his hopes and dreams for a second chance at life. Having someone to go home to was so important.

He'd been doing a course at TAFE as well as going home on weekend leave. He was ready to re-enter society. The week prior to his release, his wife decided to have a small operation. Get it out of the way was the plan. I don't know what went wrong but tragically she died during, or soon after, the operation. I cried for him. All his dreams gone and an empty world to re-enter a few days later. It taught me a lesson, yet again. Take one day at a time. It isn't over until it's over.

At Christmas time, I became the prison's tennis champion and won first prize: four dollars! It was played on an elimination basis and while my around-the-court speed was minimal given my wonky knee, I could hit it back alright and tactically was ahead of the rest. The lad I was playing in the final was much younger and fitter and I assessed his form as being much better than mine. I figured my only chance was to play first thing in the morning when it was relatively cool and I was at my freshest and maybe he wasn't. He agreed to play me at 9am and somehow I was able to win. He was so disappointed and embarrassed that a "grey-head" could beat him. In prison, anyone over 40 is considered an old man. There was an unhappy ending to this lad. He was transferred out of the Cottages after being caught with some drugs and at Yatala, he over-dosed and was found in his cell.

I could feel myself becoming stronger willed as each day passed. I felt I was paying for my sins and had nothing to hide anymore. The monkey was off my back. I was so blatantly honest, others annoyed me with all their crap. I knew I hadn't yet won the battle with gambling but I knew I was winning the battle with life.

***

THE COLES $64,000 question was whether I was still going to be with Jacky, post-prison. As hard as I knew it had been for her, I desperately wanted the chance to make the marriage work again.

Trudianne, too, was such a big part of my life. I didn't want to be in a situation where I couldn't see her.

Twelve months into my sentence, especially after that memorable weekend smorgasbord at Cadell, I'd felt that Jacky had softened a little towards me. Accordingly, I raised my hopes.

I was doing a TAFE Course in the city and would jump off the bus at a certain spot on the way in and Jacky's Mum, Mitzi, would bring Trudianne to me and I'd have a little play with her on the swings and slides before continuing my journey. There were times I think Mitzi reckoned Jacky and I would get through it all together.

As part of the home detention deal, I needed Jacky's approval for me to be able to come home for the last six months of my parole period.

Milton Bowman came and saw me and said he had some good news. Jacky had been to see him and asked him questions like what was I really like and what were the chances of me being normal. He saw it as an up. But I saw it as a down and it was.

Letters from jail
(from Terry to his sister, Laraine, in Perth)

Cadell, Wednesday, September 27: *Terry also has good points Sis, but they too can be overlooked if it's only the bad ones you're looking for.*

Wednesday, October 18: *Tonight I went to the local oval and did a bit of coaching with the Cadell team. They had three or four promising young lads unlike the trainees team. There was about seven or eight there. One bloke was the son of a headmaster. I walked up to him and asked him the name of the fielding position at which he was standing. "Mid-off," he replied correctly. Last Saturday if I told one of my team to head to mid-off they would have got lost!*

We knew it would be difficult particularly when I came home on some day leaves and felt the negative energy from Jacky. Neither of us knew how to handle the situation. On my first overnight leave pass from the prison I invited Ian Chappell around to our place for dinner. You could cut the air with a knife it was so tense. When it was time to go to bed, I was too scared to even put my arms around her. I laid there listening to the clock ticking away and eventually got out of there and went to sleep on the lounge. Some people thought I made a mistake asking Ian around but I thought Jacky needed someone else there; the thought of just me sitting there all night would be difficult. I'd been out of her life for a long time.

One of the next times she walked in for a visit, with Trudianne, I knew it was over. I had the forms there for her to sign. She walked through with Trudianne and told her to go and play. I saw her face and tears started to well up in my eyes. I can remember her sentence clearly: "I have decided I don't want you to come home."

In some ways I was half expecting it. But it was a moment I'd dreaded from the very first day in jail.

"Surely you can't leave me in here," I said. "Can't you just get me out?"

"No, I've made my decision."

I couldn't hide my anger. I'd been the one doing the time. Why was I being punished again? Later, of course, I realised just how much a toll it had been for Jacky, too. She'd brought Trudianne to see me virtually every weekend. I could not have survived the system without seeing my daughter.

I said to Jacky that she'd have to go because I was getting upset. I moved out from my seat and one of the lady prison officers who obviously knew I was struggling said to me that I had to pull myself together. It was important I remained strong. She said I could talk to her about it.

But every time I thought about it, I could feel that gut wrenching feeling. I had come a long way and there had been a lot of changes in me that Jacky hadn't been able to see because I was unable to show her.

I don't blame Jacky for not hanging in. But I was saddened and deeply hurt that she chose not to.

It wasn't a wrong decision, but it seemed on the surface to be terribly harsh.

Basically it left me with a further six month stretch to serve behind bars – unless I could find another address to go to.

It was a very traumatic time, made even more so when Jacky went away on holiday to Darwin. She'd told Milton that she was definite that we were finished. She no longer had any feelings towards me. More over she didn't wish to discuss anything. She considered the matter closed.

Despite expecting it, the pain of the heartache was absolutely enormous and I was suffering extreme stress. Thirteen years, including five-and-a-half years as husband and wife were over.

I wrote to my sister and to my friend, Frank, who I had met at Mobilong. Several times I wrote letters to Jacky in moments of anger and torment, re-read them in the morning and didn't post them.

Trudianne was two years of age when I went in and four when I came out. Throughout the time – and ever since – she has given me total, unconditional love.

I had watched other guys along the way in jail get a "Dear John" bad news letter. Some dropped their bundles completely. Others slashed their wrists.

I was so close to re-joining society. I felt I was ready. I didn't need this setback, or want it to jeopardise my immediate aim – to get out of prison.

I rang a friend, Steve Harris, who immediately came to my aid. If I needed an address, he'd help. It was very inconvenient and difficult for him as his wife Sue had just had a little baby girl. Prison officials carried out an inspection and yes I could go there.

I knew it was only temporary and that I had to look further afield as soon as I could. The problem I had was that the department didn't like lots of moves.

Not long afterwards, I met Geoff Brokenshire, a friend of Steve's. He and his wife were going to South Africa for a holiday. Would I like to house sit for them? I couldn't believe it. I could get out of Steve and Sue's hair and have a chance to adapt to life on my own.

And the guardian angel sitting on my shoulder was to come forward again. Harry Phipps returned as he said he would. However, I was a little apprehensive this time. I'd heard on the gravevine that the Golden Grove business was no longer.

When Harry arrived at The Cottages it was with another man. I mentioned Golden Grove. "It's gone," said Harry, "there's nothing we can do about it now. But let's look at the future. I've still got $40,000 of the $100,000 I was investing and this is the man we're buying the business from.

"We'll be back to see you again soon, with the details."

Eventually, as promised, the business was there. Harry had come through.

I had gone into prison with no hope and no aspirations. The judge had called me a parasite and a blot on society who had little hope of rehabilitation. Now, thanks to the kindness of all sorts of people, I had some digs and a job and was able to continue to build my self esteem.

Laraine really hung in strong for me, too. Before I went to prison, she spoke to me daily on the phone from Perth. Her phone bills must have been tremendous. She helped Mum come to terms with the fact that I had made a mistake and that I wasn't some horrific person. Afterwards she continued to play a huge role in the person I am today.

CHAPTER NINETEEN

A Very Lucky Man

"My husband wouldn't come here to listen to
you. He said you were a criminal. I can't wait
to go home and tell him what he missed."

My release date, March 15, 1990, remains etched in the memory. It was supposed to be 24 hours earlier, but there was a late complication.

Amazingly, "Yorky" Smith, the prison officer who had been so philosophic the day I initially went into the Adelaide Remand Centre just happened to be there. He'd been moved next door to the women's prison but was working that day on relief.

I walked past him and couldn't resist a dig: "Guess what Mr Smith? Remember the conversation from 18 months ago? I can tell you I have plenty (of friends)."

"What was that, Jenner?"

"You said to me that I'd find out who my friends were. And I now know what you meant. I'm delighted to tell you that I have got plenty and that I am a very lucky man."

He gave me a half-smile and said, "Look after yourself Jenner".

The home detention officer picked me up and drove me firstly to the Commonwealth Employment Office where I was entitled to an unemployment cheque. I then went straight into the job Harry had organised, with the blinds company.

My original sentence was for six-and-a-half years with a minimum of three non-parole. Good behaviour reduced the sentence by a third. It meant I was to serve two years, including the last six months on home detention. Once you're on parole, you are what's known as a "prisoner at large" – free, but with restrictions. And that lasts for the full time of your sentence, for me, a further four-and-a-half years.

Other than being able to live out of the prison environment and seek employment like anyone else, you are "free" only as far as they allow you to be. There was no drinking or going into hotels. I couldn't go to any places where gambling was conducted including Keno, which theoretically meant I couldn't even go into a chemist! They were truly draconian laws.

My first home detention officer was extremely serious. He denied me permission to even walk or jog up and down the street where I was staying with Steve and Sue Harris because he said it may upset the neighbours! This guy was obsessed with the fact that I was considered "high profile". Even if I was driving home from work, I couldn't just stop at a "deli" for a sandwich. I'd have to first obtain his permission. I tried to obey the rules but I also dared to be normal.

He told me that if I was reported as being seen somewhere and he didn't know where I was, he'd treat it as a serious breach of my home detention order and I could go back to prison. There was no room for flexibility. It wasn't going to be easy to survive.

I then obtained permission to move to the Brokenshire's house while they were away. Geoff even left unsigned, open cheques for me to pay the accounts as they came in. When they returned from their six-week trip, they nicknamed me "Gladys", after the cleaning lady. The house was immaculate.

The first night there I had a celebration of sorts and a favourite meal I can still remember: rump steak with soya and holbrook sauce, embellished by butter and grated zucchini, plus lightly-boiled carrots and cauliflower oven-browned with sprinklings of matured cheese... not quite your standard prison fare!

Theoretically home detention means imprisonment at home but you are allowed to work a genuine job. I had to say where I was going and when. If there was any change I had to report the exact details.

While the job selling blinds didn't eventually work out, it wasn't Harry's fault. He was trying to look after others and trying to make sure the whole world was happy. Harry had given me the start he promised and he provided me with new optimism. I was so fortunate, a job and a place to stay while I assimilated back into society. I had to learn many things all over again, simple things, like looking someone straight in the eye.

When the Brokenshire's returned, I was able to rent a tiny little place in Kensington Park. Trudianne called it "the little house" so it must have been small! I also had a new home detention officer called Sandy and for the next six months, she showed a genuine interest in my life.

It was very difficult coping with everything, given that my marriage had ended at a time when I was desperately trying to become familiar with the outside world.

Sandy had had problems in her own life and was able to counsel me. She gave me some sound advice. She even helped me scrub walls so that when I moved I wouldn't lose my bond.

Sandy was a very good sounding board. Some may say that she got too close to the prisoners. At the end of my "probation", she said I was one of her more difficult ones because I was so emotional. I found that losing Jacky was more difficult to overcome than gambling and smoking combined. I was playing one of my favourite CD's, by Andy Williams, and broke down when he sang the Hawaiian Wedding Song. It was *our* wedding song and brought back so many memories. How I wished she was there again.

The support of people like Sandy and Laraine and many others helped get me through. I carried around a clipping Laraine sent:

> When men speak ill of thee, live so as nobody can
> believe them – Plato.

I knew that some people were going to knock me but as long as I stayed clean and moved forward in my life, I'd earn the respect of others which, in time, would make my bad times seem less important. This time I was in control and had no wish to re-experience the downers, especially of the last 10 years. I had a strong resolve, lots of Christian friends and most importantly of all, Trudianne was there to help me stay strong.

Sandy treated all her cases in a very special caring way. She was very important to me, important enough for me to introduce her to my Mum and Laraine. Things seemed to be far more positive for me. I was having initial problems sorting out the business side of things and she helped me out there, too. She also took control in making sure that I behaved myself. And she did this in a manner that didn't make me feel like I was still in prison. Having a sense of freedom again, rather than being stood over, was so important to me.

Sandy even organised my first public speaking function, on behalf of the Liberal Party at a church hall near Yatala. All she wanted me to do was to talk about prison. She felt I could express what other prisoners couldn't. Jennifer Cashmore (Coburn) and Grant Chapman and many other politicians were among the invited guests. I spoke from the heart and at the end of it, I read my "Hard Labour" poem.

I'd written the poem in a matter of minutes. The words were flowing. It was almost like I was in a trance.

Reading it out in front of all the people was more difficult the further I got into it. But eventually I finished it. I kept breaking down. It's said that one of the "rules" of public speaking is leave them laughing or leave them crying! Lots of people came up to me after I finished and shook my hand. One lady gave me a huge hug and said, "My husband wouldn't come here to listen to you. He said you were a criminal. I can't wait to go home and tell him what he missed".

My six months' home detention was to finish at midnight and at 11pm Sandy came around and said to me from midnight I was free again to have a drink. I made it two.

***

FOR TWO years I had to make weekly visits to the nearest parole office in Norwood. It was a hell of a drain. I felt like I'd kicked a goal when the visits became fortnightly and then monthly. A couple of times I forgot, but would go in, apologise and everything was okay again.

Being on parole and trying to make my job work was a difficult mix. If I wanted to go anywhere I had to obtain permission from the parole board. All submissions had to be well in advance. It was very difficult because several times while I was working for the blinds company, they wanted me to go to Sydney where most of the buying was done and it created problems.

My first parole officer was very good, but the second was totally lacking in understanding and wouldn't give me any latitude. I was going to get into trouble with her one way or another because she wasn't giving at all. Nothing was easy. She would say, "Put a request in". I'd try to explain how I needed to know now, but she'd say I needed to conform just like everyone else. She'd deal only with written submissions. At one point I was so frustrated that I told her I was tempted to jump a plane and just go, even if it did mean going back to prison. Thankfully the parole board granted me a release from her.

The next one, John, was very good and I had him right through the remaining four years of my sentence. He understood my life was different to some other prisoners; that I was going to be back in public life and that I had to go interstate, sometimes at short notice. He organised it for me at 24 hour's notice and helped free up in my own mind that I was back in society and that I could be my own man again. I wasn't allowed to break any of the rules, but he didn't impose the rules so tightly that I was strangled.

When the last day came of my six-and-a-half year sentence, it just expired. I never received a certificate to say it was over. When you have been so controlled for such a long time, it leaves you with a slightly hollow feeling.

Important in my rehabilitation was my work with the Adelaide City Mission and Roger Bryson, a former leg-spinner who played cricket for Sturt. I had met him and Gavin Browning in my last weeks at The Cottages.

Roger invited Neil Hawke and myself to the opening of the Hindmarsh Youth Drug and Alcohol Centre and when I was there I saw Ann. She was very nice, attractive and business-like. I asked Roger who the lady was. "Leave her alone," he said. "She works for the Mission. Plus she's married!"

A week later, when I asked after her, Roger said, "Don't get your hopes up but I hear her marriage is over".

That began a period of the chase, trying to get to know her. I wasn't able to impress her early and she only allowed me to see her every five or six weeks.

I even supplied all the blinds for a centre Ann was managing. Roger arranged that. He was in there trying for me.

My lease had expired at "the little house" in Kensington Park and while looking for something else, I lived at Rostrevor for four months.

Rodney Marsh came to Adelaide to do commentary for the Test match and stayed with me. It was a very uplifting time. We drove to the cricket on the first day and the car stayed in the car-park for five days. We got a cab home each night. I was meeting people again and it was a very emotional experience. Only one didn't look me in the eye or shake hands. Everyone else was genuinely pleased to see me and share some small talk.

It was during this time that the blinds business went topsy-turvey and I had to get out of it with some sort of honour. I sorted it out with Harry and he agreed.

I moved to a unit at Campbelltown, complete with a little front garden where I could have barbecues and entertain. It became my home. And for the first time in years, not only was I settled, I was genuinely happy.

T.J. testimonials

Dr. DON BEARD

(Surgeon with the South Australian Cricket Association)

As the South Australian Cricket Association's surgeon, I was able to closely observe thousands of club, state, Australian and international cricketers with all their problems: surgical, medical and psychological.

Terry had very few injuries and always kept himself remarkably fit. He looked after the two greatest parts of a leg-spinner: his fingers and the shoulder.

It was an absolute joy to watch him bowl and particularly in tandem with Ashley Mallett. You would never miss a single ball they bowled!

It was obvious that Terry was thinking all the time. He mixed his deliveries in countless ways and was a master of spin and flight. He was obviously annoyed with himself if he bowled a loose ball. He was a fierce competitor. But he didn't expect every ball to take a wicket. He'd play with a batsman, allowing him to cut and drive and suddenly would come the master ball that had the batsman falling for his trick.

He worked so hard to get these wickets that if an lbw or a catch behind were given not out, he'd often take it out on the umpire or the batsman. Later in his career he had to work so much harder to get his wickets and when he missed out, he reacted all the more strongly.

Off the field, to me, he was always a gentleman. He always appreciated everything I did for him. When I went into the dressing room, he would stand up to speak to me. But his behaviour on the field at times wasn't good. He worried me. I felt he needed a minder, both on the field and at times, off it, when his behaviour and his statements about the administration, opponents and umpires was perhaps less than desirable. I would have liked to have been that minder.

He was such an astute tactician on the field and had such an obvious broad knowledge of the game I genuinely felt he could have become captain of the Australian XI.

With the problems of his personal life, his cricket started to deteriorate and, at times, he lost control of his behaviour. It made me shudder as I knew of his immense capabilities.

Eventually there was an incident in a District cricket match where he obviously had to be charged with behaviour not in the best interests of the game. There had never been a SACA tribunal, but one was formed and as someone completely independent, I was made the chairman. I had evidence from a number of witnesses and eventually decided that in the best interests of cricket, and Terry Jenner, a severe reprimand was in order. He appreciated the warning.

Unfortunately his own personal problems continued and at times his behaviour on and off the field was unacceptable. He was not the Terry Jenner that I had known only a few short years before. His life and his world fell apart. But in spite of it all, his friends stuck with him. Eventually he landed up in court and was sentenced to a term of imprisonment.

It was here that I met him again in my capacity as Visiting Consultant Surgeon to Her Majesty's Prison, an appointment I had taken on because no-one else would do it. It was amazing who turned up as patients, with representatives from a wide cross-section of families in the state. Some of the inmates made medical complaints in order to improve their conditions, but not Terry. I saw him, but never as a patient. I knew all about him and was given reports about his behaviour, which in prison was exemplary. He served his time and served it well.

Eventually he was released. He told me later he had been given considerable support whilst in prison, and again on release, by the Adelaide City Mission.

In turn, he was very supportive of the Mission, organising a number of sporting functions and dinners to help them with their projects. He was always spreading the good word and for this he had my admiration. He also set about improving young cricketers, particularly young leg-spinners and he did it so well that he was soon in demand all over the country and overseas as well.

Finally he started cricket commentating. He was magnificent. He had a good command of English and a good knowledge of the game. I always appreciated listening to him.

In his lifetime he has had many peaks and troughs. Perhaps the best thing that can be said about Terry is that he has tried to recompense his friends, colleagues and society as a whole for his transgressions.

CHAPTER TWENTY

A Guardian Angel

We made eye contact, only for him to immediately drop his head and look away. I was less than a metre from him. It was the type of moment I'd dreaded.

We were at the Test cricket in Adelaide and Ian Chappell said to me that Neville Oliver wanted to see me in the ABC box. "He wants you to talk about Shane Warne."

There was a pause. He could sense my reluctance. "C'mon," he said, "it won't do you any harm."

"Okay," I said, "I'll see you there. I'm going around the back of the stand."

"Pigs arse!" said Ian, "you're coming around the front with me. And not only will you come around the front, you'll look up. You've paid your price. You have every right."

As we walked together, I looked around and saw lots of familiar faces, including one guy I'd thought enough of years earlier to have given him one of my Australian baggy green caps. We made eye contact, only for him to immediately drop his head and look away. I was less than a metre from him. It was the type of moment I'd dreaded. Maybe I wasn't as accepted as my closest mates said.

It made the walk around to the ABC box that little bit longer. I ran into the guy a few years later and we shook hands and he said how good it was to see me again. I told him about the day in Adelaide when he hadn't been prepared to look me in the eye. He said he didn't know why he did it. I said, "Well it hurt a lot".

It was the only negative reaction I can recall and I can say now without hesitation that throughout my dark years, I did not lose one genuine friend.

If I was in any doubt, my 50th birthday party at *Casa Mia*, run by cricket buff Malcolm Amos, proved it once and for all. Money was tight and everyone had to put in $20 but it was a super night.

We invited 60 and all but two showed up; the couple who couldn't, Ray and Sylvia Milton, had been overseas and were stranded in Brisbane.

Mum got up and made a speech. She spoke how I'd left Perth for Adelaide as a 22-year-old, but we'd seen a fair bit of each other and that I had experienced a lot of drama and trauma in my life. Then she put her hand on my shoulder and said, "I'm very proud of Terry". I've never forgotten that.

A lot of people that were very close to me were there and it meant the world to me.

As your life progresses and you move forward, you can't take everybody with you. But you never forget them.

One man I owe a particular debt to is Bob Day, a highly-successful Adelaide businessman and philanthropist.

I'd met him originally when he played in a fundraising cricket match I helped organise for the Adelaide City Mission. I didn't realise then what an impact he'd have on my life. Over the next couple of years, Bob supported the Mission in so many ways.

When I took over as coach of Tea Tree Gully they needed sponsors. I sat down with Bob and without hesitation, he came on board. He organised a new fence to be built and became involved in other areas too, such as tree planting.

One pre-season, we were at a club luncheon and Bob said to me, "You must be pretty happy with the way things are going along now".

"Yes and no," I said. "To be perfectly truthful, Bob, I still see myself finishing up in a bedsitter at Smithfield."

"How can you say that? You're doing these functions, coaching a cricket club, doing this and that."

"Where else do I finish up, Bob? I don't even own a home."

"Why don't you buy one?"

"How am I going to buy a home? You don't go to prison with a good credit rating."

"We can fix that," he said and within 48 hours a house brochure appeared on my desk at the Mission. I couldn't believe it. I rang him and he told me where I could find this display house, which was one of his Homestead award winners.

I went that very day, but me being me, I didn't like the look of it. As much as I appreciated his help, getting an $80,000 loan seemed in the "too hard" basket and said so.

"Why don't you go down to Seaford and tell me what you think of the display houses there?" he said.

Ann came with me and the first one Bob had chosen was too small. It only had a limited kitchen area and smallish bedrooms. One next door, another Homestead home, was a lovely villa which did have a kitchen which you could work in, a larger dining area and big bedrooms. "This I like," I said to Ann.

I phoned Bob. "I've got good news and bad news, Bob. I love your house, but not the one you chose; the one next door."

"Alright, get the other one, then."

"But it's more expensive again."

"I'll send someone over and you can discuss all that and see what can be worked out."

At Bob's direction, a bank officer came and saw me. I told him my life story and the fact that I had a full-time job at the Mission but I didn't have any deposit or anything else to use as collateral. He said it didn't matter. Bob had arranged for the deposit to be paid at *the completion* of the contract!

"That surely can't be right," I said.

"Yes it is," he said, "One way or another Bob wants you to have this loan, but I will try to work out how to get it for you standing alone."

I went and saw Bob, thanked him for his generosity and told him how the bank was looking to arrange a loan which wouldn't involve him. Even though the house and land package I wanted was slightly dearer than the original one we'd looked at, he still didn't see a problem.

I couldn't get over how positive he was. He had so much faith in me.

"This all sounds fabulous, Bob, but where do I get the money to pay the $9000 difference?"

"How much rent are you paying?"

"$140."

He said he had had a little unit next door to his office. "You can have it rent free and bank the $140 a week."

I signed with the bank and by early 1993 was the proud owner of my very own house in Wynn Vale. What a remarkable man!

Bob has built a Christian Centre and accomodation places and donated them to charity. He's that sort of person. He also helps with young cricketers in so many ways. Laraine often says I have a habit of falling on my feet. In Bob's case, I'd met a Guardian Angel.

T.J. testimonials

ROSS EDWARDS
(Former West Australian & Australian teammate)

T.J. will always be one of my favourite cricketers. It was to his great credit that his career really blossomed in Adelaide after he'd battled for years fighting for recognition in Perth.

He and Ashley Mallett left for Adelaide and both kicked in, having struggled to get a game side-by-side Tony Lock, our veteran WA captain and one of the best finger spinners of them all.

Not many players were going to take the frontline spinning duties from "Lockie", given his record of 300-plus wickets for WA, the majority at the WACA, the least-condusive wicket for spin bowling in the country, if not the whole world! And it should not be forgotten that Lockie also was captain! Further complicating the picture for T.J. was the arrival of another leggie in Tony "Rocket" Mann, who spun the ball as much as him and also possessed an excellent wrong-un, one of the best around.

T.J. probably thought that Rocket was a further thorn stopping him from getting a regular game. Funnily enough in T.J.'s very last game for the State, he was one of three specialist spinners along with Lockie and Rocket. John Inverarity also bowled his slow left-arm in that game, at the WACA. Even though we were easily beaten outright thanks to "Fritz" Freeman who took a swag of wickets, it was still a memorable game for T.J. and I. We had no chance of winning on the last day but took the overnight score from 6-91 to 6-175, our partnership in total being worth 92. We both made around 50 in a low-scoring game. In the first dig we also put on 40 odd, having been lifted up the order.

After his transfer to South Australia, T.J. loved to catch up with his old mates. And for years his combination with "Rowdy" Mallett was the best going at Sheffield Shield level.

While he was excellent company off the field he was highly competitive on the ground, whether you were old mates or new acquaintances.

I well recall a match on a crumbling wicket in Adelaide with W.A. batting and I must have batted long enough to irritate T.J. With Rowdy at one end and T.J. at the other I copped a considerable amount of verbal from both of them, particularly T.J.

We toured together to the Windies in 1973, with a team which suffered from injury and illness to our main fast bowlers Dennis Lillee and Bob Massie. It was a fighting team which struggled but eventually prevailed through dogged determination as typified by T.J. and the great leadership of Ian Chappell.

I also recall our very strong team spirit in difficult circumstances in Trinidad and T.J. was instrumental in that.

In Jamaica we were given a barrel of beer which T.J. and Dougie Walters proceeded to set up on their ground floor balcony for anyone who happened to walk past.

Then he ran into trouble and had a tough time. But his strength of character allowed him to face up to the facts, see things as they were and be straight, honest and open as he always is.

After he'd paid his penalty he did a lot of charity work and for that he is to be admired. We haven't caught up for awhile, but when we do, it's always like old times. T.J. never forgets his mates.

CHAPTER TWENTY-ONE

Warnie

It was a seemingly effortless, yet a magnificent delivery. "&%#@ me," I thought to myself. "What have we got here?"

I was still on parole when I first met Shane Warne. My home detention had just finished and I was working with the Cricket Academy spinners.

Initially I'd been hesitant but Russell Vincent from the South Australian Cricket Association persisted and finally I agreed.

It was a traumatic thing for me to say "yes". I was scared the kids may not respect me. I'd never been a coach, not at this elite level anyway, and here I was trying to have credibility when, in my own mind, I didn't have credibility as a person.

I walked into the Adelaide indoor centre and not only were the kids there, so were some of their parents! I was terrified. Somehow I got through that session and Peter Spence, one of the Academy coaches, told me there was this other young spinner coming in called Warne. "You might like him but I'm told he's a bit hard to handle," he said.

I had never heard of him. Apparently he'd been in the West Indies with the Australian youth team.

The first time I saw him we were outdoors at Adelaide No.2. I looked up and saw this chubby, cheeky bloke with blond, spiked hair. We shook hands and he was genuine in his grip.

"What do you want me to do?" he asked.

"Just bowl me a leg break."

Without any real warm-up, he bowled this leg break which curved half a metre and spun just as far! It was a seemingly effortless, yet a magnificent delivery.

"&%#@ me," I said to myself. "What have we got here?"

"Bowl me another, Shane."

He did and it spun almost as far.

Our relationship began on that first day. With our first handshake, there was an immediate affinity.

He listened, I watched and he tried. I was not trying to change him but to help him *understand* what he was doing. I couldn't help but think how lucky he was to possess such an astonishingly good leg break.

I asked him what else he had and he bowled his flipper which was also very good.

He had a gift from God and I felt if his talents could be harnessed, he could be anything. What I particularly liked about Shane is that he, like his bowling, was totally uncomplicated. What you saw was what you got. When someone is as open as him, you always feel you're going to be able to get through.

He was young, inexperienced and a non-conformist. But he was willing to learn. You don't teach someone like that how to bowl. But you can help them better understand exactly what they're doing and why.

We began to experiment with a slightly longer run-up, just to see if it helped him to have more "energy" in his actual bowling action. I wasn't looking for faults, merely seeing if more momentum through the crease would also automatically trigger more dip and side-spin.

We worked for half an hour but he didn't like the extra steps. Basically Shane bowled his big leg break always at the same pace. For variation, he used his flipper. We spoke about some of the alternatives, a top-spinner, for example.

He listened intently throughout and then tried to put exactly what we'd discussed into practice.

From that day on Shane and I have maintained very close contact. I guess we were good for each other. He was the most exciting young talent I'd seen and I was someone who could help give him the knowledge he wanted.

At that time there was a change in the leadership at the Academy. Inaugural coaches Jack Potter and Spence left, to be replaced by Andrew Sincock and Barry Causby, both former Sheffield Shield players with South Australia. Barry was seconded from the Commonwealth Bank. I think he felt like he had a charter to run. It like it was a military school, when it was never designed that way.

Shane found this attitude very difficult to handle. He wasn't a loose canon. He was just a person who did things naturally. The Academy expected the young boys to live in hotels, yet not be part of an evening's activities. Shane was one of the few lads with a car and there were occasional problems with time-keeping. If Shane was late, so were the other kids he was driving.

Shane didn't enjoy the running through the sand hills. On one run he was lagging behind and was challenged for not putting in. He had been and his reply included a swear word, used in a disbelieving way. "&%#@ off," he said.

It was not taken kindly and suddenly Shane was in big trouble.

I arranged to meet Barry Causby at the Caledonian hotel for a chat and tried to explain that there was a touch of genius in Shane. Sure he had a rebellious streak, but there was nothing sinister about him. He was an unaffected kid who said what came into his mind. He was also a good kid and I related the story where Shane, Ricky Ponting and Murray Goodwin stood on a city street corner one freezing cold winter's morning to collect money for the Adelaide City Mission. At the time they were only unknown Cricket Academy boys.

I told Barry that Shane had a touch of maverick about him but he also had an ability which we couldn't afford to lose just through what I felt was a clumsy attempt to instill discipline.

Unfortunately the conversation fell on deaf ears. Shane had previously been sent home on the bus from Darwin after a party prank that had not been appreciated. That caused him to miss the youth team tour of Sri Lanka. Now they wanted to punish him again.

Jim Higgs, a Melbourne-based Test selector and former leggie, was, like me, very keen for Shane's talent to be recognised. He encouraged him to return to Melbourne and, if he was good enough, to play for Victoria. All this was happening long before he was ready; he'd taken only a handful of wickets for Glenelg. But it was a way of encouraging him at a crucial stage in his development.

Unfortunately the shift initially only fuelled Shane's frustrations. Victorian coach Les Stillman and captain Simon O'Donnell didn't seem to appreciate how best to use him; so much so that in part of our times together Shane talked about moving to New South Wales. If Shane had gone to Sydney, he could have ended up a surfie because he would have had to survive by himself, for himself. His parental influence had always been very important. Both his Dad and Mum are very good people and are as natural as Shane.

I knew that he was a Victorian down to his toenails and I used that as the angle. I couldn't believe there was something this good floating around and not being encouraged. I talked to him about his love of St Kilda, his close friend Trevor Barker and of all his mates he'd grown up with.

Shane had competition from two older spinners in the Victorian squad: the left-arm orthodox Paul Jackson and the right-arm leg-spinner Peter McIntyre, who I felt was also struggling for the recognition he deserved.

I'd become coach of Tea Tree Gully and felt "Macca" could benefit from an interstate shift to a more caring and spin-friendly environment – just as I had 25 years before. It would also end the immediate competition between the two. It was a win-win situation. Macca played some very good years for SA and also broke into the Australian side. Soon afterwards, with Jackson also moving interstate, Shane was his State's No.1 spinner.

It was during this time, in a Cricket Academy versus Victorian second XI game in Melbourne that Rodney Marsh, the new Academy coach, asked me to come over as Shane was worried about his wrong-un.

The game was at the Junction Oval and we were flicking the ball around, on our knees, seven or eight yards apart, on a concrete-floored dining room. He wanted me to help him improve his wrong-un but with the grip he was most comfortable with, it wasn't going to be easy. He bowled his leg break and it'd go "whoosh", really ripping into your hands with force. You couldn't help but get excited just working with someone who could do that.

Then we tried the wrong-un, but he was turning his wrist right over, inside-out and upside-down and it would fall out rather than spinning with any pep.

I suggested, in his case, that a change of grip for the wrong-un may be in order. "I'm not asking you to change your grip for your leg break, but let's experiment with it for the wrong-un and see what happens." He spread his first and second fingers and immediately started to get the leverage and spin the ball back sharply. I told him that I had two wrong-uns, an obvious one and one harder to detect which the old West Australian fast bowler Des Hoare had shown me. Shane has always loved anything new and he'd never ripped his wrong-un quite like this before. But after 20 minutes he stopped, examined his finger and said, "Gees, take a look at this".

He'd developed the world's biggest blister on his ring finger. Spinning a leg break three feet hadn't put a mark on it, but bowling the wrong-un had.

Having toured Zimbabwe with the Australian "B" team, Shane was chosen for his first couple of Tests against the Indians. I was watching his debut match on TV from Sydney when he first came on to bowl. There was a huge buzz around the ground. My phone rang and it was Ian Chappell, direct from Channel 9's SCG commentary box. "Listen to this, T.J." he said, turning up the effect's monitor. "And that's for a leg-spinner."

I was rapt Shane had made it, but also knew that his hard work was only just beginning, if he really wanted to make it. We were in constant touch and at the end of the season, the Australian Cricket Board ran what was called "Camp April". Shane came over and stayed with me for a few days. We worked in the nets, talked and then worked again. Shane was such a natural. But everything had come relatively easy to him. He hadn't been forced to make too many sacrifices. Like most kids in their early 20s, he enjoyed a drink and a smoke and the company of his mates.

I felt he needed to lose some weight, get leaner and meaner which would show his detractors he was serious about his cricket. It would also repay those who had shown a lot of faith in him. I'd decided to give him the big talk before he went back to Melbourne.

He came in with a slab of beer under one arm and with a bottle of Limestone Ridge red and a bottle of St George's red under the other. He asked which bottle I'd prefer. He intended giving the other to Rodney as a token of his appreciation for Rod's efforts. (Rod drank his when Shane took seven-for against the Windies in Melbourne in 1992-93. I've still got mine.)

The carton of beer remained unopened in my little place in Campbelltown and Shane said, "Are we going to have a beer?".

"No, we're not going to have a beer."

"What's wrong?"

I said, "I'm angry Shane", and launched into my speech, telling him how he hadn't made the necessary sacrifices to be playing for Australia. I didn't want him to make the mistakes that I did. There wasn't a decent wrist spinner, under 35, good enough to be playing. I wanted him to go home, put his head down and really see how good his best was.

He knew that I understood exactly what he was going through. We were so alike in so many ways. Needing to be liked was high on the list.

He looked thoughtful and said, "You wouldn't want me to lie to you would you?".

"No, I wouldn't, Shane."

"Well I can't promise I'm going to go home and do something about it."

"If you don't, Shane, you might lose some support. A lot of people have faith in you."

Next morning in the car heading to the airport, not much was being said.

"Do you mind if I light up a cigarette?" he asked.

"Why do you ask, Shane? You've never asked before. You've just lit it up."

"I won't have one if you don't want me to."

"Shane, if you want to have a cigarette at eight o'clock in the morning, that's your choice. I'd rather you had some breakfast – not because that's what I do, but because it's better for you."

There I was being a pain in the arse again.

He had his cigarette and there was silence again until we hopped out. He thanked me and caught his plane.

Two weeks later there was a phone call from Brigitte, Shane's Mum in Melbourne. "I don't know what you said, Terry, but it's working," she said. "He is running every morning bar Tuesday when he goes to golf. He has already lost four kilograms."

I thanked her for calling and said we'd have to see how long his fitness regime lasted. He had Merv Hughes' wedding coming up. That would be a challenge. But he was to have only one beer and otherwise drank nothing but water.

He trained with a football mate of his from St Kilda and went from strength to strength. It was no coincidence that his bowling grew in stature every day as he became fitter and stronger. He got more "body" into his action and in a very short time, went from being a very good leg-spin bowler to a great leg-spin bowler.

When I played I'd never bowled a flipper. I wasn't game. No-one had ever shown me exactly how to bowl it anyway.

Shane had been taught the flipper by Jack Potter when he was first at the Academy. To perfect it and to better understand it myself, I spent several hours with Rodney Marsh and his assistant Richard Done, both of who could bowl one. In slow motion they explained it step by step. The trick was the release. If the seam remained upright, it would dip and curve. Little did I realise how invaluable that afternoon was going to be, not only for me helping Shane, but also in allowing me to show others a wrist spinner's full repertoire.

Part of my plan with Shane was to introduce him to the top spinner and the back spinner which he didn't have and to get him to understand how he bowled the flipper so he could become more consistent with it.

We reduced everything to slow motion and I asked Shane to bowl his flipper as slow as he possibly could. He got a big curve going.

Gradually, I got him to quicken the delivery, so that it would be marginally faster than his leg break without being so fast it lost its element of surprise. All the time he was working on the process and *feeling* in his own mind exactly what he needed to do to successfully bowl the delivery. In time, we worked on other variations, subtle changes of pace and using angles on the crease, all in the name of keeping batsmen continually guessing.

Shane's arm was so low in the early days that it was almost impossible for him to bowl top spinners or wrong-uns. For these deliveries, he had to tell himself, "Arm high" and "Spin up".

The one thing I was never going to do was to let Shane lose that ripping, searing, signature leg break. Whatever he added to his repertoire was purely for variation. Shane was someone special and his leg break was always to remain his major wicket-taking delivery, no matter how many flippers, zootas and assorted "mystery" balls he was to develop.

Unwittingly as time went by, subtle changes crept in. Compare videos of Shane bowling in his first Test against the Indians to how he bowls now and you'll see what I mean. But Dennis Lillee and most of the other bowling greats were the same. Most of the champion bowlers refined their actions over a period. Bowling a cricket ball is such an individual art, it's almost impossible not to change at some point. Even Shane, as good as he is, can't always reproduce the same perfect action which generates the massive side-spin.

I'd see things and be on the telephone to him and try to be of every assistance.

Whenever he came to Adelaide, I'd go down before a game and there were occasions off-season when we'd have a day or two devoted purely to assessing where he was at, how he was feeling about his bowling action and his plans for bowling to a particular player.

One thing he did change after a conversation was his habit of starting his run-up with the ball in his left hand and keeping it there until the last moment. I queried him and he said it didn't feel right any other way. We compromised and suggested he start with it in his left, but then change it over early so he could actually feel the ball in his hand, thereby promoting greater control.

Along his journey Shane has quoted many of the little things we've discussed and that's reassuring.

I'm proud that Shane refers to me as his mentor. It has had a great rub-off in my coaching career to a stage where I now go all over the world helping young spinners. It's a once-in-a-lifetime opportunity for me. Then again, Shane is a once-in-a-lifetime bowler.

I was just in the right place at the right time

***

ONE DAY, Shane, Trevor Barker and I had a round of golf at Southern Golf Club in Melbourne. We went into the grill bar afterwards for a drink and a chat. Trevor was a legend at his chosen game, Aussie Rules, but he also had an absolute passion for cricket and would forever be asking questions about past players and their accomplishments. Shane couldn't tell you much about the history of the game. I'd say to him on occasions, "Shane, Test cricket didn't start in 1991. You did".

There was a period when he first became "famous" when the advertisements he was doing seemed to occupy more time than his bowling. I worried about that and I expressed that concern. We'd always be open and honest with each other. He didn't always like what I said, or agree with it, but he knew that it came from the heart.

There have been some wobbly moments in his career, but that happens. The batsman does show up and occasionally he's going to win. Wrist-spin bowling is all about taking risks. Sometimes you'll come off; other times you won't. Shane's genius was that he narrowed the percentages his way, like no-one else before him.

***

WHEN SHANE took his headlining Test hat-trick in Melbourne in 1994-95, I noted that there wasn't much spin in any of the three wicket-taking deliveries. I'd previously noted a tendency for him to be following through one side of his body and occasionally falling away at delivery.

We got to Sydney and I said, "Mate, I think we have a problem brewing here".

"Geez, you're not bad," he said. "A bloke has got 20 wickets and a hat-trick and you reckon he has a problem."

"I'm only going to tell you what I see and I see it brewing," I said. "The facts are that you're not following through across your body. It's becoming more and more apparent. Your arm is getting higher and you are following through down one side."

Shane has always been a good listener. He explained that he was trying to get more curve on the ball.

"Why?" I said. "No-one curves it like you do. Do you know what makes a ball curve, Shane? Spin. No-one spins it more than you. The more spin you put on it, the more chance it'll curve."

I'd hit a sensitive spot. Maybe I could have been a little more diplomatic. After all, he *had* taken 20 wickets in two Tests. Some of the journos were even talking about him breaking Jim Laker's Ashes record.

He struggled to make an impact in Sydney and was even dobbed for a couple of sixes by England's No. 11 Devon Malcolm.

The next Test was in Adelaide and Shane asked if we could go to the nets on practice day. He said his shoulder was becoming increasingly sore. It explained why he wasn't driving through the crease. Perhaps that was also why he was following through on the right side of his body.

It was no coincidence that as his damaged shoulder deteriorated, so did the flipper, because of the inverted way the shoulder works with the flipper. During the Test we met out the back and talked it through. I spoke to Richie Benaud and he captured one or two deliveries on video which I showed Shane. He then accepted the need to follow through across his body. He went to Perth and was a different bowler, spinning the ball like the Shane of old.

Having to make allowances and understanding his injuries has been an important part of my education as a coach, too. If the body simply isn't allowing a player to do what he wants and requires certain compensations, a coach has to be flexible in his thinking, too.

Some people may say a wrist spinner's success is all to do with the flick he imparts on the ball. But that's only partially right. The whole action revolves from the very first step a bowler takes. If something is out of alignment at any stage, there are going to be complications.

In England in 1997 when Nasser Hussain started the series with 207 at Birmingham, Shane took 1-110 and 0-27 and was so short on confidence that he felt he couldn't grip the local Duke's ball and instead, at practice, was using a Kookaburra.

With Geoff Marsh and "Tubby" Taylor's help, we had to prize the Aussie ball out of his hand and get him using the one being used for the series. His action also needed some work. Unfortunately, because of the problems he was having injury-wise, Errol Alcott, the physiotherapist, was reluctant to allow him to bowl for more than 20 minutes. Twenty minutes in and we hadn't got anywhere. Shane said he wanted to keep going and we did. I cannot remember one time when we've worked together that he cut a session short. He always wanted to work it out and finish it at that time; he never wanted to leave anything half done.

I talked him through it bit by bit. By now Ian Healy and Steve Waugh were on hand and listening in, too. Then he started to get it to happen. The problem was that he was jumping up and not forward so he had little or no momentum. We took a while to find it but suddenly he jumped forward and everything clicked. Healy said they'd been saying the same types of things to Shane as me. But it hadn't worked. "As soon as you show up, he's ripping 'em again," said Healy. "We'll have to call you the spin doctor."

I've been fortunate to see Shane play in South Africa, the West Indies and England. Wherever he is, I seem to have found a way of getting there. Shane said he wished the Australian Broadcasting Commission or Channel 9 employed me full-time so I could be at every Test, but with my work and family commitments, it's not always feasible.

For years, Shane's workload far outstripped the overs bowled by any other Test bowler in the world. It was inevitable something would give. First he had his finger operated on and then his shoulder.

As good as he was, even Shane found initial difficulty coming back from his finger operation at the start of the 1996-97 summer. He bowled long spells in Brisbane, normally one of his most successful grounds, for only moderate returns. Basically nothing really happened for him. I sensed it was a confidence problem and in the nets in Sydney we reverted back to the basics and slowly worked our way through the whole routine. Even without a batsman at the other end, he was having problems turning his leg break. He asked if "Heals" could join us. Shane was bowling off just one step and as we talked it through, finally turned one sharply. And then another. The next curved and ripped like the very first ball he'd bowled for me in Adelaide all those years previously.

"Ah mate," I said. "People would kill for that."

He turned to me with the straightest and most disappointed face and said, "Was that good was it?".

"You know it was good."

"If it was good, why didn't it *feel* good."

He'd hit the nail on the head. His feel for the ball, post-operation, was different to what it had been prior to that.

I spoke to several doctors who told me that you could not have that operation without any nerves being touched. We had to encourage Shane that there was a new feel to his big leg break. Only a genius could have re-programmed his computer so quickly. He took seven wickets in Sydney and 22 for the five Tests coming off an operation he initially feared may not have allowed him to play again.

***

A DISTINGUISHED former Australian cricketer once questioned how I, a modest performer at Test level, could be of any value to a champion like Shane Warne. "T.J. took only 24 wickets. What could he possibly teach Shane?" he said.

If you went by his theory, only Brownlow Medallists would be able to successfully coach. And, of course, that's just not right.

In the period I played I was lucky to play under Les Favell and Ian Chappell, two inspiring captains who backed their players and believed in their ability. Richie Benaud was also there at different times for advice.

Shane often refers to himself as a "soak" because he does soak up information from people. I also listened and learned from my first days of first-class cricket.

Most of what I impart is what I have gleaned from those experiences and from other people I've been fortunate enough to have met and listened to along the way. And much has been developed after retirement.

Shane has needed a confidante and someone to work closely with, if only because of his workload, unprecedented among slow bowlers of his or any generation.

The sheer number of balls that Shane bowled in the '90s triggered unconscious and quite marked changes to his action. He started to follow through down his body, rather than across as he had when he bowled Mike Gatting with the "Ball of the Century".

His delivery arm edged higher and higher. Over different periods he has bowled with his weight to his side rather than forward and occasionally, more back than forward. Often they have been injury-related faults and have cropped up through the unconscious need to nurse a particular part of his body. In the West Indies in 1999 when he was dropped, his action was flawed and for one of the few times in his career, he was unable to produce the big leg-spin which made him stand out above the rest. Few considered that just nine months previously he'd had a serious shoulder operation.

Having struggled like never before in the West Indies, Shane came out and was Australia's matchwinning player not only in the one-dayers with the Windies, but in the World Cup.

As well as Steve Waugh, who played to help the Australians make the semi-finals, it was Shane who won both the semi-final and the final with inspired spells of leg break bowling. In both these games, Shane bit the bullet and trusted his recovering shoulder. It was exciting to see him turn back the clock.

It had been a rocky 1999 for him, with the undoubted lowlight being his axing from Australia's XI for the deciding Test in Antigua in 1999. In retrospect, he may have handled it a little differently, but he was so disappointed and frustrated. Previously he'd always been able to come back from injury and bowl as if he was brand new.

It seemed to me that physically he'd recovered but mentally hadn't regained the confidence to use his shoulder fully.

It was in Adelaide earlier in 1999, when he bowled more like the Warne of old.

England's Graeme Hick had flat-batted him for four over the top of mid-on during his first over of a one-dayer. But, in-between overs, I could see him focusing on what he needed to do and how he needed to bring his shoulder more into play. His second over was excellent and eventually he took three wickets. And while there were a couple of short ones, at least they had spin on them. I was so proud he had the courage to use his bowling shoulder that half-way through his spell, I rang his mobile phone and left a message. "No matter how tonight finishes, at the end of your fifth over, congratulations. You are now Shane Warne, the *leg-spin* bowler. You are now rotating your shoulders and no matter how the rest of the night goes you will be able to think back to those initial overs, bar the first. It was brilliant."

It was a great game of cricket and the Australians won. At 12.30am there was a phone call at home. It was Shane, the old bubbly Shane. I was thrilled he'd rung.

A week or so later when Australia won the finals 2-0, Shane finished the game by trapping Alan Mullally lbw with a slow flipper. It was the best ball he'd bowled all summer.

I'm glad he has decided to play on. Cricket needs its heroes. He changed the game with "That Ball" to Gatting in '93 and he has continued to thrill and entertain crowds around the world ever since. And, if he wants to, I still believe he can take 500 Test wickets.

T.J. testimonials

RODNEY MARSH
(Ex-Test great and head coach at the Commonwealth Bank Cricket Academy)

When it was finally decided that I was to take this job, I had heard that T.J. had been doing some coaching with the boys. The first thing he said to me was, "Gee, we've got a great leggie in Shane Warne". He'd never seen a ball come out of someone hands better than the way Shane bowled them. You could actually hear the ball humming as it came at you.

In that year T.J. also looked after Stuart MacGill, who I knew pretty well. I'd played with his father and my kids had been to school with him and played in the same cricket team. T.J., as a former West Australian, was the obvious bloke to look after him.

He had a lot more time on his side then having just got out of the slammer and not only did he coach them, he'd talk to them about leg break bowling for hours on end afterwards. If I ever had a problem with a kid, T.J. would come in and take him out, sit him down beside the river and have a bite to eat with him and talk. He was really very helpful.

T.J. could talk under water with a mouth full of marbles! He's never ever stuck for a word and is a great salesman. He also takes an obvious great enjoyment in the art of bowling. I've learnt so much from him about leg-spinning. He always reinforces the importance of the basics. And that's why I like to have him coaching the boys because he continually goes through the check points. He's also excellent company to have around.

CHAPTER TWENTY-TWO

The Invincibles

"Tell young Terry to thank him very much for
all the invitations. I'd be delighted to see
everyone at Government House."

I never speak flippantly of my time in jail. It was too serious for that. But I couldn't resist a dig at myself at a cricket breakfast in Sydney one morning when I followed Sir Oliver Popplewell, the president of the esteemed Marylebone Cricket Club and a Judge of much standing. "The last time I was invited to speak after a Judge he gave me six-and-a-half years!" I said.

There was a pause, before everyone broke up. I'd been re-accepted.

There was a 20-year reunion of the 1973 team to the West Indies, a great day and night and at the conclusion, Ian Chappell called for three cheers for me. Support like that meant everything to me and kept me moving forward. It was very moving; as if it was my party. Only Keith Stackpole who was already committed and John Watkins who lived in Newcastle, couldn't attend. The Adelaide City Mission benefited by more than $25,000.

Kerry O'Keeffe gave an incredibly funny speech. Roger Bryson was the Master of Ceremonies and innocently asked Kerry how he was enjoying the reunion.

"Roger," replied Kerry, who was as merry as anyone, "if I stay any longer, instead of being a fundraiser for the Mission, I'll be a customer!"

"What do you recall about the West Indies, Kerry?"

"All I remember is sitting around the swimming pool with all the single blokes watching for British Airlines planes to arrive so we could pick up the hosties!

"We had two opening batsmen called Stackpole and Redpath who were more like Laurel and Hardy and we had a captain called Chappell who thought that PR were two letters late in the alphabet. His brother Greg with his fuzzy hair on this tour could have played for either side!

"Our wicketkeeper Rodney Marsh was eight hamburgers over par. Dennis Lillee was touted as our sex symbol. He was bald-headed, false-teethed and had an I.Q. to match his bowling average!"

Skully didn't bypass anyone. He called Dougie Walters "nicotine-stained and alcohol-riddled" and then he started on me. "And as for T.J.," he said, "he was our treasurer and our biggest complaint was that he never had any money!"

Kerry's speech was brilliantly-delivered and is considered such a classic that one of the television stations, Ace TV still regularly includes it, totally uncensored, amongst their all-time favourite highlight packages.

We'd played a game earlier in the day, but as Ian said, we were all getting too old for cricket, so again on behalf of the Mission, I helped arrange tennis and golf charity days, involving local businessmen who paid for the privilege of standing side by side some of the sporting greats. Not only was the '73 side again involved, but so were other sports celebrities including Ken Rosewall, John Newcombe, Frank Sedgman, Tim Horan and Gerard Healy. One year we featured former Australian captains including Greg Chappell and Kim Hughes. They were fun events highlighted always by a dinner afterwards.

I was working full time for the Mission, before starting to do some radio work with the ABC and extra coaching, over and beyond my duties at the Academy. It was apparent that I couldn't spend the time in the office that someone on a full-time salary needed to. So I volunteered to work for them on a contract basis. My first major project was the reunion of the Invincibles, celebrating the 50th anniversary of the greatest Australian cricket team of them all. It proved to be a fabulous success which benefited not only the Mission but other charities around Australia.

The first question people inevitably asked me when the testimonial was announced, was would Don Bradman, the team's captain, be attending? But it was impossible. As much as he may have liked to have attended, how could he choose this function above others like the opening of the Bradman Stand and dozens of other appearances he had reluctantly turned down? He was almost 90 years of age and happy to remain out of the public spotlight.

He did, however, agree to sign the memorabilia and also to attend Government House in Adelaide to meet the Governor, Sir Eric Neal, and Lady Neal and the surviving members of the team. I initially didn't hear from him, then received a message back via Barry Gibbs, the SACA's former chief executive: "Tell young Terry to thank him very much for all the invitations. I'd be delighted to see everyone at Government House."

As he'd so often been in the past, the Don was again in my court.

The whole group was very much looking forward to seeing Sir Donald again. When someone said there should be a photograph to mark the occasion, he smiled and jokingly said: "You can't go to one of these things without a photo being taken!"

Along with Sir Donald were nine of the Invincibles: Bill Brown, aged 85, Ernie Toshack, 83, Ron Hamence, 82 , Ian Johnson, 80, Doug Ring, 79, Sam Loxton, 77, Bill Johnston, 76, Arthur Morris, 76, and Neil Harvey, 69 – plus, of course, their partners. Keith Miller almost would have made it, too, but for illness.

It was important for the wives to be involved, too, and over an unforgettable four days, which included the $100-a-head, black tie charity dinner plus time in the Barossa, we had a fabulous time.

Ann, my partner, was there the whole way through, helping and caring for everyone. She was magnificent.

It was like playing your first game all over again arriving by bus at Government House, knowing you were going to meet Sir Donald, the greatest cricketer of all time.

We were supposed to be there for only half an hour, but ended up staying 90 minutes. Lady Neal escorted the ladies through the house, while the Governor, Sir Donald and the boys talked outside. One of the group photos was sent to The Queen.

I shook Sir Donald's hand and realised just how frail he was. I asked him how his golf was going and he said he wasn't hitting the ball far enough to be competitive. He was using a golf cart to get around, yet his handicap was still 23, a mark many would be proud of, let alone someone in their 90th year!

The team had gone through the entire 34-match tour undefeated and the bond they shared was still clearly apparent. They joked and played around like kids, signed memorabilia and had one heck of a time.

The dinner was held on April 16, coinciding to the very day, 50 years earlier, that the Strathaird carrying the team landed at Tilbury.

The dinner, at the Adelaide Oval, which held so many memories for so many of the team, was an enormous success, with 505 in attendance. Beforehand, they all stood out and looked over the oval, marvelling at the beauty of the place and of St. Peter's Cathedral.

Two more dinners were held in their honour in 1998, one at the Brisbane Sheraton after an old mate of mine from Perth, Leon Larkin, had asked if another dinner could be arranged. The players were unanimous. They were having too good a time not to again be in it! September 19, the very last playing day of the tour was chosen and almost 400 attended. Mike Coward hosted each of the nights and did a splendid job. His research and detail was something else.

At the end of the night, several of the Victorians were in debate; Harvey, Loxton and one or two others saying that the original 17 had included seven from Victoria. Was there any chance of a Victorian function? It was only eight weeks to the Boxing Day Test match yet we were able to arrange a third and final dinner, at the Hotel Sofitel, again with the hearty endorsement of the '48 boys, who were now quite used to being in party mode!

The guys did a lap of honour in open cars and were guests of the Melbourne Cricket Club, the Victorian Cricket Association and the Australian Cricket Board. It was a fabulous finale, the only downer being that we'd lost Ian Johnson along the way. He hadn't been able to make it to Brisbane and died shortly afterwards. Ernie Toshack, too, was quite ill along with his wife, Kath, but both were able to come. It wouldn't have been the same without them.

Just a fortnight before the Melbourne event we had only just over 200 confirmations, but with the support of David Emerson, the VCA's marketing manager and the general backing of the Lord's Taverners, 568 went, ensuring another wonderful night. Ronny Hamence and Doug Ring sang their famous little ditty about being "Groundstaff bowlers" and at the end of the night, the wives joined their husbands on stage for a version of *Now is the hour when we must say goodbye*.

Being the emotional person I am I had tears running down my cheeks. It was such a special part of my life which I'll never forget. Again Mike Coward was involved, along with Tim Lane and Jim Maxwell. We went well past midnight but no-one seemed to care. Every time an Invincible ventured outside to the men's room, he'd be engulfed and asked to sign autographs by many of the people who couldn't get in. They were still signing well past 1am! We even ran out of programs.

The signed and framed team photographs and bottles of port, each in limited editions of just 48 all sold out. Overall, combining the three events, well over $120,000 was raised for charity which was very gratifying.

Having such a close involvement with the team reminded me of how cricket used to be played. No wonder the guys were loved everywhere they went. It was a privilege Ann and I will never forget.

CHAPTER TWENTY-THREE

New Beginnings

"Mate," I said, banging the door with my fist.
"I have got to get out of this bloody plane." It
was a grade 1 panic attack.

The day I met Shane Warne was the day my life really turned around. The ABC took me on board to describe leg-spin and doors started to open.

I was talking with Bob Zadow, the former South Australian batsman who for years had been involved with Tea Tree Gully, one of the newest of the Adelaide clubs.

The club had been in the district competition for almost a decade and hadn't played in one final.

Bob was keen for someone else to take on more of the load. He knew of my work at the Academy and asked me if I'd be interested to coach. I was and the club appointed me, I must say with some reluctance in certain quarters and a lot of enthusiasm in others.

From the day I took over, I had almost unequivocal support from the players but a conflict in the hierachy. It was going to be a tough job. Nevertheless I needed the money as much as I needed the job.

I was standing with Bob at the first practice at the indoor centre and said, "Bob, tell me the 'A' grade side isn't training here tonight".

"I'd like to," he said, "but they're here." I knew we were starting at rock bottom.

We worked it through and as the season unfolded, I found some good allies in some of the young guys and the team started to win throughout the grades. "B" grade made the grand final. So did "D" and "E" grades and we finished fourth in the club championship.

The club had gone from having no success at all to having three teams in the finals in the one year. While the "A" grade side finished second last, some very good young kids had been blooded and were better for the experience. At the end of the year I went and recruited two cricketers from Victoria, leg-spinner Peter McIntyre and pace bowler Brad Wigney. Both proved to be great recruits – and again Bob Day proved incredibly generous, allowing both to stay rent-free, just as I had done, at his unit.

In the second year, the "A" grade side improved and "B" grade made it through to the grand final again, only to be beaten.

Off the field there were ructions, but the new president Ian Berry supported me loyally. He said, "You look after it all on the ground. I'll look after it off it and keep the others at bay".

Each year we got better and better. The kids who had been successful in the "B" grade side progressed through to "A" grade. Some of the Under 16 kids also progressed. We had a youth policy and it was working.

By my fourth season, my radio commitments and some television work with Fox were intruding into the time I had for coaching. I was initially reluctant to do a fourth year, but as the club had been beaten in the semi-finals the year before, I felt I should hang in for one more season.

I did that and we made the finals again. We'd lost a couple of players but we had a terrific team spirit.

Tea Tree Gully played an important part in my rehabilitation and my understanding of people.

I'd learnt years before on the bus between Cadell and Waikerie that you don't actually have to like each other to form a team. But if everyone respects each other and the role each person plays, you can build a team spirit and encourage success which at the outset, doesn't seem possible.

The year after I left, they won the "A" grade premiership which was a tremendous thrill.

Ann and I had also become more of an item and on return from co-hosting an Ashes tour group to England in 1993, she told me how much she'd missed me. From that day onwards, we have been very close.

Ann is an intelligent, attractive lady with great strength. She's good company and has always been very supportive of me. I enjoy being with her. She cares for me and also for Trudianne, which is very important.

I moved into Wynn Vale in June 1993 shortly before the trip to England and from that time onwards haven't taken a backward step. The challenges have been there and have been met, one by one. I started to work full-time at the Mission and continue my media work.

The opportunity to have high profile commentary, coaching and overseas tour leader roles wasn't even an option pre-prison. I was simply too busy running away. So embarrassed was I with my lifestyle that I shunned virtually all of my old cricketing mates. I didn't want to look them in the eye, or answer any questions, like, "What are you doing now T.J.?".

"Well, actually I'm about to go to prison."

I was stronger for the experience of doing time. I knew I'd never re-travel the steps which got me there.

Going on the tour with "Jar" (Barry Jarman) in 1993 was a fabulous opportunity. Some of the tourists have now been on three or four trips with me. They are real allies. We have a reunion each year on Jar's houseboat. Most of the crew are there: "Fairway" Burns, "Over-the-odds" Moyle, "Carrots" Ferguson, "Tight shorts" Tom, "Talbot Smith" Harrison and of course, "Bent-arm" Barry. The stories get taller, I can assure you!

The most eventful tour, by far, was in 1995, after "Fritz" Freeman was unavailable. I took a group to the Windies, one-out. It was an amazing experience, unfortunately not for all the right reasons.

It was a small group of just 10 and we all applied for an overnight visa in America, having intended to fly to Los Angeles and Miami before heading down to the islands. However, my request, which should have been automatically stamped was rejected on the grounds of my criminal record. Simon Lane from the travel company was also a lawyer and was so incensed he tried to have the decision overturned by the United States Consulate in Australia. It meant I had to go and get finger-printed again. The prints were circularised around Australia and they came back with a misdemeanor from Perth years previously when I'd been an innocent victim after Rowdy Mallett and I had come to a girl's assistance. After all these years, it shouldn't have even still been on the files. But it was coming back to haunt me.

The U.S. Consulate was notified of my "prior" and again I was knocked back. Simon asked when would I be allowed to land on American soil and they said not for another five years!

My tour group was clear. They headed off through L.A. and Miami and onto Antigua while I went the opposite direction, through Hong Kong, Anchorage and Toronto. Finally, five days later, I made it to Antigua!

I was pretty stressed when I arrived as the cricket had already started. One of the group members, with an obvious sense of humour, had left the entry tickets I needed at the prison gates, directly adjoining the St John's ground! As soon as I arrived, the group burst out laughing. "You obviously found the prison front door alright."

"Yes," I said, "It's amazing how visiting rights are so transferable. Hopefully my accomodation isn't!"

After a couple of days I double checked that everything was in order with our return back, as the group had had some problems coming through Los Angeles. The lady at the agency was very sorry but said she didn't know anything about the tickets we held. It took two days to unscramble that hassle and finally we followed the Australian team to St Kitts.

We arrived but there was no welcoming party. I asked a travel lady there if she knew a woman called Doris because she was the one who was going to meet us.

"I'm Doris," she said, "but I'm not expecting you."

She dropped what she was doing and organised us for the night and came back the next day and said everything was going fine but she couldn't get us off the island! We were due to head to Barbados and then onto Trinidad for the third Test. It was Easter and all the inter-island flights were chockers. She had room for three of us, but not for all 10.

We went to the cricket down at the St Kitts ground and would you believe it but there was another prison at the end of the ground! I couldn't get away from them.

Doris suggested the only way we could keep our itinerary and make Port-of-Spain would be to charter a plane ourselves.

Nothing had gone right since I arrived and as the group leader, I was getting more stressed by the minute. I was phoning home, but All Purpose Travel was closed because of the holiday break. Luckily, Ann had Simon's mobile number. We made contact and arrangements were completed for us to hire two six-seaters to get us off the island. It made for a 4am start to make the airport by 4.30am but by now we were all pretty united. One of the guys, Andrew Thiele, even advanced the $US700 we needed himself as I didn't have enough money.

I reassured everyone that it was a piece of cake and that we'd have no problems at all. It didn't cross my mind how claustrophobic it would be in there. It was just like being back in prison again. We'd got the first plane off and I hopped into the second one. The door slammed. I looked around and saw how I was absolutely surrounded by all this luggage. There was literally no space at all and I was gasping for breath.

The pilot was starting to crank up the propeller. I yelled to him, "I've got to open this door!".

"What? Don't be so stupid."

"I do," I said, "I've got to get out of this plane."

"Don't be so ridiculous."

"Mate," I said, banging the door with my fist. "I have got to get out of this bloody plane." It was a grade 1 panic attack.

The door was opened and out I went for a walk. One of the group, Peter Johnson, who is now a good mate, had no idea about my claustrophobia. "&%#@in' well grow up," he said.

I was walking around the tarmac thinking how am I going to do this? I have to go.

We re-arranged seats and I wasn't as sandwiched. Andrew went and sat with the pilot while I faced away from the front of the plane. Jane, one of the girls on the tour, was a nurse and she was talking to me all the time trying to take my mind off it. I felt I couldn't breathe while we were taxiing. But once in the air I settled down. We got to Barbados without a hitch where Gillian Cozier, Tony's wife, expertly looked after us. We saw some great cricket, including the Curtly Ambrose-Steve Waugh confrontation when Waugh made the best 63 you would ever wish to see. The Test finished early, we had a day-off, then left, the group going back through the U.S. and me heading in the opposite direction, stopping all stations.

We went to the West Indies again for the Brian Lara show in 1999 and I was there, too, with a tour group when Australia won the World Cup several months later in London.

If you would have asked me in 1989 when I was sitting in a prison cell what I would be doing in 1999, I would never have included being at Lord's, watching the world's best play cricket. I would have hoped to have still been with Trudianne and having served my time, be doing something positive again. I genuinely thought if my marriage fell over, so would I and that I would never find happiness again. It's amazing how events occur to pick you up again.

The most enjoyable trip of all was to England in 1997 with another group. It was a good unit and it was obvious from the day we set out that it was going to be a fun trip.

I was looking after all the blokes, plus one lady, Carolyn Ridings. Eric Freeman's group had all the couples.

I got an invitation early in the trip to play in a Lord's Taverners cricket match at Windsor Castle. I didn't really want to play and didn't respond. On the morning of the game, a fellow arrived at the hotel and said, "Is Terry Jenner here?".

I was standing right in front of him. "That's me, how can I help you?"

"I've come to take you to the cricket."

I did a quick re-think and after being assured that two of my mates, Andrew Thiele and Peter Johnson could come too, I grabbed a pair of joggers and away we went. I was rather surprised to learn that the Duke of Edinburgh was going to be there. He was actually our 12th man for the day. We were having some pre-game Pimms and I found myself standing next to the Duke and chatting away. He was so natural.

The day before we'd watched the ceremonies at Buckingham Palace and I said to the Duke, "Were you actually riding behind The Queen?".

"Oh yes," he said, "my word I was."

"Was Charles there too?"

"Oh yes."

"I couldn't actually see you under your helmet."

He said they were "plurry difficult" to see under and also were so very heavy. I grinned and said, "Did you see me there? I was standing just near that light pole as you came around the corner".

He looked at me, realised I was being mischievous and had a bit of a chuckle.

"Actually, sir," I said, "I remember you in 1962 at the opening of the Perry Lakes stadium in Western Australia. You'd been out to the game's village and as you were driving around with your parade of cars behind you, there were a lot of sprinklers going across the road.

"Your car stopped suddenly and at that very moment, all the sprinklers squirted over all the cars behind you!"

"Oh no, that couldn't be right," he said, "but there was a time when my job at the opening of the Chelsea Flower Show was to press the button which turned on the sprinklers.

"As I was walking along, the manager of the show said to me, 'Sir, if you wanted to get back at the media, this is your chance, as if you press the button right now, they are standing directly under the sprinklers!'."

The Duke laughed and said, "but I couldn't do that and I didn't do the thing at Perry Lakes either".

It was a memorable day even though I never got a wicket, thanks to "Rosco" Edwards who deliberately kept dropping catches off me.

Come the last over of the game, I was bowling to Robert Powell, the actor, and a gentlemen wearing an MCCish type cap. He didn't look like a young man but he could handle the bat.

I tried to get Robert Powell out and he skied it high into the deep and took a single – again no-one made a serious attempt at the catch.

I turned to the umpire and Robert and said, "This guy is going to cop the whole repertoire now!".

I came in and bowled as quick and as hard-spun a leg break as I could and he missed it by a foot. The follow-up was the hardest, quickest-spun wrong-un I could bowl and as he went across to cover it, it darted back and hit him in his chest!

I completed the over with a series of deliveries, all of which either beat his bat, or hit him in the body.

Last ball of the over, I bowled my trademark ball, the slider. He flashed at it, nicked it and David Cowper, our 'keeper, took the catch.

"Howzzattt, umpire?" I said.

The umpire, an Englishman, looked at me and said, "No, not out. And I hope you feel proud of yourself son. The guy you were bowling to is 73 years old. Over. And time".

Postscript

"Daddy, bad people go to jail, don't they?"

Little Trudianne, my pride and joy, then just five years old, was talking to me.

"Not bad people," I said, "People who do bad things."

"No, Daddy. Bad people go to jail."

I said, "Is Daddy a bad person?".

"Have you been to jail?"

"Yes."

"Why?"

"Because I stole my boss's money."

"Why?"

"Because I was silly."

"But you're not silly now, are you Daddy?"

It was an absolute tear-jerker. I just fell apart. That's how honest it has always been with Trudianne and I. She has been my strength and focus throughout.

I talk to her about what happened to me. She listens and learns.

Sometimes I wish I could have a 25th hour in the day so I could have more time with her. I've tended to be away a lot lately, but most school holidays, I try to plan at least a week where I can be with her. I like taking her places like the movies and giving her my time.

If prison did one thing for me, it reminded me how important loved ones are. And there is nothing more precious than a Dad's relationship with his daughter.

Trudianne lives with her mother, but she also has her own room in our house now, her own dolls to play with and everything else that a father likes to bestow on a daughter.

I think there's some of me in my daughter and I would be disappointed if there wasn't. Trudianne has a lovely nature, is terrific with kids and is developing into a very elegant young lady – much too quickly, incidentally, for her Dad's liking!

Ann and I and Jacky and Redmond (Trudianne's stepfather) have sat together at the same school concert. I know that Redmond loves Trudianne and would do anything for her, but it is a difficult situation.

I have been married only once and that took 10 years. I know that Damian, Ann's son and Trudianne will be happy if Ann and I were married. We've known each other for a long time now and maybe that will happen one day. If it does, it will be a bonus. But then again, everything is a bonus when you've been where I have.

Statistics

Terry Jenner Season by Season

Season	M	Inns	NO	Runs	HS	Ave	50s	Ct	Runs	Wkts	Ave	BB	5wl	10wM
1963-64	8	15	5	215	37	21.50	-	3	629	7	89.85	2/75	-	-
1964-65	3	5	-	50	20	10.00	-	-	116	2	58.00	2/14	-	-
1965-66	10	17	4	347	69	26.69	1	7	1007	20	50.35	4/49	-	-
1966-67	4	7	-	148	45	21.14	-	1	373	6	62.16	2/91	-	-
1967-68	8	11	-	118	37	10.73	-	7	594	23	25.83	5/32	2	-
1968-69	9	11	4	158	33	22.57	-	7	773	26	29.73	5/75	1	-
1969-70	8	14	1	230	43	17.69	-	6	929	34	27.32	5/49	2	-
1969-70NZ	7	7	1	100	26*	16.67	-	6	625	32	19.53	7/84	1	-
1970-71	12	17	5	233	60*	19.42	1	9	1360	42	32.38	4/22	-	-
1971-72	11	17	3	264	73*	18.85	1	4	982	43	22.83	5/88	1	-
1972-73	6	7	1	69	18	11.50	-	5	581	24	24.20	5/67	1	-
1972-73WI	10	14	5	234	48*	26.00	-	3	1026	36	28.50	5/90	1	-
1973-74	9	17	1	547	86	34.18	3	6	1077	30	35.90	7/127	2	1
1974-75	11	20	3	458	74	26.94	3	7	979	27	36.26	5/110	1	-
1974-75SA	3	4	1	106	57	35.33	1	1	266	6	44.33	2/26	-	-
1975-76	11	14	4	290	50*	29.00	1	12	1108	27	41.03	5/73	2	-
1976-77	1	2	-	13	12	6.50	-	2	93	4	23.25	4/73	-	-
Total	131	199	38	3580	86	22.23	11	86	12518	389	32.18	7/84	14	1

Test Record

Season	M	Inns	NO	Runs	HS	Ave	50s	Ct	Runs	Wkts	Ave	BB	5wl
1970-71 v England	2	4	-	36	30	9.00	-	2	176	6	29.33	3/42	-
1972-73 in West Indies	4	6	3	66	27*	22.00	-	-	347	13	26.69	5/90	1
1974-75 v England	2	3	1	100	74	50.00	1	3	136	3	45.33	2/45	-
1975-76 v West Indies	1	1	1	6	6*	-	-	-	90	2	45.00	2/75	-
Total	9	14	5	208	74	23.11	1	5	749	24	31.20	5/90	1

Game by Game Test Record

M	Date	Versus	Venue	Batting	Ct	Bowling
1	Nov 27- Dec 2, 1970	England	Brisbane	c MC Cowdrey b JA Snow 0	- 1	24-5-86-1 4.6-2-9-1
2	Feb 12-17 1971	England	Sydney	c APE Knott b RGD Willis 30 c KWR Fletcher b DL Underwood 4	1 -	16-3-42-3 21-5-39-1
3	Mar 9-14 1973	W Ind.	B'town	not out 10	- –	28-9-65-3
4	Mar 23-28 1973	W Ind.	POS	lbw b LR Gibbs 2 b LR Gibbs 6	- -	38.3-7-98-4 15-2-46-0
5	April 6-11 1973	W Ind.	G'town	c Al Kalliacharran b KC Boyce 10	- –	7-0-15-0
6	April 21-26 1973	W Ind.	POS	not out 27 not out 11	- -	32.2-9-90-5 17-7-33-1
7	Nov 29- Dec 4, 1974	England	Brisbane	c P Lever b RGD Willis 12	2 -	6-1-24-0 16-5-45-2
8	Jan 25-30 1975	England	Adelaide	b DL Underwood 74 not out 14	- 1	5-0-28-0 15-4-39-1
9	Nov 28- Dec 2, 1975	W Ind.	Brisbane	not out 6	- -	4-1-15-0 20-2-75-2

Overall Test Record

	M	Inns	NO	Runs	HS	Ave	50s	Ct	Runs	Wkts	Ave	BB	5wI
In Australia	5	8	2	142	74	23.67	1	5	402	11	36.54	3/42	-
Overseas	4	6	3	66	27*	22.00	-	-	347	13	26.69	5/90	1
Total	9	14	5	208	74	23.11	1	5	749	24	31.20	5/90	1

First Class Record in Australia

	M	Inns	NO	Runs	HS	Ave	50s	Ct	Runs	Wkts	Ave	BB	5wI	10wM
Tests	5	8	2	142	74	23.67	1	5	402	11	36.54	3/42	-	-
S/Shield	87	141	20	2537	86	20.96	7	60	8124	234	34.71	7/127	8	1
Tour games	14	19	7	319	50*	26.58	1	9	1606	53	30.30	5/32	4	
World XI	5	6	2	142	73*	35.50	1	2	469	17	27.58	4/63	-	-
Total		111	174	31	3140	86	21.95	10	76	10601	315	33.65	7/127	12	1
Overseas	20	25	7	440	57	24.44	1	10	1917	74	25.90	7/84	2	-
Total		131	199	38	3580	86	22.23	11	86	12518	389	32.17	7/84	14	-

Sheffield Shield Record for Western Australia

Season	M	Inns	NO	Runs	HS	Ave	50s	Ct	Runs	Wkts	Ave	BB	5wI	10wM
1963-64	7	13	5	194	37	24.25	-	2	614	6	102.3	2/75	-	
1964-65	3	5	-	50	20	10.00	-	-	116	2	58.00	2/14	-	
1965-66	8	14	3	329	69	29.90	-	6	709	13	54.53	4/49	-	
1966-67	4	7	-	148	45	21.14	-	1	373	6	62.16	2/91	-	
Total	22	39	8	721	69	23.26	-	9	1812	27	67.11	4/49	-	

Opponent	M	Inns	NO	Runs	HS	Ave	50s	Ct	Runs	Wkts	Ave	BB	5wI	10wM
NSW	5	10	3	97	22*	13.86	-	1	448	7	64.00	4/49	-	
Qld	6	8	2	117	37	19.50	-	6	535	7	76.42	2/32	-	
SA	6	12	1	310	69	34.44	1	1	413	5	82.60	2/14	-	
Victoria	5	9	2	197	42	28.14	-	1	416	8	52.00	2/91	-	
Total	22	39	8	721	69	23.26	1	9	1812	27	67.11	4/49	-	

Sheffield Shield Record for South Australia

Season	M	Inns	NO	Runs	HS	Ave	50s	Ct	Runs	Wkts	Ave	BB	5wI	10wM
1967-68	6	8	-	83	37	10.38	-	4	503	17	29.58	5/66	1	-
1968-69	8	10	4	148	33	24.66	-	6	659	19	34.68	4/38	-	-
1969-70	8	14	1	230	43	17.69	-	6	929	34	27.32	5/49	2	-
1970-71	8	11	3	157	60*	19.65	1	7	896	30	29.86	4/22	-	-
1971-72	6	11	1	122	48	12.20	-	2	513	26	19.73	5/88	1	-
1972-73	5	7	1	69	18	11.50	-	5	468	19	24.63	5/67	1	-
1973-74	8	15	-	494	86	32.93	3	5	911	26	35.03	7/127	2	1
1974-75	7	13	-	287	55	22.07	2	3	560	13	43.08	4/83	-	-
1975-76	8	11	2	213	42	23.67	-	11	780	19	41.05	5/73	1	-
1976-77	1	2	-	13	12	6.50	-	2	93	4	23.25	4/73	-	-
Total	65	102	12	1816	86	20.17	6	51	6312	207	30.49	7/127	8	1

Opponent	M	Inns	NO	Runs	HS	Ave	50s	Ct	Runs	Wkts	Ave	BB	5wI	10wM
NSW	18	26	4	495	67	22.50	2	9	1707	55	31.03	5/66	2	-
Qld	16	22	3	440	86	23.15	1	10	1557	58	26.84	5/67	4	-
Victoria	15	26	3	316	50	13.73	1	11	1567	42	37.30	4/22	-	-
WA	16	28	2	565	60*	21.73	2	21	1481	52	28.48	7/127	2	1
Total	65	102	12	1816	86	20.17	6	51	6312	207	30.49	7/127	8	1

Against All States in Sheffield Shield

Opponent	M	Inns	NO	Runs	HS	Ave	50s	Ct	Runs	Wkts	Ave	BB	5wl	10wM
NSW	23	36	7	592	67	20.41	2	10	2155	62	34.75	5/66	2	-
Qld	22	30	5	557	86	22.28	1	16	2092	65	32.18	5/67	4	-
SA	6	12	1	310	69	34.44	1	1	413	5	82.60	2/14	-	-
Victoria	20	35	5	513	50	17.10	1	12	1983	50	39.66	4/22	-	-
WA	16	28	2	565	60*	21.73	2	21	1481	52	28.48	7/127	2	1
Total	87	141	20	2537	86	20.96	7	60	8124	234	34.71	7/127	8	1

Half Centuries in First-class Cricket (11)

69 For Western Australia v South Australia in Perth, 1965-66
60* For South Australia v Western Australia, Adelaide, 1970-71
73* South Australia v World XI, Adelaide, 1971-72
67 South Australia v New South Wales, Sydney, 1973-74
59 South Australia v Western Australia, Adelaide, 1973-74
86 South Australia v Queensland, Adelaide, 1973-74
74 For AUSTRALIA v ENGLAND (5th Test), Adelaide, 1974-75
50 South Australia v Victoria, Melbourne, 1974-75
55 South Australia v New South Wales, Adelaide, 1974-75
57 For Derrick Robin's XI v President's XI, Cape Town, 1974-75
50* South Australia v West Indian XI, Adelaide, 1975-76

5 Wickets in an Innings in First-Class Cricket (14)

5/66 For South Australia v New South Wales in Adelaide, 1967-68
5/32 South Australia v New Zealand XI, Adelaide, 1967-68
5/75 South Australia v West Indian XI, Adelaide, 1968-69
5/49 South Australia v Western Australia, Adelaide, 1969-70
5/83 South Australia v Queensland, Adelaide, 1969-70
7/84 For An Australian XI v A New Zealand XI, Christchurch, 1969-70
5/88 South Australia v New South Wales, Sydney, 1971-72
5/67 South Australia v Queensland, Brisbane, 1972-73
5/90 For AUSTRALIA v WEST INDIES (5th Test), Port-of-Spain, 1972-73
7/127 South Australia v Western Australia, Adelaide, 1973-74
5/105 South Australia v Queensland, Adelaide, 1973-74
5/110 South Australia v MCC, Adelaide, 1974-75
5/135 South Australia v West Indian XI, Adelaide, 1975-96
5/73 South Australia v Queensland, Adelaide, 1975-76

10 Wickets in a Match In First-Class Cricket (1)

11/170 For South Australia v Western Australia, Adelaide, 1973-74

Wickets Taken As Follows

		%
Caught	230	(59.12)
Caught & bowled	28	(7.20)
LBW	33	(8.48)
Bowled	63	(16.20)
Stumped	34	(8.74)
Hit wicket	1	(0.26)
Total	389	(100.00)

Batsmen Most Dismissed in First-Class Cricket

Six Times: PH Carlson, JH Edrich, HB Taber, GD Watson

Five: AR Jones, A Turner

Four: RI Charlesworth, BE Congdon, JRF Duncan, R Edwards, R Fredericks, RB Kanhai, CH Lloyd, AL Mann, AJ Seiler, RF Surti.

Sources:

(1) Ray Webster's Australian first-class matches, Vol. 2

(2) Cricketer & Australian Cricket Annuals (1970-77)

(3) Wisden Cricketers' Almanack (editions 1965-78)

(4) South Australia in the Sheffield Shield, John Winter

Please note the following descrepency:

The Oxford Companion of Australian Cricket suggests Terry Jenner made 10 fifties took 87 catches and conceded 12520 runs. After exhaustive checking I believe the figures, as shown, are correct – LAWRIE COLLIVER.

E DIVISION YATALA LABOUR PRISON

DAILY UNLOCK (A.M.) AND (P.M.)

1   CELL TO BE CLEAN / INCLUDING TOILET AND HANDBASIN

2   KNIFE FORK AND SPOON SET TO BE LAID OUT ON TABLE

3   STAND BY DOOR

4   CELL INSPECTION WILL TAKE PLACE

5   MAIL AND REQUESTS HANDED TO OFFICERS

6   RUBBISH AND FOOD TRAYS OUT

CELL CLEANING

MOP AND POLISH ETC. - DURING MORNING -

SHEET CHANGE

EVERY THURSDAY - SHEETS AND PILLOWCASES
ARE TO BE TAKEN OUT OF CELL ON THE A.M. UNLOCK
AND PLACED IN THE UNIT CIRCLE. THE UNIT CLEANER
WILL RE-ISSUE CLEAN LINEN IN THE A.M.

NOTE

ANY DAMAGE TO CELL OR DEPARTMENT EQUIPMENT
WILL BE PAID FOR BY THE PRISONER RESPONSIBLE.

PRISONER'S REQUEST

To The SUPERINTENDENT

No.................... Name........ JENNERS T

Date.................. Cell.......... Gang............. Sentence....................

REQUEST

REQUEST TO BORROW

MORTONS T.V. FOR THE

NIGHT. *thank you*

approved for 1 night
must be returned on A.M
unlock and take full responsibility
for T.V.

Referred to—

Date.................. Superintendent........

SAGPD R4761

General Index

Inmates Index